For Mary Bluh.

My mother, my sister, my friend.

THANKS FRIENDS

STAROGUBSKI PRESS is named after my grandmother, Anna Fox Steinberg. Starogubski is the real name. Steinberg* is the name the immigration officer picked.

The first thankyou is for my grandmother Anna, who like me, was a writer, but unlike me was born in the wrong time. And to my mother Mary Bluh, who will never be the same after all the editing and proofreading.

To my sisters in Philadelphia. The CR group. Jean Ferson, Dorothyanne Peltz, Judy Abrams, Fran Rose, Marie Dunleavy, Suzanne Haney, Jackie Richlin and Jean Zaleski.

For help in editing and proofreading my thanks and gratitude to Mary Bluh, my sons, Craig Lowy, Kenn Lowy and Brian Lowy. To Morton Cohen and Jean Zaleski.

The typesetting was done by Frances Anderson and Lucinda Cisler, who were both a great help in other ways too.

Thanks to Elliot Berd who designed the cover and whose advice was unfailingly good.

Although everybody was marvellous during this first publishing venture there are three people who made this book possible. Craig Lowy, my son, who gave up his own art to help me with this book. Jean Zaleski who encouraged me from the beginning. Morton Cohen who did everything but write the actual book. All three are beautiful people and wonderful friends.

Woman to Woman

european feminists

Bonnie Charles Bluh

STAROGUBSKI
PRESS
New York, N. Y.

Copyright © 1974 by Bonnie Charles Bluh
All rights reserved

Library of Congress Catalogue Card Number: 74-20184

Manufactured in the United States of America by Book Crafters, New York, New York. No part of this book may be reproduced in any form without permission in writing from the publisher, except by a reviewer who may quote brief passages in a review to be printed in a magazine or newspaper.

Book designed by Bonnie Charles Bluh
Typesetting by Frances Anderson and Lucinda Cisler
Cover designed by Elliot Berd
Cover illustration by Jean Zaleski

Copies of *Woman to Woman* are available by mail for $4.50 (US) each, postpaid, from

    STAROGUBSKI PRESS
    Post Office Box 46
    General Post Office
    Brooklyn, New York 11202

Please send only prepaid orders.

CONTENTS

Introduction 3

Preface 9

Ireland 15

England 57

Holland 109

France 155

Italy 203

Spain 251

Brooklyn 297

Women's Centers and Groups 315

INTRODUCTION

INTRODUCTION

IN AUGUST of 1971 I left the United States for Europe. I left my three sons, my mother, all my friends, the life I knew in search of myself. Because in Europe I would be alone. I would have time to think. To write. To be. I went with the idea that I'd finish a feminist novel. In Ireland I changed my mind and began writing this book.

For one year I lived with my sisters in Ireland, England, Holland, France, Italy and Spain. I wanted to record the second feminist movement in Europe. The feminists and I shared together, ate together, attended meetings, spoke about our deepest feelings. And as we talked, I found myself creeping more and more into the dialogues until I began to realize I was very much a part of the book.

In Spain where I lived and was putting the book together, I contacted Mary Yost who became my agent. Here is an excerpt of her letter: (All letters are on file.)

— I have now read [the book] and find it fascinating all the way. I like the way you have injected the personal note throughout. I would like to start it on its rounds right away. I don't think we'll have any problem placing this manuscript even though the market is beginning to look glutted on the subject of liberation here in the U.S. So far I haven't seen anything announced about foreign countries and we'll keep our fingers crossed. —

The first rejection came from a major publisher. — I don't feel that *The Seventh Rib* [the title at that time] promises to be a book . . . could run with. Maybe a balanced objective analysis of where the women's liberation movement is, world-wide, sounds too dull, but on the other hand I find Bluh's treatment too one-sided, too subjective and personal to attract significant sales. —

Another publisher held the book for three-and-a-half months, refusing to send it back. Finally they said they were in deliberation and would let us know within twenty-four hours. Three days later they called. No. Too angry. Too personal.

Mary Yost was puzzled by the reactions. While she kept encouraging me, it became apparent something was wrong. After nine months I left Mary Yost to go with Hy Cohen of Lanz-Donadio. There we met with similar reactions. The book is too angry, too personal, not academic enough. And the topper: Where will we find the market? Who's interested in the European feminists?

There was, however, a different reaction from the women at the publishing houses.

— It is, as far as I know, the first [book] to report in this fashion on the international scope of the movement and to offer a progress report on its status in the various countries. —

— I think it's fine, a good job of reporting and of reinforcing the ties women increasingly feel as one another's sisters, regardless of country, occupation, life experience, etc. —

— Do try to put it in as many hands as possible. I am confident that you will find not only sympathetic eyes, but also, a contract behind one of those doors. —

— This is a kind of personal journalism in which she uses her own point of view and recollections from her own past experience freely, bringing these to the interviews she records with the women in the various countries. The book then has something like a novelistic life at the same time that it informs. —

— Tell Bonnie Bluh not to be discouraged. She has written a fine book and when it is published we (many here) feel it is bound to make a major contribution in each person's investigation into identity.

TIME PASSED. I decided to forget the book. There were so many changes in the feminist movement in Europe. But if the book wasn't published I would be letting the women down. And myself. And what if there were changes? Those changes wouldn't invalidate the beginning of the second feminist movement.

And it was a time of excitement.

In Ireland the feminist movement was less than five months old. The women smuggling contraceptives from northern to southern Ireland were jubilant.

England. In 1791 Mary Wollstonecraft wrote *A Vindication of the Rights of Woman*. And now in 1971 feminists from all over were crowding into two little rooms at their tiny headquarters in London.

In Holland I heard women discuss homosexuality openly for the first time (in Europe) and I had to face my own sexuality.

France. The feminists had recently published their *352 Abortion Manifesto*. The first signature was Simone DeBeauvoir's. France where Mijo and I were followed by the police.

Italy where I marched with my sisters in a freezing Rome in the first international abortion march.

Spain where I lived for eight months and saw *machismo* first hand. Spain where I found some of the most dynamic feminists. Women who didn't dare have headquarters or use their real names; where I was followed by the police and drugged.

Yes feminism has changed in Europe. But nothing can take away from the excitement of that time. This then is a living document of the second feminist movement in six countries. It is the truth of that time.

I AM publishing this book because I am positive there's a world of women who want to know how feminism got started in Europe. And because I think it is time for women like me to take responsibility for their own lives. The women in this book stood behind what they believed. I think it's time for me to do the same.

This is a gut level book. My authorities are the women themselves.

* Where this appears in the text, it means the person's real name has not been used.

** the real name

Bonnie Charles Bluh
September 1974
New York, N.Y.

PREFACE

PREFACE

AT THE airport I sat shaking. Ran to the ladies' room and swallowed a tranquilizer. In the airport lounge, mouths were moving without faces, blurred words swimming round me. I sat with my friend Jean Zaleski and told her I'm not going. I can't leave my children. It was a stupid idea. I'm going home. But where was home? I'd given up my apartment, sold everything. I no longer had a job. My ex-husband had the children. Jean, I'm not going.

In the midst of my cries, we heard the music of bagpipes. The vacuum sounds came toward us. Jean said, — Oh look, they're seeing you off. — Very funny. Nothing was funny. The group was going to Ireland to play in a competition but I knew I wasn't going anywhere. The call for my flight came over the loudspeaker and I stood, not knowing what to do. Jean pushed me toward the gate. — Go, get on that plane. — I moved slowly. Like a wind-up toy I moved, hearing the unreal sounds of the bagpipes, looking backward at Jean, and suddenly I heard her yell, — Right on Bonnie and write that book. —

My legs felt like balloons about to lose their air as I boarded the jet. Sitting in my seat, I stared outside at the runway. Numb, unable to move. Fasten your seat belts. The roar of the jet jolted me. You can't go home. It's gone. You sold everything, remember. People picking at things, bargaining for all you possess. Take it, oh take it.

The jet was silently floating above the earth. I looked at the black sky, the blinking stars that swept by the window. Eight months ago, I looked at that same sky and thought, no it can't be. My former husband had called from his office in Florida. I lost my job, he said. Eight months later, I watched everything I had leave the apartment. And still he didn't have a job. The phone calls from friends, relatives. You can't leave your sons. He'll never get a job. Nobody's hiring engineers. How will they live? Going back to work while they carry your furniture out. Nobody at work knows anything. How marvellous they say. You lucky thing, going to Europe for a year to write a book. Smiling back, I say yes, I know.

The stewardess came with a drink and I drank it down. Remembering how I went home that night to a half-empty apartment, cooked dinner with my children, with my former husband who was now living with us because he had no other place to go. Talking with my sons, laughing with them, and all the time thinking what the hell is going on in your head? What kind of a mother are you? At 8:00 pm I left to be with eight other women, as I had done every Wednesday night for eight months.

Consciousness raising they call it. Understanding what it is to be a woman in a patriarchal society. Every one of us, in speaking of our lives, our day-to-day experiences, learned we'd thoroughly absorbed the socialization imposed upon us. We started with the idea it was happening to me and gradually discovered it was happening to *us*. In discovering ourselves, we discovered each other. And in discovering each other, we learned sisterhood.

I can't go, I told them. Why not? He's not working. Then he'll have to find a job, they told me. The children are his responsibility too. I know, I said, but when? I have to leave my apartment in a week. One of the women turned to me. Look, your ex-husband had twenty-three years to discover himself. Don't you think you're entitled to one year? But you don't understand, I replied. I'm not even sure anymore.

Nine of us left at midnight. They hugged me. And once again I thought yes, no matter what, I'm going. When I arrived home, my ex-husband informed me that the job he'd hoped to get was his. The next day I went to work and he drove with two of my sons to Connecticut to look for a house. At 11:30 pm I received a phone call. His car had blown up. Don't worry. Nobody's hurt. I called Jean. She drove over and sat up all night with me while I explained why I wasn't going. Last year my oldest son Craig was critically ill in the hospital. Incident after incident piled up, making it a nightmare year. Now the accident with the car. How can I go? Something terrible will happen.

Three days later I waved goodbye as my three sons left with their father for their new home. Everything gone. Now my sons. I looked around at the almost empty apartment. Another feminist came with friends and together they bought the remaining furniture. As the van took off, she grinned at me and yelled, — Right on Bonnie. —

Fasten your safety belts. We are approaching Dublin Airport.

Little did I realize then how freely feminists were communicating, travelling from country to country, forgetting their differences. These feminists learned that women are natural friends. That although nationality, politics, economy and ideology may differ, they are united together in their life experiences.

The International Women's Liberation Movement was not a dream.

I am deeply grateful to my sisters in Europe who taught me the true meaning of sisterhood. It is they who made this book possible. And it is this love and sisterhood that binds me to them.

Benidorm, Spain
July 1972

IRELAND

BALLSBRIDGE

AFTER CHECKING in at my pension at Ballsbridge, a suburb on the way to the Irish Sea, I ask my landlady about the women's liberation movement in Ireland. She never heard of it. I take the bus to O'Connel Street, buy the newspapers. Nothing. I look in the telephone directory. No listing. I begin to ask people. Yes, there was a group of women who went from Dublin to Belfast and brought back contraceptives, but that was months ago. Wherever I ask, I hit a dead end. The one name I have in connection with *The Pill Train* is Mary Kenny, but I learn she is now working in London.

I go through the same routine the next day and again, nothing. The bus takes me to the Irish Sea, where I sit and wonder if the action was just an isolated one, built up by the press in the States. After all, Ireland does not have a feminist history, and now with the war in Belfast....

The next morning at breakfast I meet Member of Parliament Pierce Butler, who invites me to sit in on a debate in Parliament. That afternoon, I walk past Brendan Behan's house, and on to Anglesy Road. Bus 7A takes me past the Sweepstakes Office, past the American Embassy to O'Connel Street. From there I walk past Trinity College, past the Irish Castle to the Parliament Building.

One of the guards at the gate telephones Senator Butler to announce my arrival. From the entrance of Parliament, one block from the gate walks Senator Pierce Butler, a smile on his face that lasts the long walk. He shows me around. A picture of President John Kennedy hangs on the wall. You know him of course, he says. And sitting next to him in the Senate chambers, I listen to a debate on the Forcible Entry Bill, of little importance to me then. Where is women's liberation I ask? Gone he says. Gone? Yes gone. Where's Mary Kenny? She's in London writing for the *Evening Standard.* Why? Oh, she was fired from *The Times.* They lost too many readers because of Mary's connection with women's liberation. And the other women in the liberation movement? There isn't any now that Mary's in London.

I am introduced to members of Parliament. How cute. Women's liberation. Did you say women's bib, one asks, smiling his vote-winning smile. Another, my isn't she feminine for one of them. Ha! Ha!

I give him my nastiest remark. Senator Butler doesn't react. Don't you ever get angry, I ask him. Oh no, never. Violent fantasies are giving me a marvellous time. Tomorrow the headlines on the trouble in the north will be hidden by AMERICAN FEMINIST HITS SENATOR PIERCE BUTLER ON THE HEAD. *Senator Butler replies, 'It's all right. I never get angry.'*

I leave Parliament and walk. In front of the main post office on Upper O'Connel Street are crowds of people. Irish men and women, some from the IRA, are screaming about forced internment in Belfast. Caps are extended for donations. – Help your brothers and sisters. – They sell the IRA paper. I buy all the newspapers: *The Irish Times,* the *Irish Press,* the *Irish Independent.* They are full of the war in Belfast, the internment of the people there, the Irish Republican Army, buildings burning. Lifeless eyes stare up from their death beds on the street. There are photographs of British soldiers rushing forward with guns, smoke everywhere. I find a news story of a beauty contest but not a word about women's liberation. Convinced that the movement is dead in Dublin, I head for Cork.

CORK

IN CORK I hear, – Women's liberation here? Never! – I go to *The Irish Times* office. They hand me a copy of *The Times* story covering *The Pill Train,* and inform me that Mary Kenny was not fired. She left because the opportunity in London was too good to pass up. Women's liberation? The women behind the desk don't know anything about it. At the *Irish Press* I meet Jean Sheridan, a journalist, who covers the women's pages. Women in Cork are not interested in liberation she says. They're happy. I think about the blacks singing in the cotton fields and

I smile. Happy? She gives me the names of two feminists in Dublin and tells me that the feminists are causing a lot of trouble, particularly in Parliament, where they recently picketed against the Forcible Entry Bill. Hello Senator Butler.

I remember his one-block smile and rush out to a phone booth and call Dublin. At *The Irish Times* I ask for Nell McCafferty. I call June Levine of the *Irish Press.* Of course we're here. Of course women's liberation is here. Welcome sister. Welcome.

I buy a ticket that will take me back to Dublin the next day. On Patrick Street, I enter Easons, which is the largest book store in Cork. There isn't one book on women's liberation on the shelves, not even Simone DeBeauvoir's *The Second Sex,* although they have other books by the author. The booklet *Irishwomen, Chains or Change* is not available. Why I ask the saleswoman? I don't know to tell the truth, except only one other person has asked for it. What do you think of women's liberation? Ridiculous she says. We're happy in Cork. Of course, we'd like to see widows get more benefits and we do have women's groups here. I talk about the feminist movement in the States. Her answer is another, we're happy. Motherhood is the most important role for women.

THE BUS taking us to the Ring of Kerry had an assortment of people, mostly Irish. Every seat was occupied except the one next to me. The bus driver was endowed with the innate Irish loquacity, his humor permeating the bus. He told the people sitting directly behind him, – Oh good, you're the first to go after me, when the bus crashes. – His tour was not the usual bombardment of dates and historical information that only a computer could digest, but a series of jokes, stories, poetry and folklore, with a little data thrown in. – Do you see that castle, no not there on your left, on your right. That's where what's his name once . . . oh, I know his name as well as I know my own. Well, don't worry. It will come to me. –

The bus drove past lush plains with so many shades of green it staggers the imagination, past hills, mountains, inlets, lakes, bays that touch the core of your being. And then Dingle Bay, where *Ryan's Daughter* was filmed, more beautiful than the movie. The bus driver says, – All right then, everyone who wants to go out, go, but only for two minutes. – I run out with my camera, look over the deep blue of the water, to little alcoves, a sky that protects the bay, the soft sloping hills. I stand outside of the bus, not wanting to get back on. Passing villages, thatched homes, cows, sheep, countless churches where all the Catholics on the bus cross themselves, castles that whisper of another time. People then as alive as I am now.

In a small village, overlooking a bay, the bus stops and the empty seat next to me is filled. Diana O'Mahoney has been visiting her mother and one of her children. She pays for two tours, as it is the most direct way to get to this remote village. — Diana, that's a Greek name. —
— Yes I know. Diana the huntress. —

Diana tells me she has four other children in Cork. The church granted her a legal separation four years ago. This means her husband is not allowed to come back. It also means that Diana can never marry again. Article 44 of the Constitution gives the church a special position. Therefore there is no divorce in Ireland. She crosses herself as we pass a church. Then says she received the separation because her husband was an alcoholic and her home was ridden with fear.

She feels three children would have been enough, but there is no contraception in Ireland, let alone abortion. — Say I was having an affair. I wouldn't have the slightest hesitation at having an abortion. —

Diana O'Mahoney studied to be a doctor. After three years she quit because she felt it would take too long. — I told my father and he let me quit. Actually he should have said no, you can't quit. But girls in Ireland really don't think about professions. It was the mistake of my life to quit school. —

She worked as a manager of a hotel for eight years, then married. At the time of her separation Diana brought her four year old child to live with her parents, who are in their eighties. Things would have been different, she says, if there had been day care centers that she could afford. Her six and ten year old sons sent to the local school and were completely on their own when they came home. Her daughters, eight and eleven, boarded at the convent school. And Diana went to work.

— In the beginning I would have taken anything. I would have washed floors. I got a job selling for five pounds a week [$12.00]. Ridiculous isn't it, but I thought aren't I lucky. I didn't feel fit for anything, even though I did quite well before I was married. I thought, who'd want me? What am I suited for? —

Her present position in an antique shop is one she likes, and her salary made it possible to purchase a home. — I bought my own home, pulled myself together. And now that I'm working, I wouldn't advise any woman to stay home. I used to be very shy. I think more of myself now and I know it's due to my working. It's given me much more confidence. —

Diana hasn't dated since her separation. — Well, the way I feel is, they wouldn't have any interest in me. I feel if I was attractive once I've lost it. — As for the pub, which is really a place for social gatherings as well as drinking, she feels that although women can go in alone, they aren't comfortable when they do. — The thing is there isn't any place to meet men. And it would be nice if women could go in and out of places as men do. —

Diana O'Mahoney wishes there was women's liberation in Cork. There are no feminists to talk with, no action groups to join. She awakens early to get her sons ready for school, works, shops for food on her lunch hour. She comes home to cook, clean, do all the household tasks. Then sits alone. She tells me she is close to her brother who lives nearby but it would be impossible for her to talk to him. — He thinks I'm finished. He wouldn't understand my desire to date and lead a normal sex life. — She's certain her children would be thrilled if she went out.

Diana would like to return to school but she can't afford it. As for her daughters, — I would make a supreme effort to have them finish school. Girls should have something they can work at. I'm trying to fire them with ambition. My own experience is responsible for this. —

In the feminist group I belong to we were getting scholarships for women Diana's age; we placed the children in day care centers. We have been working on a commune for women in transit and so much more. As I looked out at the darkening Irish countryside, I thought, how different it would be for Diana if there were a feminist group in Cork, if there were inexpensive nursery schools or free ones, if there were divorce. If . . . if. But what good were all the ifs?

THE NEXT morning in my pension, at breakfast, I meet Mr. and Ms. Short, tell them about my book. Ms. Short gives me her daughter's address and phone number. She is Constance Behan, artist, married to John Behan, Ireland's leading sculptor. Call her she tells me. Constance would love to talk with you. Another name.

On the train to Dublin I meet a man who plays rugby for the Cardiff Wales International team. Fascinated with the feminist movement and totally oblivious that it's in his country as well, he says, — They shouldn't have women's liberation. They shouldn't need it. God made men and women equal. He bloody well did.

— The women in Wales fight like men, with their fists. When my sister argues with me, I say you're right love, you're right pet. I wouldn't argue with her for anything. —

Ah here it comes. The male concept of liberation. He's all for us fighting with our fists. Next he'll give us permission to get on top when we fuck.

His grandmother who lived to the age of ninety-seven worked in the mines in South Wales, stoked the boilers in the pit. He tells me they had two women on twelve hour shifts. — Now there are two men on eight hour shifts. It takes three men to do the job of two women. Love, those women were really something. My grandmother hit me once and I never will forget it. She knocked me cold like a light only once. I never went to see her again. My father would say to me, I'm going to visit Grandma. Want to come with me? Me! You must be joking. —

DUBLIN

FROM THE Houston Street station I took a bus to O'Connel Street. There I called Nell McCafferty's office and left the phone number of my guest house. When I arrived my landlady informed me that Nell McCafferty had called and asked me to meet her at the Pearl Bar on Fleet Street.

The Pearl Bar is the hangout for journalists and the Abbey Players. All the tables were occupied with people talking animatedly, waving to people at other tables. Some moved from table to table, talking to their friends. A conversation at one table joined the conversation at another. — Read your story on the squatters. Loved it, really loved it ... I hear Larry's covering Belfast ... Sean doesn't even know there's a war going on. Every day he gives me a new beauty contest to cover. If I write another 36-24-36 I'll scream. What do you think of ... — I interrupted a conversation at a table and asked if they knew Nell McCafferty. — Everybody knows Nell. — Apparently she'd been there and gone, but they were expecting her in five minutes. I moved through groups of people to get to the bar, where I ordered a pint of Guinness and waited. Forty-five minutes later she walked in.

NELL McCAFFERTY

Don't ask a prophet for a blueprint

THE MOMENT you see Nell McCafferty you are aware of a fighting determination. She is completely nonconventional in dress and speech. I told her what happened at Parliament. Angrily and in the thickest Irish brogue she said, — The bloody bastards. We stormed Parliament ten days ago. Oh we're here all right and they know it. — She handed me the booklet *Irishwomen, Chains or Change* and told me she was sorry but she had a 7:30 appointment, and would see me tomorrow morning at 10:45 at Bewley's Oriental Cafe on Westmoreland Street.

The following morning I entered Bewley's, the one place in Dublin to get a good cup of coffee. I asked the hostess if she knew Nell McCafferty. Yes she did. Would she tell her where I'm sitting when she comes in? Yes. I ordered coffee and waited. At 12:00 no Nell. I searched the other rooms, then walked across Westmoreland Street to the offices of *The Irish Times*. No, they didn't know where she was, she hadn't called, didn't have any appointments until the afternoon. Really, this is impossible, I told them. I hung around the offices for a while, then went back to Bewley's for more coffee. At one o'clock as I was getting ready to leave, Nell entered, like a gush of wind, her eyes darting from table to table. I yelled, — Nell, here. —

— Oh I'm sorry Bonnie really. — Her face was taut, her eyes swollen. — A friend of mine was killed in Belfast. I had to make the funeral arrangements. — — Here, let me get you some coffee Nell. — — No, — she said, — I know this place, — and before I could reply she was at the counter.

As we sat sipping coffee, I told her how sorry I was. She shrugged, it's nothing, it happens every day in Belfast, but her expression told me something else. I took out my pad and Nell told me that in March 1971, in Dublin, they read about the women's liberation movement in the United States. Twenty women, many journalists, got together and began discussing the plight of Irish women. This was the start of the Irishwomen's Liberation Movement. At the same time M.P. Mary Robinson was trying to get contraception legalized. The Senate wouldn't allow her to read the bill. They said, 'We will sink into a sea of filth.'

The irony is that there is contraception in Ireland, but they call the pill *cycle regulators*. If you can prove you're having menstrual irregularities, the doctor gives you a prescription. The pills are very expensive and only the middle class and rich can afford them.

Disgusted with the situation and determined to bring it to the public's attention, twenty-two women set off on May 22, 1971. They took the train from Dublin to Belfast, and there they bought the pill, the intrauterine device, diaphragms, jelly. Nell's eyes light up when she talks about this. The train headed for Dublin and the Customs officers. The twenty-two women got off the train, marched to Customs and declared the contraceptives. The officers were prepared for them, were ordered to let them through. When the twenty-first woman put down the contraceptives she said, — Here's my jelly. — Nell yelled, — You can't let her through. She's breaking the law. Arrest her. — The Customs officer looked bewildered. Nell laughs. — We expected maybe ten people, but there were crowds, hundreds and hundreds of people behind the barricades screaming, — Let them through. Let them through. — Hundreds of people cheering twenty-two women who expected to spend the night in jail. Suddenly they began throwing the contraceptives through the barricades, to the cheers of the crowds.

The next day they were denounced from the pulpit. A few of the feminists expected this, were in church and yelled back at the priest, — Nonsense! —

Nell talks very rapidly in her fascinating but hard to follow Bogside brogue. — We have eight hundred members, two hundred very active, extremely active, six hundred give us support.

— There are no halls available in the city, so we meet in each others' homes. After the booklet, *Irishwomen, Chains or Change* came out, Parliament actually accepted sex. Sex has been officially recognized this year. Before you couldn't even mention the word. It has always been banned in books. We're considered a radical movement and any time there's a radical movement in Ireland, they call it a communist movement. It works like a charm. —

She discussed a meeting where the women got up and introduced themselves. — They'd say I'm Mary so-and-so and I have three children or five children. Then suddenly it dawned on them, why do we have to say we have children. Fine, we love them, but there's more to us than kids. — In Ireland girls must get married early. The average girl leaves school at twelve, works in a factory. Less than 1% of the higher professionals in Ireland are women. As for abortion, it's an unquestionable word.

Nell discusses consciousness raising. There were sixteen women. None could speak more than three sentences. — It nearly wrecked them. Actually it did wreck them. — They haven't done any consciousness raising since.

Consciousness raising. I tell Nell about the first time our group in Philadelphia got together. Nine women, mostly strangers to each other. Strangers to ourselves. Hesitantly they begin to speak. Does anybody care? Will somebody listen? Two weeks, three, four weeks. Sometimes quietly, other times in a fervor they reach inside themselves, and begin to learn what they feel as women. All of us are learning a new awareness, while I throw in bits and pieces of the surface me. When the room becomes choked with tension, my humor jumps out, and all nine of us laugh. I constantly joke.

On the fifth week I'm funny to everyone but me. Suddenly I realize I've become my own victim. You idiot, you're laughing at your own expense. Talk. Say something. But where do you begin?

My childhood, where I fought with my fists, played handball with a hard black ball and no glove, where I ripped my clothes climbing fences and trees, foundations of buildings going up. Little girls playing with their dolls, and you smash yours on the side of a building. I hate it, I don't want it. All around me I hear she's impossible. School, where notes went home. She asks too many questions, talks too much. Then she's a dreamer, doesn't pay attention. And I hear, what's wrong with her and the answer, she's stupid. In class . . . Now girls, we'll learn how to sew. We'll make a skirt. Looking at the material, wondering what I'm supposed to do with it. Cutting, cutting until the material is so reduced it becomes a skimpy blouse. Everybody has a nice new skirt except me. What will we do with her? She's impossible. Can't sew, can't cook. She's terrible at typing, shorthand. I withdraw into a dream world, write stories in my head, create my own world, live in the movies. Periodically I think, what am I going to do with me? I join girls' clubs and fight. I join mixed groups and fight. Wherever I go, there is a battle and the words she's impossible become a reality.

Where do you begin? Marriage at nineteen, children, taking a marriage counselling test and discovering your husband is so placid he could live with anyone, but he got stuck with you. Being told you have the highest score for aggressiveness ever recorded. Aggressiveness!

Male. Penis envy my brother called it. Envy? That marvellous male organ that gets in your way when you climb trees, fences, ride a horse. I do all of those things unencumbered by a protrusion that flops around and needs protection. Penis envy? Dear Dr. Freud, you lived in a fool's paradise. Who wants it? You may have the instrument, but we are the orchestra.

While eight women listen, I talk, and for the first time I leave the fantasy world that saved my life. No, not saved but negated it. And each week, we all grow and learn. And when I joke, it's no longer as a cover up.

I turn to Nell, ask her about herself. She tells me she's twenty-seven years old, born in Derry, in northern Belfast. She's from a working class family, lived in the Catholic ghetto with her mother, father, two brothers and three sisters. Her father has a civil service job, her mother is a homemaker. Nell finished secondary school at sixteen, continued her education at the University of Cork. There she majored in English, French and psychology.

— When I was in school there was one girl in the engineering faculty. She was thought of as a freak.

— In Belfast, you're marginally better off if you're a Protestant, but it's actually an economic problem. The situation is ridiculous. In the slums, on one block there are Catholics, around the corner are Protestants. They both have nothing. Yet they convince both blocks that the other block is better off. And they believe it. —

Nell McCafferty has always been a maverick. Her father calls her a communist, a pervert, a lesbian. Yet, she's the only one in her family to graduate from a university. — The only thing I could do was teach. I couldn't teach in a Protestant school because I was a Catholic. I couldn't get a job in a Catholic school because I wasn't a good enough Catholic. You had to go to the bishop to offer your services, not qualifications. — She snickers. — Your services!! I wouldn't go because of the humiliation. Finally I said, why aren't I getting a job? —

The bishop answered that *A:* Psychology is a dangerous and dirty subject. She should have asked permission to study it. *B:* She appeared in a review on stage at the university. It was a play by Synge and in it she took the Lord's name in vain without bowing her head. [the words she spoke were not hers but Synge's] And *C:* She once wrote a poem about lesbianism when she was eighteen.

In the two years after graduation she worked a total of three-and-a-half months. She taught six weeks in a Catholic school, two months in a Protestant state school, each time replacing pregnant women. To collect unemployment insurance she joined the Dole. If you haven't earned money you collect as well. This is similar to welfare in the States.

In 1966, she spent six months teaching in France. At that time she read *The Source* and was so impressed that she went to Israel for eight months. There she lived and worked at *Kibbutz Maayan Baruch* in the Upper Galilee. — I loved it. It was the greatest experience of my life. I loved it but picking apples nearly broke my back. — In between her travels, she came home to find jobs. On October 6, 1968, the day after the first riot in northern Ireland, she came home again, after spending two months in England. Shortly after that, she became a journalist with *The Irish Times*.

We speak about the very beginning of Irishwomen's Liberation. The three most active then were Nell, Mary Kenny and June Levine, all three journalists. They refuse leaders, don't want to run the movement as a bureaucracy. She tells me the socialists haven't really infiltrated but are trying. — Why not a people's party they ask? —

Nell talks about Mary Kenny. — The movement misses Mary. She was a colorful person, a fighter. People identified Mary Kenny with the movement. — But, she adds that Mary is a career woman and her position as features editor of the *London Evening Standard* was a good opportunity.

Nell drinks more coffee, chain smokes as she talks. The quickness of her speech is a contrast to the bent weariness of her body. — The first demand of our movement is 'one family, one house'. Ireland has the worst housing record in all of Europe. The only country with bigger slums is Turkey. We base this demand on the constitution which says, 'The family is the basic unit of society'. —

Nell tells me people who are homeless are moving into empty houses that are scheduled to be demolished. Although these homes stand and the people haven't anywhere to live, the Forcible Entry Bill argues that they are on private property. That they are homeless is of no concern to anybody but the homeless. It is quite common for three families to live in one house. The state figures in Dublin show that 5,000 families are in need of housing. The women's liberation figures soar to 10,000. They base it on the number of people who do not apply for housing because they are either ignorant of their rights or because they're discouraged. — Women's liberation is the biggest single threat to the Forcible Entry Bill, — she says.

On Benburb Street, there are state corporation flats. Nell points out that the people living there are the dregs of society. Thoroughly disgusted, with no hope for employment, they turn to drink. She talks about a woman who lived with her six children in one room. Her husband managed to find a job in England, so she and the children followed. When his job didn't work out, they returned to Benburb Street, only to discover their room was taken by another mother and her children. — There they were, two women fighting over one room, for the privilege of sharing a bathroom with fourteen other families.

— Then there's Griffith Barracks, a halfway house for homeless people. They use this case all the time. The man died. The corpse wasn't even cold when a family moved in. It's such a hard life, most people aren't compassionate. —

I ask her why Ireland doesn't declare a housing shortage. She shakes her head. When I ask Nell what the solution is, she looks at me and smiles. — I'll give you my pat answer. Don't ask a prophet for a blueprint. —

IN EASONS, the largest bookstore in Dublin, I find they have Betty Friedan's *The Feminine Mystique*. *Sexual Politics* is banned. They are out of *The Second Sex* which was formerly banned but is available when available. They don't have *The Female Eunuch* in hardback but they may have it when the softback version is released. Shulamith Firestone's *The Dialectic of Sex* they never heard of. As for *Irishwomen, Chains or Change* they don't have it.

It is virtually impossible to get into the post office on Upper O'Connel Street. People jam the street, talking amongst themselves. Irate speakers, their voices cutting through the frenzied atmosphere, tell their audience about the deplorable situation in the north. Part of the crowd responds angrily, their tempers short; while others mill about, listening to conversations, to the speakers, their expressions bewildered, incredulous.
— Murderers, killers, — shouts one outraged speaker. They talk about a deaf mute, a young boy who was killed when a soldier ordered him to halt. En masse, enraged citizens of Belfast turned out for his funeral. Here is where Nell McCafferty's friend died.

That night in Liberty Hall there is a meeting opposing the Forcible Entry Bill, forced internment and the war in Belfast. The poster on the platform states: KILL THE BILL BEFORE IT KILLS FREEDOM. *To Comment, To Protest Freely, To House the Homeless.*

On the platform six men and two women talk among themselves. They represent the trade unions, socialist organizations, a students' group, the Londonderry Civil Rights Organization in Belfast and Irishwomen's Liberation. I introduce myself to June Levine and she takes me to where the feminist group is sitting.

The speakers take their seats on the podium. The first speaker maintains that Parliament has dogmatically refused to recognize the crucial housing shortage. — The Forcible Entry Bill protects the property, the rights of the landowners, but what about the rights of the homeless. Aren't they entitled to decent housing? — Another spokesman is infuriated with the passage in the Forcible Entry Bill which will curtail freedom of the press. — We have little enough say as it is. That isn't enough for them. Now they want to censor what we read. —

We hear a speaker tell us that Parliament has always been indifferent to the problems of the masses, while they pride themselves in being guardians of the minority rich. — When are we going to wake up to the facts? These people have no right to be on private property they say. Where are they to live, I ask? Why should our M.P.'s worry about these so-called trespassers? They go home to their nice warm houses, while hundreds of homeless wander the streets. —

One man talks about internment, the war in Belfast, the never ending negotiations prolonging—the barbarous violence. While homes are burning, Irish men, women and children are dying, our great leaders fly back and forth between Belfast and London. There's no need for them to rush when we all know their homes are safe, their bellies full. Are their families being interned like animals? Who is to speak for us? It's time we did something to stop these injustices. —

Madge Davidson, representing the Londonderry Civil Rights Organization, has made the trip from Belfast to Dublin, in order to attend this meeting. Her impassioned speech draws outcries from the audience. — The city reeks with violence. Nobody is safe. Although everybody knows we are a nonviolent organization, our members are being arrested daily. Today when I left we printed our last newspapers. We're completely without funds. We can't even buy the paper for printing. Our offices have been without lights, without heat for over a week. But I assure you, nothing will stop us. We will print our paper, we will demonstrate, we will continue working until the last person is taken. — As she sits down, an outraged member of the audience rises and maintains that they must continue. Everybody digs into their purses, their pockets so that Madge Davidson will have money when she returns to Belfast that evening.

Derry McDermott from women's liberation speaks about the feminist position on the Forcible Entry Bill. In keeping with their first aim which is 'one family, one house', and as the main force opposing this bill, IWL will continue fighting until the bill is killed. She goes on to say, — The Irishwomen's Liberation Movement stands behind our men. — I turn to Margaret disgustedly. What does she mean behind?

I spot Nell McCafferty standing in the doorway of the hall. After the meeting I move towards her, only to find she's gone. I make arrangements to see June the next day, and go with Derry McDermott and Margaret Kelly to the Paradiso Restaurant. As we wait for our food, Derry asks me if I thought her speech was all right. This is her first time before an audience and she claims she was very nervous. I tell her she appeared self-assured, that her delivery was forceful. — Who wrote the speech Derry? — I ask. She answers she wrote it herself. Why did you say we are behind our men when women's liberation is the main force blocking the bill?

She shrugs, can't explain why she said it. It just seemed natural. I ask if the feminists have aligned themselves with the socialists, who were essentially responsible for the meeting tonight. She replies that it is almost impossible for them to disassociate themselves since so many of their aims are identical. A socialist herself, she would like to see the IWL have their own actions, but feels they need all the support they can get. She points out that IWL may be supporting the socialists' actions, but they in turn were supporting them. For example, when they went to Belfast to purchase contraceptives, the socialist groups, within hours, arranged to have hundreds of their members at the train station in Dublin to show solidarity. She says it is imperative that they receive backing wherever they can get it. This bill must not get through, or it will set the feminists back, not only in the housing situation, but in a free press, free speech. She admits she's aware that the feminists took a back seat at this meeting, but doesn't know what they can do.

— In Ireland it is difficult to separate feminist aims from the politics of the country. Everything is political here. And the politics of Ireland regards women as second class citizens.

She substantiates this statement by pointing out that soon she'll be forced to leave her job. Civil service employees are compelled to resign when they marry. This naturally only applies to women.

Derry has travelled, lived in other countries, which has made her more aware of the inequality women suffer in Ireland. Like Nell McCafferty, she too lived on a *kibbutz* in Israel. Her inspiration was another book. *Exodus.*

Margaret Kelly is married, has one son. She says that since she's a feminist her attitudes have changed, resulting in a more equal relationship at home. Although there isn't any consciousness raising in Dublin, Margaret and Derry, close friends, have one to one CR sessions often. They discuss their feelings, role playing, the influences of the society and the church.

It is 2:30 am when I leave them. The buses have stopped running. The streets are deserted. As we hail a cab for me, they say, — Tell him you're one of the Kennedys. He'll love that. — Their faces smile as I wave from the moving taxi.

JUNE LEVINE

Everybody in favor of abortion is already born

FROM BALLSBRIDGE, I walked to June Levine's office, past the beautiful Presbyterian church on Elgin Road, past elegant homes with new cars parked in front. Past old brownstone homes that look very much like the houses Sean O'Casey describes in his autobiography. A half-hour later I ring the bell at 6 Waterloo Bridge, where the Irishwomen's Liberation Movement is located. In another part of the building I sit in June's office.

— You'll have to forgive me. I can't think of anything but the war. Look at what they're doing to my people. It could tear your heart out. Look at this photo. —

As she scans the paper she gives me bits of information. Her mother, who can trace her family origin to an Ireland centuries ago, converted from Catholicism to Judaism when she married June's father who emigrated to Ireland from Lithuania. She has three brothers, one sister.

June Levine started as a feminist but is now involved politically.
— In a Tory capitalist government, women haven't a chance. In Ireland, you can't separate the government from the church. The government has wooed the church. Here we have divorce Irish style. The women are deserted, abandoned. The priests encourage them to take their husbands back. The men come back and the women become pregnant. The woman is conditioned for centuries to believe her life should be close to the life of the Virgin Mary. Blessed Mother. Virgin. The virgin life is typical of Irish women. She's of no concern before the child comes. She's *his* mother. She reveres *her* sons. *Her* daughters polish the boys' shoes so they'll be ready for Mass. The ghastly thing about living in Ireland is that we have a patriarchal society that seems to be chivalrous but there's actually a lack of chivalry. Women have to be independent and they're terrified. Half never finished school. —

June Levine left school before she was fifteen because there wasn't any money for her to continue. She immediately apprenticed at *The Irish Times,* where she remained for five years. At nineteen, she met her husband, a Canadian who was studying medicine in Dublin. Within six months she married him. The first year she worked for the *Irish Press.* And she gave birth to her first son. For the next six years, while her husband finished his studies, she freelanced and studied.

— My marriage was wonderful. I got excited when I heard his car drive up. — Her husband, a psychiatrist, abandoned her when she herself was a patient in a mental hospital, suffering from endogenous (organic) depression. He claimed he had enough mental disorders to cope with in his professional life. — I thought I had an ideal marriage, but it wasn't real. I had invented the man. —

Up until the time of the marital breakup June was living in Canada with her husband, where she worked as a journalist for the *Winnipeg Free Press* and the dailies; as a sub-editor for the St. Boniface newspaper in Regina. In 1963 she drove ninety miles round trip twice a week to take a literature course in London University in Canada. She had two more children, first a daughter, then a son.

Seven years ago, realizing her marriage was finished, she returned to Ireland. She weighed eighty-five pounds, was depressed, felt responsible for the termination of her marriage. Her sister advised her not to stay in Ireland. But June felt differently. — I love Ireland. I love the people. When I came back, I came home. It's an open air lunatic asylum but I love it. —

As one of the founders of Irishwomen's Liberation, she believes the movement will either swing towards lesbianism or man-hating. She showed me the book *Irish Beauty* which she wrote in 1969 when she was a beauty editor, and was published early in 1971. — I don't know how I could have done that. —

June Levine is aware that her sensuality is a strong part of her life. Yet another part of her rejects this. At the time of this meeting she was sharing her home with a man who is separated from his wife. However, he still sees her publicly for appearances' sake. June knows divorce is impossible in Ireland, but when she asked him if he would get a divorce if he could, he gave her a blunt 'no'. She doesn't want to marry again but his answer infuriated her and she answered him with one word. 'Bastard.'

Last year she had a hysterectomy. It disturbs her that she can't have any more children. She says she loved having them, bringing them up. June is adamant that women have the right to have as many or few children as they wish. But she is just as adamant about abortion. For her, abortion is out of the question. For a half-hour we argued back and forth, but I never made a dent in her thinking. June Levine has read the books, she knows the arguments, but nothing can convince her that abortion is right. In the middle of my impassioned discourse, she turned to me, gave me a funny half smile and said, —Everybody in favor of abortion is already born. —

Then as if nothing were said, — The Irish woman doesn't realize that sex is her trap. She cannot begin to think of the concept of being a full human being, independent of her sexuality and of its exploitation of her. Irish men have a peculiar attitude about sex. Sex is to be saved for marriage. They have sex, feel guilty, go to confession, then back again to sex. Irish men must be the hardest bachelors in the world to pin down. We have the highest number of bachelors in Europe. Irish men are supposed to be the only men in the world that will step over a bunch of Playboy bunnies to get to their beer. —

June has a friend who's a priest. Recently he asked her what he could do for women's liberation. She answered, — Leave them alone. — — Won't you talk about it June? — Her reply, — The woman upstairs has fifteen children. She wants to use the pill. She needs your permission. Will you give it? — No was the priest's answer. June ended the conversation with, — Then there is no dialogue. —

On March 16, 1971, June Levine, Mary Kenny and others took over the *Late Late Show,* a weekly Saturday night talk show. It was the first time Irishwomen's Liberation was brought to the public via TV.

Since then they have picketed for jury service for women, to have them called to serve as men are. They are trying to bring information on contraception to the public, but this is literally impossible, since contraceptive literature is banned. They were successful in bringing the plight of the unmarried mother to the public's attention and in October 1971, the government officially recognized these women, and they now receive children's allowances.

June and I walked to the Pirate's Den Restaurant near Baggot Street. It was a very chilly day and I ordered soup. June said, — I'm sure it's one of those damned packaged soups, like Mother something-or-other. — She turned to the waitress who assured her it wasn't. We ordered our lunch, and discussed the movement in Ireland. I told her I was disturbed that the feminists were more concerned with politics in general rather than sexual politics. She told me she believed this was due to the newness of the movement in Ireland, and that eventually the women will learn to fight exclusively for their own causes.

— Bonnie, before I forget, I called Mary Anderson and told her your feelings on feminism. She's anxious to talk with you. I think you should call her. —

After lunch we went to the Irishwomen's Liberation office where I met a number of feminists who talked enthusiastically about the movement. How did you find out about us, they asked? I told them about the newspaper coverage in the States. Wonderful they said. Where do you go from here? I answered England, Holland, France, Italy and Spain. Listen, say hello to our sisters and tell them we're here. We read that the movement in Italy is pushing for abortion. Wish them luck. Tell them we're next. We discussed WL in America and then turned to the problems of sexism in Ireland.

THE REPUBLIC of Ireland is a country where marriage reigns supreme. The government is married to the church, the church is married to the government, the people are married to the church, the women are married to the men, and the men are married to the pub.

Article 44 of the Constitution gives the Catholic Church a special status. As a result, contraception and abortion are illegal. A woman may be a Protestant or a Jew; still she cannot obtain a divorce in Ireland.

A man may desert his wife, and return when he wishes. He automatically resumes all his marital and parental rights. A woman who deserts immediately forfeits all her rights, her marital home and her children.

The father is the legal guardian of the children and has the sole right to decide on their education, religion and domicile. The government grants a children's allowance, which the father can use without question. However, the mother cannot draw from these savings. The father must consent to an operation on his children. He can have the children placed on his passport without the mother's consent, and take them abroad whenever he wishes, without her permission.

Article 40 of the Irish Constitution promises equal rights, before the law, to all citizens of the Republic of Ireland. Approximately one million, four hundred and thirty-five thousand Irish citizens are women. They are not accorded equal rights. They are not called upon for jury service. A woman may apply, providing she is a householder, but she is blocked by judges and lawyers, who are suspicious of ulterior motives. Only one woman has succeeded in being accepted.

If a wife pays tax on her income, her husband is entitled to the rebate. He is entitled to scrutinize her tax forms, but she is not entitled to see his. He is not required to support her above and beyond what he considers her needs. If she saves from the household money, it is still legally her husband's money, not hers. She cannot claim these savings.

She must have his permission for pledging any credit, almost any kind of financial arrangement, and lastly if she needs a gynecological operation, he must give the ok.

One third of all employees in the Irish Republic are women. Less than 1% are classified amongst the higher professions (doctors, lawyers, etc.), 6% work in administrative, executive and managerial positions. 12% hold positions in the lower professions (teachers, nurses, etc.), 81% work as salespeople, factory workers, clerks, telephone operators, barmaids, domestics and so on.

The average woman in the Irish Republic earns only 54.9% of what the average man earns. It is interesting to note that in 1938 they earned 55.6% of men's wages. In the spring of 1971 the figures for northern Ireland show that women's earnings were 62% of their male counterpart. These figures, published by the Central Statistics Office show that on the average a woman-hour is worth five shillings, three newpence, whereas a man-hour is worth nine shillings, six newpence. There is inequality in the trade unions as well. About two-fifths of all women employees are in trade unions. The figure for men is two-thirds.

The Deserted Wife: It is her obligation to prove that she has made every effort to patch up the marriage. She must further prove that her husband left of his own volition, that in six months she hasn't received any money from him, that she is less than fifty years old and has at least one dependent child. All this to receive public assistance.

Nursery Schools: There are no state or local authority nursery schools. Private nursery schools are too costly for the average worker.

The Widow: A contributory pension is paid to the widow, but only if her husband has paid a required amount of employment contributions; and only if four or more years have elapsed since his entry into insurance. The State considers it a man's responsibility to provide for his widow. If he has not provided, she must go through a means test to receive money. The money allotted guarantees her a life of poverty.

Education: It is compulsory for boys' schools to provide a full course. Not so in girls' schools, where only 10% provide mathematics. This automatically disqualifies the girls from professions such as medicine, science, architecture, etc. In 1968, only 161 girls took honours math at Leaving Certificate. The figure was just under 2,000 for boys. Corresponding numbers for physics were: 91 girls and 1,452 boys. In 1969, University College Dublin had 4 girls majoring in agriculture, 15 in dentistry, 16 studying veterinary medicine out of a total of 3,494 female students. The rest went for their Bachelor of Arts.

I looked over clippings of the feminist movement in Ireland and realized the movement here is unique, because so many of the feminists are journalists. The editors are not particularly happy about this, but since journalists are unionized there isn't much they can do other than gripe.

COLETTE O'NEIL

So many self-made martyrs

AT THE IWL headquarters I met Colette O'Neil, a vivacious woman who was never at a loss for words.

Colette, June and I walked to Searson's bar on Baggot Street where we sat at a table and ordered pints. Colette, twenty-eight years old, was the woman who marched up to the Customs officers on May 22 and read the Constitution. She stands up and dramatically re-enacts the scene. — Article 44 of the Constitution claims freedom of conscience as a human right to every citizen. —

Colette O'Neil was positive that all the feminists connected with bringing contraceptives to Dublin would be arrested, but she didn't care. — It's drummed into your head you're going to die if you take the pill. God will strike you. —

She'd hoped I'd brought contraceptives with me. Four children is all she wants, and she's petrified that without contraceptives she may get caught. Travelling from Dublin to Belfast is now impossible. Why hadn't I brought contraceptives with me? Why hadn't I brought women's liberation buttons? — Why didn't you? — she asks. I catch a glimpse of my reflection in the pub mirror and wonder if just bringing me was a mistake.

Colette grew up in a corporation house, a house subsidized by the government. She received primary school education, had to quit when she was fourteen. She was brought up as a religious Catholic.

Her husband runs a social gossip magazine and disapproves of Colette's connection with the feminist movement. That she is an active member is no secret. She manages to get her picture in the newspaper whenever there is an action. Her husband's biggest complaint is that she may affect his business, his magazine. Colette does not discuss her husband or her children, but women. — So many self-made martyrs walking around. They call themselves women. They want to be slaves to themselves and their husbands. They think they're martyrs. That's typical of Irish women. I say to the women, leave the lot, leave the children to the men. —

She believes the feminists must fight for contraception, and that abortion will naturally follow. — Women are slaves to their bodies without it. — She admits that until recently she never connected contraception with women's liberation. — But how can you be liberated without it? — She is aware that changes must come from the individual but is positive that these changes will not have any impact unless feminists actively fight for equality. — There must be equality for women in every sense; in mind, in body. She must be able to think for herself and make her own decisions. To choose what she wants, instead of allowing others to choose for her. —

She claims that the movement would be more effective if it stressed education. — We need education and communication with one another. The movement will lie dormant until we see and talk with other women and begin to realize a common experience. There's so much to be researched in Ireland. Politically we're attacking the system for the first time, what it stands for and is supposed to stand for. — Colette looks at me and grins. — Martyrs are on their way out. — Before I get a chance to ask why that remark is directed at me she turns serious. — We're 52% of the population. How many realize we have the power in our hands? —

Moira Woods joins us. She is one of the original members of IWL, a medical doctor and the mother of six children. Like June, she is adamant that abortion is wrong and contends that she cannot consider this a feminist aim. She is in complete agreement with every other feminist goal, but to her abortion is morally wrong. As we argue back and forth our dialogue is periodically interrupted by a woman at another table who keeps baiting June. Moira seems unduly agitated. In the middle of an exchange, the woman comes to our table and demands June speak with her. Moira is infuriated by the interruption. She explains to the woman that she specifically took time out of her busy schedule to be with us. June promises her she'll speak with her shortly, but the woman refuses any excuses. Exasperated, June and Moira join her at her table.

I ask Colette why Moira seemed so upset. Was it because of our disagreement on abortion? She says no and reveals that Moira not only has her medical practice and her children to care for, but her husband is in the hospital, critically ill with cancer. Finally, the three return.

The woman tells me she made the mistake of leaving her husband, taking her son and daughter with her. She doesn't want to return to him, but even if she did, she couldn't. Her husband, a wealthy man, refused to support her. Her son decided to go back to his daddy, who could give him all the material things his mother could not. This woman still had her daughter, although she had no means of supporting her. She could work, as she was well educated, but was so overwrought work was impossible. She wanted a divorce, but this was out of the question. She wanted her son back, but even this wasn't allowed. She thought of running away to England with her daughter, but was petrified she'd be found and brought back.

Not long ago, completely distraught she moved to a hotel with her daughter. The owner, an old man, offered to help. Apparently his help was not the help she sought. — He practically raped me and all the time

I had to act sweet and pretend I didn't know what was happening. —
Somebody questioned her word rape. — Well, he didn't actually do anything. How could he? We were in the hall. But he kept touching me saying you poor thing. You're going through a terrible time. What can I do for you? And all the time he was trying to get me in his room. They're beasts. They don't see anything but themselves. — Her eyes burned. — My father said I could do anything, then I married the wrong man and I can't do a damned thing. I'm a professional nobody. —

JUNE'S FRIEND drove me back to the office where I picked up some material and took a bus for O'Connel Street. I wanted to go to a movie and relax. I walked into the Gresham Hotel where John Behan's sculpture was displayed. Against the wall were angular metal shapes, bordering on the abstract, Don Quixote-ish in character. They were interesting, much to my liking, and for me very un-Irish.

While looking for the coffee shop, I was found by an Indian Indian. — Are you lost? — he asked me. — No, I'm not. — — Oh then did you think I was lost? — That I refused to answer. He persisted. — What made you think I was lost? Would you join me for a drink? —

I explained that I had an appointment, not mentioning that my appointment would go on in half an hour and if memory is accurate, it was called *The Raging Moon.* He smiled at me. — Do you work here? — — I'm writing a book. — — How interesting, — he replied. — And what is your subject? — — Women's liberation. — Smiling, he informed me he was most interested in that subject and then, — Would you be so kind to join me for a drink? I only ask ten minutes of your time. It is a joy for me to have a conversation with an intelligent woman. —

We ordered and he spoke softly, telling me he was a professor, came from New Delhi, he liked Ireland. How nice I was a writer. With the social amenities finished, he turned to the main business of the day. — That's a woman's liberation button isn't it? What is your position on sex? —

— Which one? —

Ha ha, he laughed. — Don't you think it necessary? I find sex most important. I like you. You're very intelligent, very lovely. — Wow, my intelligence must be oozing from my pores. I had hardly said ten words. Professor continued in his soft voice, sipping his drink, his sensuality much louder than his voice. He assured me he liked sex, he would like to have sex with me. He understood I had an appointment but wouldn't I break it, and if I wouldn't, any time would be fine. How marvellous for two intelligent people to meet. Ah I thought, Spinoza and fucking.

My Indian friend was getting all worked up. He reached for my hand. As he held it, I gazed into his eyes and told him I hated sex, especially with birdbrains who espoused superintellect. — Professor, the feminist movement is not handing out free sex this year. I would suggest you read some of our literature and enrich your otherwise unenriched brain. —

This sensitive creature became very upset, not by my refusal but because he was afraid somebody might hear me. His dilated pupils darted from table to table. — I'm known here. They know me. Please speak softly. What will they think? —

I left this cultured Professor at the table, where he was doing his best to act nonchalant, while his body slumped in the seat. Cuing up for *The Raging Moon* I pacified my own rage with a chocolate bar. This man undoubtedly believed that his set of organs gave him the right to propose jumping in the sack and then had the audacity to criticize my NO. Speak softly he said. Softly? I should have kicked him in the balls.

CONSTANCE BEHAN

It's a medieval religion

I TOOK two buses and walked on Bobins Mill Road to get to the Dublin Art Foundry. The area is a slum. There I saw children, not more than babies themselves, wheel their baby brothers and sisters. I walked with two little girls who were pushing a carriage with their three month old brother. They were very proud of him, showed him off to me. Apparently he was the sixth. The oldest girl, who was in charge, was seven years old and already playing mommy. The flimsy houses looked like the cardboard houses we built when I was a child. Inside the doorways, in the hallways leading up narrow stairs, toys spilled over entrances of crumbling stone. Mothers and children looked out of first floor windows, so close to the ground, they didn't have to go out the door but just step out of the windows.

The Dublin Art Foundry was at the dead end of the street. A tremendous steel door dominated the stone wall of the foundry. Constance and John Behan wiped their hands on their aprons and greeted me warmly. They had just finished firing sculpture.

Constance Behan is secretary of the Independent Artists, a group of professional painters and artists who have an annual exhibition in Dublin. As late as 1960, indigenous Irish art was not represented in the Irish exhibitions. Thirty women and men got together and decided that rather than look abroad or to America, they would do their own work, have their own gallery. They put the thirty to forty percent commission, normally given to gallery owners, back into their own gallery, making it a cooperative venture. There they have poetry readings, play readings, as well as displaying the art. The Independent Artists are mainly socialists involved in politics. Other artists believe that art should be above politics. But according to Constance, it is impossible for artists to divorce themselves from the politics of their country.

Constance Short Behan was born in County Armagh, sixty miles north of Dublin. She has three brothers. Money was saved for the boys to go to the university. — I accepted it. — From thirteen to eighteen she went to a convent school. — That should be done away with because it leads to terrible confusion. — At fourteen she became a *Pioneer,* which is a total abstinence association. She laughs. — The slogan was abstain for the honor and glory of God. —

For Constance the facts of life were all very vague, — really way out there. You know, touch me knickers. — I learn that knickers are underpants. She says she never heard words like lesbian until she was nineteen and living in London. After that, whenever she heard lesbian, she thought of two horns.

Constance came from the country to Dublin when she was eighteen, — totally unprepared, — in her own words. She took a course in advertising, publicity, worked at an advertising agency. — I was a commercial artist. I had my doubts about many things before but I didn't think freely. It was a progression. I lost my virginity at nineteen-and-a-half. We're so conservative in Ireland that it would horrify people to think of sex before marriage. You're unclean. The church is responsible. We should try to get women away from the apron strings of the church. Rosary beads are their aids in childbirth.

— I believe in marriage because I'm old-fashioned. I have almost two thousand years of Catholicism behind me. Our preoccupation with the past is ridiculous. — Yet, she and John married in the State Registry Office on Kildare Street, rather than in church. She describes herself as a former Catholic.

Constance Behan lost a baby recently, says she nearly went out of her mind. — John had this foundry so I was lucky that I could work. — Her daughter, two-and-a-half, goes to nursery school. Recently her daughter was ill and she stayed home with her. I ask if she feels she could do this if she were employed elsewhere. She tells me she is aware that her freedom is directly connected to her choice of husband and the fact that he has the foundry. Other freedoms will not be hers or her contemporaries' until feminist aims are achieved.

— Women are paid to be baby machines. They get children's allowances, yet they can't collect the money. And it irritated me that I couldn't get a passport without John's signature. Did you know the father must sign for the children's allowance? We have tongue-in-cheek Catholicism here. The cycle regulator, which everybody knows is the pill is one example.

— The church is a capitalism. They own the best land in the country, the best homes. They have to keep women in submission. It's unreal. It's a medieval religion. —

Constance handed one of the workers money, asked him to buy bread, cheese and milk so we could have tea. She took me around the foundry, showed me some of John's sculpture, the molds, explained that she is a metal worker, working on the castings until they are finished products.

— I can't say I'm truly liberated because I'm not. I could never be as liberated as you, because your society is more liberated. I don't believe in God, but I must admit to having Catholic influences. Our conflict is trying to get out of this.

— You have a womb. What is it for? I want babies. I need babies. Why are we made the way we are? Why do we have breasts? Why do I have to give up things to be something. I think every woman needs a baby. Maybe I'm centuries behind the times, but this is what I honestly feel. —

John and three of the workers joined us. Six of us sat at a wobbly table, with wood shavings, eating bread and cheese on pieces of paper, drinking huge cups of strong hot tea.

MARY ANDERSON

It was classified as a mortal sin

MARY ANDERSON, journalist, met me in her office at the *Irish Independent*. After a few minutes there, with constant interruptions, she suggested we go to a pub. We ordered shandys and talked.

Intimidated by her own lack of experience, her recent hostility towards men, she appeared intense, angry. — It's impossible for change in this country. We're brought up on love. Love of country, church, husband, children. If you've been brought up on this, it's difficult to tell everybody that they're wrong, you're right. I can't do this until I'm educated outside of the country, away from the influence of the church, school friends, family and the politics of republicans. —

Mary Anderson was not born in Ireland. Her father, once an Irish republican, became a communist. Born in Ireland, married in Ireland, he decided to move to England by himself. There he met and lived with a woman who bore Mary. She says her father was idealistic, stubborn, proud, arrogant, — and I admired him tremendously. — When Mary was thirteen he died and her mother decided to move to Ireland, a country she'd never seen but had romanticized. — Romantic, — Mary snickers, — I'm considered illegitimate. You don't know what it's like to be illegitimate in Ireland. —

According to Mary, she had a traditional family life, traditional if you're a Catholic. — The first thing you learn is Hail Mary, Mother of God. Mother. Female. Child. —

In a private Catholic school run by nuns, sex education was classified as *The Formation of Chastity in the Diocese of Dublin*. A student in this school she states, — Eighteen year old girls were told not to use tampax because it would make you interfere with yourself. Imagine, interfere with yourself. It was classified as a mortal sin. —

She talks about the poverty in Ireland, particularly the poverty of women, asserting a social revolution is essential for women's liberation. — You can't discuss the function of a woman's body and mind, how she thinks and feels. You can't analyze the indoctrination she's had right from the beginning when she doesn't have the basic needs. — She continues telling me the basic need is 'one family, one house'.

I retort. — I'm sure you know I've argued about this demand with everyone. Your situation in Ireland is the worst in Europe, next to Spain, so your fight will be the hardest. Feminists are contesting the family structure and you're fighting to maintain it. Why? Let the socialists fight for housing. As long as you press for equality for people and not women, you'll continue being linked with the socialists and their goals, which have nothing to do with feminism. —

She nods, tells me that at a recent meeting of IWL when she suggested they educate the women they replied, fine, let's educate them on housing. — I think it's only now that we realize we're going about women's liberation in the wrong way, that we're not a feminist movement yet. —

Mary Anderson joined IWL a few months after it was formed. She'd read about the feminist movement in the States three years ago, was pleased that it had spread throughout Europe. We discussed the International Feminist movement, the difference in the Irish movement but somehow we kept going back to housing, social reforms, socialism.

QUESTION: If you get social reforms, if you manage to change the system, will that alter women's position in Ireland?
ANSWER: No. Women's position will never be altered until we get rid of the church.
QUESTION: How?
ANSWER: A social revolution.
QUESTION: Then who will control?
ANSWER: The socialists.
QUESTION: Then will the status of women change?
ANSWER: No.
QUESTION: Now what?

Mary turns to me and reflects. — That's why I wanted to talk with you. There are feminists who are fighting for feminist aims but we've had no political experience and the socialists win in every debate. The rank and file have come up through labor unions, most are socialists. — Her views have changed since joining IWL and she too is more politically aware, not only of the politics of the country, but of sexism that is constantly practiced and fostered.

As we talk, a man enters the bar, nods to Mary, who gives him a begrudging look. She says she liked him once, can't like any man now that she understands the damage done to women in the female-male relationship. Once again, she mentions leaving the country, but adds that she's tied to Ireland as long as her mother remains. — I don't think women's liberation will work in Ireland until we've broken away from nationalism and study the International Movement. —

After the *Late Late Show* where the feminists got a countrywide platform, the women arranged to have a public meeting. On April 16 they agreed that Irishwomen's liberation must become a reality. A number of women were very excited when Kate Millett offered to speak at their first meeting. They took a vote and it was decided they wouldn't have Ms. Millett. Their reason: What she had to say wouldn't have any relevance within the context of Irish society. Mary Anderson was one of the feminists who wanted Kate Millett. However, she understands why she was turned down. — Kate Millett presupposes we've read Miller, Mailer and Lawrence, and she further presupposes we've analyzed the books. Not only are the books banned in Ireland, but women don't read that much. They're educated to read romantic fiction. —

Her secretary enters the bar with a visiting male reporter who has an appointment with her. She says in a minute and they go into the other room.

Mary believes, without a doubt, that the movement has made people uncomfortable, but it has also made them more aware of women's problems. She maintains too much emphasis is placed on the married woman, the mother, the widow. That feminism in Ireland is mainly concerned with home life. — To use the word spinster is an insult in Ireland. —

I ask Mary Anderson what she writes on women's liberation in her column and am told she isn't allowed to write about the movement. I mention June Levine, Nell McCafferty, others. — I'm considered too involved. My boss objects to my being in the movement. He thinks I'm a hothead. — Her secretary motions to her, tells her she's way behind schedule. Mary stands up and continues. — Look, I can't be fired because I'm in the union but I have been threatened. — She says goodbye and goes into the next room to the waiting reporter.

I WALKED to St. Stephens Green, sat on the grass and watched the children play. What are my sons doing now? I moved from the park to O'Connel Street where I took the #8 bus to Dun Loughaire, a forty minute ride to the Irish Sea. Sitting on a rock alone, I saw on the horizon the ferry that would take me from Ireland to Hollyhead and on to London.

The sea lashed against the rocks, a grey green sea that spilled mounds of white foam over the rocks, only to return to the sea. The sky was a cold grey. I sat, pulling my coat over me, drawn by the desolate sea, the isolation I felt sitting there.

Motherhood. So important in Ireland. I could hear Nell McCafferty's words, — sure we love them, but there's something more to us than kids. — Months before I left the States, a friend of mine asked if she could interview me. A psychologist and feminist, she was writing a book on mothers, why they became mothers, how they felt when they conceived, etc. I sat in her living room answering her questions and then the question, if you could do it over again would you have children. And my answer no I wouldn't and the tremendous pain I felt when I heard my words. Quickly I added, but I love them, they're wonderful. I was annoyed that I felt so compelled to assure her of my love.

Would I have them? I remember the words, women who don't have children are selfish, they live for themselves, they're incapable of giving.

So I became one of the unselfish ones. After six years of marriage my former husband and I decided to have a child. Four months later, without a sign of pregnancy, I figured something was wrong with me. Believing the erroneous tale that when you have sex for years without trying to conceive, you can't conceive, I rushed to the doctor. When the examination was over I blurted out, — What's wrong with me? — Not a damned thing was the answer. If you don't become pregnant within three months, I'd suggest your husband get a thorough checkup.

Within three months, an egg and sperm connected. Unexpectedly the sole interest in me is my stomach, whether it's high or low, round or not so round. People who formerly looked at me as that selfish career woman now see me as one of them. Hands I never shook pat my stomach. — My it's big. Ooooo, I felt it kick. Doesn't that make you feel marvellous and terribly creative. — They are suddenly concerned with my diet, my exercise, my health, my sleep.

Bets are placed on its arrival date. Rings with strings attached swing above my stomach. To the right it's a boy, to the left a girl. Bets are placed on its sex. What are you going to name it was a question that drove me wild. I finally announced if it's a girl, Chloe Lowy (my married name which I promptly returned when I divorced) or Louie Lowy if it's a boy. That was the end of that question.

Finally hatching day came and Craig was born. Now let's look at the new mother honestly. You give birth, a little stranger is brought to you, cute as hell (mine was anyhow) and you've convinced yourself motherhood is natural. Only to discover you're clumsy holding him (he moves), your fingers become pin cushions when diapering him (again he moves), you're afraid you'll break his arms when you put on a shirt. (How come he moves so much?) But within a short time what is supposedly natural is learned. And for three to five days in the hospital you are the center of attention. You receive flowers, candy, perfume, bath powder, bath oil, books, magazines, all the modern day offerings for the mother of the new messiah.

Now you're home and the interest in you has switched to *him.* Isn't he lovely. What a bright little face. He looks like the mother, the father, like Great-Grandpa Bluh. He couldn't possibly look like himself. And while all this talking is going on, your fun begins. Between feedings and burpings, you're dunking diapers in the toilet bowl. (How can that little thing have so many bowel movements?) You sterilize the bottles, make the formula, another feeding. Clothes to wash, meals to cook, house to clean. God forbid the neighbors should see a dirty home.

After approximately three weeks you sigh with relief as you enter the outside world with your baby, only to find you're forced back into the inside world. — How long does he sleep? . . . Does he see yet? . . . What's his formula? . . . Is he on demand? — To this one I answer, no I'm on demand. — Does he have a lot of b.m.'s? Mine does. Does he? — Tomorrow I answer, I'll keep count and let you know.

Out there, you're with women just like yourself because other women are working way out there, in the world you left when you became a mother. The discussions are utterly fascinating. Every little burp is talked about in minute detail. You ask yourself, is this what I went to college for?

At night the sperm carrier comes home from that other world, which is his birthright, and you eagerly grab at him for news. — What's happening out there? Really . . . really. Tell me more, more, more. — From a singer, an actress, a feature writer I become a mother. From an engineer, the father remains an engineer.

Conversations with others become almost impossible. Your limited life gives you little to contribute, so you think, and you become convinced your mind has stopped functioning. You're dull, a bore. And the stimulating conversations on the street continue. They spread to shops, to other homes, to parties where the men gather on one side, the women on the other. You're asked, what does your husband do? Does your son walk yet? Does he talk? What does he say? Is he toilet trained? Nobody asks what I'm doing. They don't have to. I'm still dunking diapers in the toilet bowl.

They segregate us into rose-covered ghettoes, put us in competition with one another with such statements as — She didn't let herself go to pot after she had a baby . . . marvellous how she manages to keep such a spotless home and take such good care of her child too. . . . We're in competition as cooks, housekeepers, mothers. Even our children are pitted against each other. Reference is made to all the menial tasks, to surface appearances, but never once do they mention our minds or personal achievements. That's the private property of the husbands, the sperm carriers, who shoot their load and continue on with their lives.

No dreams for us, no wide horizons. And if we dare express dissatisfaction, we're told women are impossible, unreasonable, who could live with them. Well the truth is, you don't live with us. You feed off us, you suck us dry. As for my children, and my answer but I love them, they're wonderful. Yes I love them, but the problem is nobody bothered to tell me I should love myself too.

Sitting here in the dark of night, with stars and moon framing the angry Irish Sea, these words lash out at me, — Bonnie, you've been duped. We've all been duped. —

THE NEXT day I call June Levine to say goodbye. I am greeted with, — Come to my house. I have a country girl living with me, an unwed mother. I think it's important that you speak with her. —

On the bus I sit next to Alison Kaye. She is a teacher, a handweaver, and has the reddest hair I've ever seen. Alison Kaye, single, in her twenties, is not from Ireland. She emigrated from Cornwall, England two years ago, and says she loves Ireland, plans to stay. — Either you fit in here or you don't. People in Ireland take the time to talk. They didn't in England. —

As the bus stops on O'Connel Street, Alison tells me she must catch a bus and meet her friends. I rush along the street with her. — I have mixed feelings about women's liberation. You hear all the wrong things and these things put me off. Things such as bra burning and the militant attitude. There are women who would join but they're afraid because of the wrong publicity. I should go to a meeting. It's not fair to criticize unless you know. —

She believes in equal pay and would like to see divorce legislation in Ireland. It disturbs her that if she ever gets married in Ireland she couldn't get a divorce. — We don't have rights here. Of course it bothers me. It's too easy not to think about these things when it doesn't affect you. —

Alison is equally unhappy about contraception which was available in England but illegal in her new country. — I have mixed feelings about abortion. In certain cases, yes it should be permitted but I think you could be too lenient with it. It must be a bad experience to go through. —

The bus driver tells her he's leaving in two minutes. She places one foot inside the bus. The bus driver, amused with the scene, asks me if I'd like his opinion.

Alison continues — Women's liberation has a left wing feeling. It's socialism in a sense. I think there are so many problems it must be connected with socialism. I should read more of the women's liberation books. I've read magazine and newspaper articles on the subject but I haven't really been influenced because I have thought of these things before. But now I feel I want to know more facts about the actual injustices. —

As the driver starts the motor Alison yells out, — Oh yes I did read *Irishwomen, Chains or Change* and yes, I will go to a meeting. — We wave from both sides of the bus as Alison Kaye, new emigrant leaves and I run for the 47B bus and more June Levine.

— TAKE THE 47B bus to Rathfarmers, beyond the yellow house. Get off at the first stop after the tuning fork. — The tuning fork? I don't understand. — It doesn't matter. Tell the bus driver. He'll know. —

I sat in the living room with June and her sister-in-law Maureen. Her son Michael and his friends rehearsed their rock group in another room. The unwed mother came in with her child and quickly left to buy groceries. June told me she was glad I came because she was dissatisfied with her interview and had more to say.

— If you compare the pace of life here to that of America, you'll see the way of life here breeds laziness into people, so it's easy for a woman to be lazy. When you're in a society where everything is active, it's easier to move. —

I asked why she voted against Kate Millett. — I voted against her because I felt it was much too fast for Ireland. If somebody got up and said your body is your own they wouldn't understand. They wouldn't accept it. I want to say I think Kate Millett is superb and I would go anywhere just to hear her speak. —

I question divorce, tell her I understand Irish people have received divorces in England. She agrees but explains you must be a resident of England for three years, that only the rich can afford this. June Levine, who is divorced discusses her chance of marriage in Ireland. — If I were to meet a single man here, the chances of his marrying me at the registry is remote. We have a famous saying in Ireland, 'You can take the man out of the church, but you can't take the church out of the man'. The marriage to the church is as unsatisfactory as the marriage of the woman and man. —

June would like more organization in IWL; study groups, sub-committees to handle different aims of feminism. To her, consciousness raising is most important. Yet she admits that when they tried it she herself couldn't speak, only cry. For the past six months she's tried unsuccessfully to get CR started but believes Irish women aren't ready for this experience.

— I could use women to lean on. I can't get that support from a man. He can't understand what he's already done to me. —

Maureen Levine turned to me, — I think women's liberation is the greatest thing since sliced bread. — She's not a member, heard about IWL when June became one of the founders. She claims she would like to join but she's shy. Contraception is important and she would like to speak about it but doesn't because she can't speak publicly.

Maureen has been married for three-and-a-half years. She is on the pill, which she got from a Jewish doctor. As a Catholic, she had to get special dispensation from the church when she married her husband, a Jew. She plans to bring up her children as Catholics. — It's as handy to bring them up Catholic as anything else. As a matter of fact easier in Ireland. —

She wouldn't hesitate to divorce if she were unhappy but adds,
— If Norman and I were divorced tomorrow, the first thing I would do is leave this country. —

Maureen is a secretary and claims she would like to work after she has children but points out that it would depend on circumstances. She believes that happiness is most important but when I asked her to define happiness she couldn't answer. However, she insists the way things are, much of a woman's happiness is related to the man she's with. — I think a woman is a wonderful creature and they put up with a hell of a lot from a man. Men are selfish. Their lives revolve around themselves. —

We discussed lesbianism which is rarely mentioned in Ireland. June joined the conversation. — Last year I was charitable and kind about lesbians, but lately I think if the ultimate goal is to have children and there aren't children, what would be the difference. I think eventually I will become asexual and find women amongst my best friends. —

Maureen complained she was taxed more because she's married. — We should be allowed to take home more of our salaries. The majority of women work because they have to, not because they want to. —

During much of the dialogue, Maureen's husband would enter the room and leave. One time he told me I needed his opinion because surely women didn't understand anything about women. He did concede that men didn't know much about men either. Finally he refused to leave and asked his sister, — What do you want to be free of June? —

JUNE: I want to be free of male oppression.
NORMAN: I would believe that of anybody but you. Nobody could ever oppress you from the time you were born.
JUNE: In a male society, they decide my potentiality.
NORMAN: What fields have you ever decided on where you were oppressed?
JUNE: I've been oppressed as a human being which is the worst oppression. Can you buy a part of a man's life? Yet you steal the whole of a woman's.
ME: Norman, would you like to be a woman?
NORMAN: No. Men have more physical strength than a woman so I'm glad I'm a man. I enjoy the physical strength. But I always regard the man as the weaker sex because he regards the woman as the weaker sex and any man who feels that is an idiot.
JUNE: That's only a sexual thing. When a woman loses her teeth, her hair, her body, where is her strength?
ME: What do you mean by weaker sex anyhow?
NORMAN: I don't know. I bloody well don't.

PEGGY O'CONNELY

I didn't want to become pregnant

PEGGY O'CONNELY* and her baby daughter live with June temporarily. She is an unmarried mother who tells me she will soon marry the man who fathered her child. Peggy is extremely shy, does not speak unless spoken to, so I am forced to ask questions.

BONNIE: Why didn't you marry?
PEGGY: Because we didn't have enough money.
BONNIE: Are you treated badly because you're an unwed mother?
PEGGY: You could say that.
BONNIE: If there had been contraceptives, would you have used them?
PEGGY: No I don't think so. People want to enjoy themselves and not take responsibility.
BONNIE: Do you believe in planning your family?
PEGGY: Only by the rhythm method.
BONNIE: How about women who have children every year?
PEGGY: I guess I believe in contraception for women who'll have children every year. I didn't want to become pregnant but when I was, I was glad I was having the child.
BONNIE: How would you feel if you had twelve?
PEGGY: If I could support them I wouldn't mind. If they were happy and I was happy.
BONNIE: What if you couldn't support them?
PEGGY: Then I would try not to have them.
BONNIE: Would you take a cycle regulator?
PEGGY: Yes.
BONNIE: You know that's a birth control pill.
[Peggy looks at me quizzically]
Would it bother you?
PEGGY: No, not really.
BONNIE: You mean if the church says it's all right you would use them?
PEGGY: Yes, if the church says it's all right.
BONNIE: If the church said you couldn't use it, would you still use it?
PEGGY: Yes.

BONNIE: Peggy, you said you didn't believe in contraception.
PEGGY: I didn't but now since the baby is born, I think differently.
BONNIE: How many children would you like to have?
PEGGY: About six.
BONNIE: Why six?
PEGGY: I like children.
BONNIE: If you could give two children a good education why not have two?
PEGGY: I'd like six.
BONNIE: Can the man you're going to marry support six?
PEGGY: He thinks he can only support two or three.
BONNIE: Where's your future husband?
PEGGY: In another city.
BONNIE: Do you get support from the government?
PEGGY: I get over fifty newpence a month [$1.25] children's allowance and I get money from the father of the baby.
BONNIE: Did you work before?
PEGGY: Yes, as a cook and waitress.
BONNIE: How much schooling have you had Peggy?
PEGGY: I went to primary school.
BONNIE: Did you want to go further?
PEGGY: No.
BONNIE: If you weren't getting married, what would you do?
PEGGY: I'd get a job if I could, and I'd keep the baby with me.
BONNIE: Would you have wanted the child even if you weren't getting married?
PEGGY: No.
BONNIE: Do you believe in abortion for any reason?
PEGGY: No I don't.
BONNIE: If your life were in danger?
PEGGY: Yes I would have it.
BONNIE: If you were healthy and had nine, ten children?
PEGGY: No I wouldn't.
BONNIE: Peggy, is love enough for children?
PEGGY: No you have to have means to support it.
BONNIE: Do you mean food and clothing?
PEGGY: Yes and an education.
[At this point June entered, sat down and listened]
BONNIE: University?

PEGGY: Well I haven't thought of that yet.

BONNIE: What do you think of women's liberation?

PEGGY: I think it's good they're fighting for women's rights. If women don't get up and fight nobody will fight for them.

BONNIE: Peggy, God teaches you love, isn't that so?

PEGGY: Yes.

BONNIE: Do you think that means loving yourself too?

PEGGY: Yes.

JUNE: Let me talk to Peggy. She's inhibited with you and she knows me well. She trusts me. Peggy, you enjoy being held and loved. Do you enjoy the sex part?

[Peggy looks bewildered]

BONNIE: Peggy, I think June is saying that sex is not just for having children, but for pleasure as well. Then why can't you have pleasure and carefully plan your family?

PEGGY: I suppose I could.

BONNIE: If I were to say you should take the pill now and have pleasure in sex and only have two children what would you do?

PEGGY: I'd take it.

BONNIE: If I were to say the opposite?

PEGGY: I'd use my conscience.

JUNE: Oh really Bonnie, she's just saying what she thinks you want to hear. Peggy, please tell her what you really feel. There are no right and wrong answers.

PEGGY: I am saying the truth. I would use my conscience.

JUNE: And would you take the pill?

PEGGY: Yes.

JUNE: [smiles at Peggy, her expression unbelieving]
Peggy, you know you wouldn't take the pill. We've talked about this before.

PEGGY: I've been thinking a lot June . . . about what you and your friends have said.

BONNIE: Peggy, do you believe in divorce?

PEGGY: Yes I do. I think if you're married and unhappy, why go through the rest of your life unhappy when life is so short.

BONNIE: Would you have sex if you were divorced?

PEGGY: Yes I would.

BONNIE: Would you marry again?

PEGGY: If I loved the man I would.

BONNIE: Peggy if I asked these questions a year ago, would you have answered the same way?
PEGGY: No. I never thought about any of these things then. But I think no.

June leaves the room. I put my pad down. Peggy and I sit and talk. She feels freer when I'm not writing. She talks about children, then looks at me, her face sad. — Maybe abortion is good. God couldn't have put children here to suffer so much. —

MAUREEN ENTERS the living room with a friend. She tells me she's decided to join IWL. The phone rings and June yells out it's Colette. I take the receiver, say goodbye. June is in the kitchen cooking a mixed grill. The man she's living with complains that she does too much. Aside from IWL she helps the squatters, works with drug addicts. June leaves to answer the phone and comes back very upset. Moira Woods' husband has just died of cancer.

By now there are eleven of us. We eat in shifts. June's friend offers to drive me to my rooming house and then to Dun Loughaire. When June who is exhausted and upset offers to see me off, I ask her not to. Relieved, she says she'll stay home and get much needed sleep.

At my guesthouse my landlady helps me pack and kisses me goodbye. At 10:00 pm I wave to June's friend and board the ferry.

We sat up on deck until 2:00 am; a young man whose name I've forgotten, his girlfriend and me. In the bitter cold we sat, like painted statues unable to move. While he played the guitar and sang I searched my bag for my ski socks. Jean said in New York, — Ski socks? In Europe? In the summer? —

We watched Ireland slip away, or was it us, and at 2:00 am we went into a boat that I'm sure resembled the refugee boats of the early 1900s. We stepped over people; old, young, babies crying, children whining. No seat for me. I took my bag and somebody else's bag and my typewriter. I bunched up my coat for a pillow and stretched out in the aisle.

In the morning I stepped over sleeping bodies to stand on deck and watch the sun come up. The mountains still grey and white with early morning sleep joined the sea. The sky moved in grey rushes. Slowly rising from the mountains was a hesitant light yellow sun. The sky turned from grey and white to pink and blue. The gulls and sea moved to a morning song.

ENGLAND

LONDON

I ARRIVED at Euston Station early in the morning, checked my bag and took the tubes for the bed and breakfast houses suggested in *Europe on $5.00 a Day* by Hope and Arthur Frommer.

In New York City, where I was born and raised, the subway was my means of transportation. I'd put my coin in the slot, go through the turnstile and move in the direction of my subway train. Other kids sometimes put the coin in and two bodies would press together and go through for the price of one. Some would run like crazy and sneak under the turnstile.

In the London Tubes you put your coin in the machine with the direction printed on it and out pops a ticket. You pay for the length of your ride. Before leaving the tubes you put your ticket in a machine that eats it. This means you can't ride all day on the tubes as you can in the New York subway system and you can't go for free.

Although I've spent more than half my life in New York, I still get lost on the subways. This is virtually impossible on the London tubes. On the N.Y. subways you psyched yourself up for the big push during the rush hour and you either pushed with everybody else or stood there watching your train leave without you. In the London tubes one cues up moves in an orderly manner into the train. Sitting in my seat I was faced with newspapers attached to bodies. These newspapers were replaced with faces only seconds before the individuals departed from the train.

At Sussex Gardens I walked past row upon row of bed and breakfast houses. For an hour-and-a-half I went from street to street, area to area in search of a single room.

Dear Arthur and Hope:

Sussex Gardens was full up. The incomparable Cartwright Gardens likewise. Russell Square; you must be joking. As for Belgrave Gardens; forget it. So I went to Kings Cross Station (less expensive in your book) and I hope you won't mind my saying it was not less expensive and for more expensive I was thrilled to find a room to share.

The owner of the bed and breakfast house told me there was a slight chance that by evening she might have a single room. I walked to the Kings Cross Station and took the tubes to Piccadilly Circus.

London is an alive bustling city that is both cosmopolitan and small town in atmosphere. People rush to and fro, their eyes pointing straight ahead. Yet when you ask for directions they politely stop, and go out of their way to be helpful. The conversation ends there and the person rushes off. If there is a curiosity about the foreigner it is rarely shown in the reserved Londoner. Walking from Piccadilly Circus to Soho, to Carnaby Street, to Regent Street, Bond Street, Oxford Street and back again to the Piccadilly Circus area I felt anonymous if not downright invisible.

What aren't invisible are the countless stores that deal and thrive on flesh. Although I know these sex shops are in the States, Amsterdam, the Scandinavian countries, etc., I somehow couldn't connect this with the conservative London I saw.

The usual pornographic books were displayed from soft pornography to superhard pornography. The hard porno books showed in great detail photographs of sex acts which are usually regarded as deviant. This is intensified in the superhard porno books where nothing is barred including animals and humans shown in bestial sexual acts.

There are books, magazines, newspapers and sex films for sale. Among the sex gadgets and aids were vibrators, electric stimulators, creams and lotions. To activate sexuality in females there is a liquid called *Play Drips.* The instructions on this bottle suggest adding ten drops of this love potion to any drink. I noticed that regular condoms are unhip in these stores. There are specials with Mickey Mouse or Dumbo on the head.

At Bennet and Company and Modern Marital Aids, Ltd., Helga is for sale. She is a substitute woman, measuring 35-25-35, equipped with lifelike breasts, pubic hair and an artificial sex organ. Made of cushioned latex rubber, she is pumped up to life size by a valve in her finger and her price is seventy pounds. [$168.00].

There is a less expensive substitute that sells for seven pounds, fifty newpence. Her measurements are 36-24-36, but she doesn't come equipped with a vagina.

Cheaper still are the torsos. If the man doesn't require a body he pays less for an artificial vagina.

What does all this mean? Any comment would be anticlimactic.

BACK AT my bed and breakfast I learned that a single room was impossible. My landlady took me to a room, unlocked the door with her key and informed a young woman who was peacefully sleeping that I was her new roommate. Laura's sleepy eyes registered surprise as she had assumed the room was hers. With a cheery cheerio our landlady left.

Laura sat up in the bed, told me she had shared the room with her boyfriend but he'd left that morning. Within minutes a man knocked on the door, stuck his head in and the three of us talked for a half-hour. When he left she told me her story.

In Chicago, where Laura and her boyfriend lived, they'd arranged for a vacation in Europe. Determined not to be trapped like her mother, she wanted to be free economically and sexually. It had to be share and share alike or it was no go. Her boyfriend agreed, but somehow something went wrong in England, the first stop of their planned trip. After three days he told her he was leaving because she did things that grated on his nerves. She talked too loudly, expressed her emotions too freely, was too uninhibited in their sexual relationship. His parting words were, 'I never feel like a man with you.'

Crushed by his hasty departure, she immediately latched on to Bill,* the man we'd spoken with. Wasn't he nice, she asked me? — You know I went to bed with him today and maybe that sounds strange to you but he gave me back my confidence. You don't know how hurt I was when my boyfriend left. I mean, no matter what he said, he did dig me sexually but he'd turn cold when I talked or made sexual demands. He'd stop right in the middle and say shutup, you're killing everything. Bill's not like that. He thought my boyfriend was nuts. I mean, he liked my honesty in bed. —

Bill left the next day without saying goodbye which left Laura more depressed than ever. The following day, planning to leave for Paris, she said goodbye to me. Five minutes later she rushed into the room all excited. Bill had left her a note which the landlady had forgotten to give her. It said, 'Laura, you're a great girl. I'm glad I met you. Maybe we'll see each other again. You never know. Bill.' She beamed and asked, — Do you think I'll meet someone in Paris? I mean, what fun is it if you're alone. But he's got to be free like me. — Exit Laura.

Enter Phyllis.* Phyllis started her European tour on a chartered flight from New York to London. She was on her own, that is she and her best girlfriend. In Amsterdam she met an American man she 'flipped for'. She parted with her girlfriend and they arranged to meet each other in London to get their scheduled flight back to New York. Phyllis spent four glorious days with her love in Amsterdam, sharing bed, board, sights, everything. She was thrilled because one night he insisted he pay for dinner. She tearfully left him in Amsterdam because he still had eight days to go and she had to get back to London. Her tears grew in London when she learned her chartered flight was delayed two days.

This also opened up certain possibilities. Should she take the next flight back to Amsterdam and surprise him? After all, it wasn't far. Or should he come to London and spend two days with her? Unable to come to a decision, she decided to call him. She came back to the room and told me the desk clerk in Amsterdam said he'd checked out. Bewildered she turned to me, — There must be a mistake. He asked me to call tonight. He said he'd wait for my call. —

Positive the clerk didn't understand, she called once again and was told the same thing. Phyllis was convinced there was a misunderstanding. She and this man planned to get together in the States. They even discussed marriage. Was there a time difference? Had she called too late?

In the time I spent with Laura and Phyllis we discussed everything. No subject was taboo. Both felt marvellous they were of this generation. Never were women so liberated. Each one discussed their mothers and their words were almost identical. In essence, their mothers were dominated by their fathers. They were totally dependent even though both worked. And they couldn't talk to their mothers because they just didn't understand. How could they? Laura and Phyllis were both in their early twenties, were university graduates, held responsible positions. And both definitely wanted to get married but they weren't going into marriage with their eyes closed. They were going to live first.

This is the liberated woman, aged nineteen to twenty-five, travelling through Europe, confident that she's escaped the fate of her mother. Confronted with subjugation, she quickly recovers and moves on to bigger and better things. Sometimes, overcome with loneliness, she latches on to a man for a time. Sometimes she takes a chance and responds to the signs in front of American Express like, — Wanted, chick for travelling. —

Both Laura and Phyllis were interested in the women's liberation movement, but neither belonged. They didn't need it I was told. — We're the new woman. We know what we want. — However, both asked me for a list of feminist books and Laura even took the name and phone number of a feminist group in Chicago.

Talking with both women it was apparent how the times have changed except for one thing. Both generations connected sex with love or deep feelings of affection. After all, one can be liberated just so far. Sex as an animal act is still, in the main, unpalatable. Men use women but women don't want to get used up.

Therefore, whoever the woman's love happens to be receives a whole new personality, which she gives him. He is suddenly witty, brilliant, fantastic, handsome. Imagine the disappointment when this great person turns out to be a shit, which is what he was in the first place.

Women in my generation were locked in a box. Unbelievably naive about our bodies, including the basic functions, we entered into sexual relationships totally ignorant. This generation has escaped that box, but somehow I see another box. Why??

MARY KENNY

At last

THE FIRST phone call I placed was to the *Evening Standard* and Mary Kenny. As soon as I mentioned I'd just been with the Irishwomen's Liberation Movement, a warm smiling voice sounded in my ear.
—Hello Sister. — We were both anxious to see one another and arranged to meet that evening at a bar on Fleet Street, the street for the thriving London newspaper business.

Sitting at a table with Mary I was transported back, by way of her verbosity and brogue, to Ireland. For the first few minutes she spoke with journalists who were at our table.

— Oh yes, on that story I think it would be a good idea to ... That's a marvellous idea. You will do that the first thing tomorrow, won't you love ... Yes, I'd like that. ... —

Sitting at the table, just the two of us, she turned to me and asked, — Have you met Anne Sharpley yet? — When I shook my head she said, — Oh but you must. She's an excellent journalist. Actually a legend on Fleet Street. Do call her. You'll not only love her as a person but she'll be wonderful for your book. —

Then seriously, — How are things in Ireland? The news is dreadful. How's Nell? Is she working herself to the bone? ... I knew it. She doesn't know when to stop. She's too dedicated. Does she still smoke so much? ... You do know her family lives in the Bogside where all the trouble is ... How's June? How's Mary? ... I felt like a bit of a rat going, but there are movements everywhere for women's liberation, aren't there? I feel I'm raising the consciousness of people. Perhaps I'm doing more for women in journalism but not in my private life. I was very identified with Irishwomen's Liberation so of course I feel badly because these women look for leadership.

— In Ireland I was offered this position as features editor. It is an interesting executive job in terms of careerism and I'm obviously a career girl. Although I felt very committed in Ireland, I also felt very suffocated. Professionally London is more exciting than Ireland. —

Mary Kenny was born in Dublin twenty-seven years ago. From age eighteen to twenty she lived in Paris, — bumming around. — From twenty to twenty-five she was a journalist in London.

The beginning of women's liberation in Ireland was in Mary's words, — terribly stimulating and funny. We came under terrible flack. We were told, how dare you attack Holy Motherhood, you slut. — She laughs and tells me she's reminded of something Christabel Pankhurst said when she was on a hunger strike. 'What shall we do, trust in God? She will provide.'

She discusses women who are still convinced other women are their competitors. — When you see a woman making it, it should be a marvellous thing. A friend of mine, a director on television, feels all women are her rivals. This woman's whole attitude is male oriented. Women have been taught to have this hostility towards each other. Yet women in the liberation movement were very kind and helpful when I came here.

— In my professional life I was privileged. I had it hard as a woman but I got out of that. There comes a moment in every journalist's life when he's around forty-five, that he'll never be the editor. But it came to me at twenty-three that as a woman I could never be the editor and it never occurred to anybody or me that the next person would ever be a woman.

— I was a feature writer at twenty-four. Before that I worked as a reporter. I got some nice breaks because I was a woman. You know, the little girl's viewpoint. I used to write articles like *Is Aristotle Onassis really an attractive man?* I thought I'll never be any more than a feature writer. —

Mary explains that the pattern for a woman journalist is writing women's features for a few years, then copping out and marrying a rich successful man. — After that the women generally do freelance writing on the side, or else go on with the same crap for fifty years.

— I will not have any of this crap of interviewing the woman behind the man. I have a fair amount of freedom in my position but I think it important to eliminate the falseness, the lies about women. One automatically does things to please one's editor. —

When Mary was asked if she would do a story on Miss United Kingdom and told to follow her around she responded with, — No, I'm with women's liberation and I disapprove of this sort of thing. It degrades, exploits and brutalizes the girls. — Mary sent a reporter and photographer out and they did a human interest story and only took a photograph of the girl's head. — We treated her as an ordinary person, not as a body or an object. It's not unkind to the girl because she's an ordinary girl who needs the money and is being exploited. —

Mary Kenny lives and works in London but she is still very involved in the political situation in Ireland, and infuriated by the war. She admits that it's difficult for her to be impartial not only about Ireland but about feminism. One journalist's report angered her.

— It was a story written by a woman, obviously not a feminist, criticizing the northern Irish women for letting their children out on the streets. Mary says, — As if she knows anything about living in the ghetto. It was definitely slanted against all working mothers. --

As I leave Mary Kenny she informs me she plans to become involved in her local feminist group and will also work with Media Women.
— Bye Sister. Sisterhood is solidarity, loving all women. I tend to be

prejudiced, in favor of women, but I feel I'm balancing the economy. — She breaks out into a broad grin. — After all there are more men working and you must encourage your sisters. —

WOMEN'S LIBERATION WORKSHOP

THE WOMEN'S Liberation Workshop at 12-13 Little Newport Street, near Soho, is small in size. However, it functions as a vast information center not only for feminists in all of Great Britain but for feminists throughout the world. The shelves are virtually bursting with every feminist book, leaflet or pamphlet from every country.

During my visits to this office I met feminists from the U.S.A., Canada, Holland, France, Italy, Germany, Belgium, Norway, Sweden and Denmark. There were also women who were not part of the movement but were interested in dialogue, in reading the literature. Feminists from the workshop groups dropped in with papers and information. Since almost all the workshops are open to all feminists, we were welcome to join any group for as long as we wished.

I also met a number of journalists who were with various newspapers and magazines. Some were Americans. All were bewildered, angry, annoyed that the British feminists didn't wish to be interviewed. They couldn't understand why I was having dialogues and they weren't. They acted as if my feminism was incidental. As far as they were concerned a story was a story. One woman became infuriated and asked me, — Does being a feminist make you a better writer than me? — I retorted she might be far better but my motivations were different. Her answer was, — shit — and she told me the next time she would say she was a feminist. I told her it wouldn't work and that the feminists would know as soon as she opened her mouth and began the interview. — Bullshit, — she said. But bullshit or no, she never got any interviews.

The Workshop office has one paid worker. The rest are volunteers. They are unbelievably swamped with work. Trying to keep up with their own Workshop was impossible with visiting feminists, and the constant phone calls that kept coming in. They couldn't speak to any feminist for five minutes without interruptions. All were trying to help women in the jampacked offices. I received the following information and was told to call Sue Cowley of the Tufnell Park group for anything else I needed.

The Women's Liberation Workshop has forty-four autonomous groups in and around London. The Workshop meets monthly, the small groups weekly. The small groups function as action groups, workshops or CR groups. The Special Interest Section consists of Family Study, Medical, Psychotherapy Group and Street Theatre. The feminists in questioning women's roles and redefining the possibilities, seek to bring women to a full awareness of the meaning of their inferior status, and to devise means to change this. Convinced that bureaucracy is detrimental, they have established their own leaderless groups. By closing the meetings to men, the women run their own movement and eventually hope to help other women be in charge of their own lives.

All members, whether they're experienced politically or not, must learn to make their own decisions, both political and personal. Since there isn't any Speakers Bureau, or trained speakers, it is up to the individual group to decide who will give a talk. Every feminist is considered a speaker.

Their magazine *Shrew* is produced monthly, each time by a different group and reflects the interests and activities of the particular group.

COMPARED TO Irish women the women in Britain are relatively liberated. Contraception is legal. Abortion is legal. Divorce is granted to women. Women are represented in most professions.

Unlike Ireland, the Church of England does not rule the government. However, there is not one ordained woman priest in the Church of England. And the plight of the working woman in England is very similar to that of her Irish sisters.

In the professions: 94% of the barristers are men; male doctors have a representation of 85%. Only one in 500 engineers, scientists and technologists is a woman. 65% of all elementary school teachers are women. Yet, of the forty-four people on the executive education committee, only three are women.

In management positions in business and industry: There are 18,060 women executives compared to 397,380 men. Although one-third of the full-time civil servants are women, only 8% work in administration.

Women representing Britain: There are 635 Members of Parliament. Twenty-two are women. 12% of local government councillors are women. There is only one woman who serves as a High Court Judge. One woman is a Country Court Judge.

Women in the diplomatic services must retire when they marry. Ditto for air stewardesses. They don't have to retire as pilots or flight engineers since they're not employed in these positions. There isn't one woman who is a member of the Stock Exchange or the Baltic Exchange. You can be a musician but you needn't apply to two major London orchestras since they refuse to employ women as regular members.

Earnings: Women in Great Britain make up 40% of all employees and on an average they receive only 75% of male earnings. In the 2,000 to 3,000 pound income range [barely middle class] men outnumber women by twenty to one. This rises in the higher levels where it's thirty to one.

The Equal Pay Act will come into effect in 1975. But as a large portion of women's jobs (secretarial, nursing, etc.) are done by women, it will do little to change this inequality.

An Irish Jig to English music: A woman must be a householder to serve on a jury. This disqualifies married women generally because the husband is usually the householder. The few women who do serve on juries are either widowed or wealthy, hardly a representative group.

The father is the legal guardian of the children. He has the right to decide on their education, religion and domicile. If he deserts his family he may return at any time and reassume these rights. The father can take the children abroad without the consent of the mother. Not so for the mother who must have his consent to do likewise. The mother can obtain a passport for her child only if the father cannot be traced. If both are on a joint passport, he may travel where and when he pleases but she stays put unless her husband decides to take her along.

The father can draw on the post office savings of the children. The mother cannot. The father is the only one who can consent to an operation on their child.

A wife is compelled by law to reveal her income to her husband but this does not apply in reverse. A wife is not automatically entitled to an equal share of the home, goods, and income.

A man supporting a wife who is physically dependent may receive a tax allowance toward the cost of a housekeeper. Not so for a woman.

A man may change his name by legal process. If a married woman wishes to do the same she must have her husband's permission.

Strictly an English tune: She may obtain an intrauterine device if she obtains her husband's written permission.

Education: A familiar story. Ministry policy recommends that less provision be made for science teaching in girls' and mixed schools than in boys' schools. University students are 72% male. Only 16% of the places at Oxford and Cambridge are granted to women. Although there is a desperate need for doctors in Britain, British medical schools restrict women students to approximately 15%, regardless of their qualifications. Out of 1,000 people receiving training in Government Retraining Centers, 999 are men. There are 518 representatives on the Industrial Training Boards; eleven are women.

Nursery Schools: Out of more than 2.5 million children between the ages of two and four, only one in ten is at a State Nursery School.

Abortion: This is not only legal but free as well. Free if the woman's doctor agrees to it. When the doctor doesn't, which is often the case, the middle class or rich woman can hire a high class abortionist for 100-200 pounds while the woman who has little money is still forced to use dangerous backstreet methods. One problem she doesn't have. She won't be arrested if she survives.

Dear Arthur and Hope:

Tonight I went to your recommended Indian restaurant on Sussex Street. I took your advice and ordered half portions, an opportunity you said should be seized whenever eating in an Indian restaurant.

Dear Hope and Arthur:

Tonight or rather this morning at 2:30 am, according to my iridescent clock, I staggered to the bathroom, down two flights of stairs, where your highly recommended dinner came out of every opening. Furthermore, Frommers, in case you think I'm the type that easily loses meals, I had three children without even a burp. I've eaten rattlesnake steak and survived. . . . At 3:30 in the morning I crawled back into my less expensive Kings Cross room.

Signed: An infuriated reader.

ANNE SHARPLEY

Sometimes one is inhibited about total honesty

ANNE SHARPLEY met me in the lobby of the *Evening Standard* and immediately ushered me into the most plush, lush restaurant I've been in since my trip began. French, with all the magnificent aromas of French cookery filling the room. All those aromas would go no further than my nose. Do to my highly recommended Indian restaurant I sipped wine, picked at *quiche lorraine* and watched Anne eat.

England has a strong history of suffragists and Anne Sharpley talks about these women. The movement started by Ms. Emmeline Pankhurst, involved the imprisonment of thousands of women from 1905-1914. These early feminists were sent away for six months, nine months. In prison they went on hunger strikes which resulted in forced feedings. A tube was thrust up the nostrils by one doctor and the food was poured in by another. At least one prisoner was driven insane by this method. Sylvia Pankhurst, daughter of Emmeline, withstood ten hunger strikes in one year, during all of which she was fed by a stomach tube twice a day.

In their fight, which was primarily for votes, they used homemade bombs, broke windows, set fire to buildings. One woman chained herself to the railings in Downing Street and while the police tried to cut the chains with a hacksaw, she kept shouting *Votes for Women*. While she was attracting attention outside, one of Ms. Pankhurst's lieutenants managed to enter 10 Downing Street and shout the same *Votes for Women* inside the Prime Minister's house. There were constant marches, constant strikes.

Anne explains the suffragists — were brutally treated by the police. In Bow Street Court, you'd get fifty women in batches. In my view, it was the most sustained internal unrest between the 17th Century Civil War and the Irish troubles after the First World War.

— The Suffragist Movement is a daunting and disparaging thing to have in your past. I think this has led to the period of apathy and exhaustion. In England that is recent history. Any period around the First World War is recent history.

— England has always had its extraordinary woman who never married, who goes off to Africa shaking her umbrella at leopards. I must explain about spinsters in England, of which I am one. In the Middle East I am an English *mees* and that would get you through and out of situations. In the Middle East and Africa, the spinsters have established a figure who is acceptable, honored and trusted.

— Everything in England is understated. It's the thing of gentleman and lady, and mind you, you must be successful but understated in attitude and behavior. I think America finds it hard to realize we are a vast polyglot, the pilot polyglot before America. We've always taken in people, waves of immigrants since the beginning. Therefore, anything anybody does is all right, providing they don't make too much noise. Consequently the Women's Liberation Movement as it is now is tolerated.

— And then our press is a very volatile press and you can't pursue a theme for too long because people become bored. —

When Anne Sharpley first encountered women's liberation, she wasn't interested. Then it suddenly struck her. — Take what you have in a newspaper . . . the cleaners and the secretaries and a few reporters and that's where women were in our industry. The reporters so totally unpromoted. The male printers earn approximately 100 pounds a week, five times what a shorthand typist gets. —

Anne Sharpley received an award as *Woman Journalist of the Year* in 1965. This was followed by *Descriptive Writer of the Year* in 1966. She refuses to discuss her other awards, dismissing them as minor. She is one of the forty established journalists who constitute the Media Women.

The Media Women monitor the media, then pass on the information to the Workshop. At the moment they're studying magazines, newspapers, wireless and television. When they find something to criticize they write joint letters to affect direct action.

— Women aren't used sufficiently as front women on TV. They're used almost exclusively in the back rooms. We never see women used as authoritative and impartial sources of information, so whenever anything important is announced it's always some bloody man, which is absurd.

— We had a situation after the Second World War where women could have taken over. We had developed all sorts of skills. The women worked at everything and then when the war was over women yielded all the work to men. —

Last November, during the Miss World Contest, the feminists staged a big demonstration. They threw fire bombs, stink bombs, fire crackers. Six of them were arrested and brought to trial at Bow Street (the same court where the suffragists were taken).

— They absolutely turned the place upside down. The trial took five days. The six feminists received fines. In covering it I had such a rough time. They didn't want to know about the capitalist press. They'd say, 'piss off'.

— Here you have a deep split. In Leeds, where they had a bimonthly meeting, the entire weekend was taken up on left wing wrangles which are such a bore. I think we don't have more professional women in women's liberation because of the left wing movement. Not because it's left wing but because it's timewasting and quarrelsome. There isn't a single luminary woman in the movement. It's not chic here.

I asked Ms. Sharpley about the new divorce law. She informed me that since January 1, 1971 one can get a divorce without the consent of one's spouse. This law, however, does not work to protect women who are nonworking wives. — In the States you have alimony and child support. Here we don't. The attitude is that women can live on little money. —

I asked Anne if she felt women in Britain were aware of their legal rights. She thought many weren't and explained that the legal provision for women to appeal against discrimination is called the Sex Disqualification (Removal) Act. This has rarely been invoked. However, Ms. Florence Nagle, a famous horse trainer did bring a suit against the Jockey Club, which wouldn't allow her to practice as a horse trainer. Ms. Nagle took her application for a horse training license to the Court of Appeal in 1966 after she had been turned down by a lower court. Ms. Sharpley points out. — She was a very wealthy woman and could afford to fight. —

The Abortion Law, which sounds liberal, is dependent upon the interpretation of the local authorities and the doctor. Anne tells me, — I have no doubt that unless you can provide a good home for the child, and two good parents, that you shouldn't have a child. I myself had two abortions and I haven't thought about it again except in those terms. In fact, everything since has confirmed these views. —

Anne claims she is hesitant to discuss her abortions. — Sometimes one is inhibited about total honesty because when one is inside the system, one has seen people victimized. —

I asked her how she felt about Mary as features editor.

— When Mary came, in effect to be my boss, I was in many ways very much her senior. I was a very established journalist and I used to do all the big stories all over the world. And I think a number of the men at work expected fireworks. But in fact one of the things you learn about women's liberation is that all this supposed antagonism between women not only doesn't exist but you can get on very well. I feel great about Mary as features editor. As it happens she's a very intelligent woman and one accepts her on that basis. —

Mary Kenny joined us too late to hear the compliment. Nor was Anne Sharpley around to hear Mary praise her, but it was unnecessary. Both women were very open in their admiration for one another.

We sat for some time just speaking in general. Anne gave me the phone number of Joan Shenton of BBC and M.P. Joyce Butler, who introduced the Equal Rights Bill in Parliament. — I'm certain they'll be glad to talk with you, — she told me.

I left Anne and Mary and took the tubes for the Tufnell Park section and Sue Cowley.

SUE COWLEY

I don't know any liberated women

I DON'T know any liberated women. For me being liberated means somebody working and involved in the fullest sort of way. I don't think we'll get totally liberated women in this society. —

— Why? — I asked.

— That means going into a heavy political rap. In this society we're bound to be repressed in one way or another. Capitalism and socialism oppress women. In Russia it's obvious women aren't liberated as women. They might be a step closer to liberation. I'm very interested in China. I've spoken to people who've been there and read a lot and it seems they've gone a long way in starting the process of stopping the oppression of women.

QUEST: What do you think of the nuclear family?
ANSW: Everything you think about in relation to women's liberation is negated by the nuclear family. Feminism is fraught with contradictions. I think the nuclear family fucks people up. I like to think of a community kind of thing, not a commune but a sense of community and we'd build from there.
QUEST: Are you saying you're not interested in equal rights in this society?
ANSW: Yes. When I fight for women's liberation I see it in the perspective of a total change, ultimately a people's liberation. I don't want to be equal with men as they are now. I'm certainly not willing

to go along with some male left wing organization. They've never taken women's oppression into account before and there's no indication that they will now.

QUEST: Are you interested in the total women's liberation movement?
ANSW: Yes, particularly in the States. Maybe because I came from there and it fascinates me. But I have friends from the Scandinavian countries and Italy and I'm interested in what's going on there. I would like to see feminists from all over the world get together but that would have to be tremendously organized. I've been to meetings with South Vietnamese and North Vietnamese women. The South Vietnamese women say the conditions are terrible for women but they think they'll get economic equality by throwing out the Americans. Fundamentally they only think of economic equality. The South Vietnamese women were very warm. We hugged each other and had tremendous rapport. The North Vietnamese women were more formal but they also had this warmth. They essentially said the same thing about the economy. But both groups said they were organizing themselves as women.

Sue Cowley is an American who came to London when she married a Londoner. She has been in the new feminist movement from the beginning. She explains that four incidents were responsible for the start of the movement here.

In the winter of 1968-69 there was a strong equal pay campaign for trade union women. This culminated in an Equal Pay Rally at Trafalgar Square in the spring of 1969.

During this same period there were a number of small women's groups who were meeting. Sue Cowley's group was one.

A new magazine called *Socialist Woman* came out on the stands. At that time the magazine identified with the trade unions.

Lastly, Essex University had a weekend workshop entitled *The Festival of Revolution!* One of the workshops was on feminism. Approximately 150 people participated during the weekend. Sue Cowley was there.

She tells me that — Two weeks later we met in London in somebody's flat and by word of mouth 70 women showed. We were high. It was all very new. We'd had no publicity at all. —

After this meeting they formed the Women's Liberation Workshop, meeting every other Sunday. They immediately began campaigns. One was against the temporary workers employment agencies who are notorious for placing women in offices at low wages. Their stickers read, *So-and-so traffics in cheap labor.*

For some time, while the small groups continued and grew, they struggled to find a new definition for women, a format, some plan. In September 1969 the political women dropped out and formed their own groups: Socialist Women, Maoist Women, International Socialist Caucus.

The women decided that these small groups would be the basis of the Workshop and they further agreed that the best area to act would be in one's own locality. It was also important that everything remain flexible.

Sue Cowley tells me they are working hard on the abortion issue maintaining there isn't any abortion on demand except when you have money. You still need the signature of a doctor who refers you to a hospital. There you must get an appointment to be seen, then given another appointment to go before a board of doctors. If they refuse you, you have the option to go to another hospital but since time is of the essence in safe abortions, this is unsatisfactory. Sue explains the biggest excuse used in refusing to do abortions is that the hospital is overloaded with patients. I wonder if they'd refuse to deliver babies for the same reason.

The Tufnell Park group is working to help the women night cleaners who are not unionized. A few of these women cleaners joined the unions but were blacklisted by their companies and they received no help from the unions. Although the Socialist Women had broken away from this feminist group, they immediately joined in action with their sisters. The International Socialist Group and Socialist Women began picketing and leafleting and eventually forced the companies to reinstate the women. The union was also forced to come to terms with them.

In 1969 the Workshop started with two groups. Before the spring of 1971 there were thirteen small groups in London. By the time the Workshop was two years old it had forty-four groups and was growing rapidly.

Although they have the center at 12-13 Little Newport Street, Sue Cowley and others would also like regional centers within the movement. The Tufnell Park group is starting one in their area. It will be rented for one day and one night a week, which is a start.

I am told there will be a meeting of feminists from many groups who will try to coordinate the various workshops, which is almost an impossible task at the center, since new groups are constantly forming. Sue Cowley is one of the volunteers.

Formerly a teacher, she claims she will probably return to work when her youngest child is three years old. The shortage of day care centers presents a problem, but primarily Sue Cowley is motivated by her dedication to the feminist movement.

I asked if she thought her husband understood women's liberation and she replied, — Let's put it this way. He's trying. I think his job is suffering because he doesn't spend as much time as he could but I don't care. I'm not a martyr. If you both decide to have kids, you both have the responsibility. —

I left Sue Cowley's in the early evening chill, wearing her sweater. She smiled and said, — You're welcome to come here any time but if you're too busy just leave it at the Center. I'm always there anyhow. —

JOAN SHENTON

It was an appalling example

I PHONED Joan Shenton at BBC just as she was leaving for home. She told me she'd gladly see me, gave me directions and we arranged to meet at her flat in an hour.

Joan Shenton majored in modern languages at Oxford. And at Oxford she decided she would like to be a performer. She grins. Tells me she's an exhibitionist at heart. Joan began her television career as a secretary for BBC. Her goal was not to be a secretary but when she tried for bigger things at BBC she was told, 'My dear girl, in the first place there's a problem with women's voices and accents and in the second place you can't possibly interest anybody until you have more weight of experience in your looks.'

Not one to give up, Joan Shenton worked as secretary and then received a job as reporter for the Central Office of Information Films, which broadcasts all over Latin America. At that time she was twenty-one years old.

— I tried to break into British television and was out of work for eight months. I realized opportunities for women in TV were very limited so I tried persuading people that they needed me. I was told, 'I don't think I want a woman because you won't be neutral enough and will distract the viewers.'

Joan Shenton disagreed and eventually got a job on Anglia TV in Norwich, Norfolk, reporting the six o'clock news daily. She stayed there for three years, still determined she would break into national TV.

In 1968 she tried again for the BBC in London and this time she succeeded. — I was interviewed but they never asked to see my work even though everything I did was either taped or filmed. I was hired only because I persevered, was around at the right strategic moment. —

Ms. Shenton, the only woman reporter on BBC I, works with the BBC *Current Affairs Group.* This involves all the current affairs programs: *Nationwide,* which airs at 6:00 pm; *Twenty-Four Hours,* late evening and equivalent to the old Huntley-Brinkley program; *Panorama,* a weekly current affairs program; and *Money Program,* a weekly program about finance.

Her working day begins at 9:00 am, and often continues on into the night. At one time she co-hosted with a man but now she has a portion of *Nationwide,* a segment which can last ten minutes or more. She covers, on an average, four topics a week.

One of her programs covered the practice of sexism in Wimpy Houses. When Joan heard that a group of women from women's liberation tried to gain admittance and were refused service she decided to go and see for herself. Rather than discuss this show Joan suggested I meet her at BBC and see the filmed program for myself.

Another example of discrimination, according to Joan Shenton, is the Saddle Club. Although she is a member of this private club, she is only welcome when she goes there with a man. However, this welcome is short-lived if she should decide to come alone. She laughs, then shakes her head in wonder at the Saddle Club's reasoning. — They say I can't come in because I'd disturb other clients. For instance if a man asked me to dance. —

Joan Shenton is with Media Women because she feels it is important. They try to improve opportunities for women in all areas of media work. They act as career advisers for women and produce an annual magazine informing women about careers in the media.

— In this country we don't have the respect of the woman's role.

We're not responsibly linked with the larger society. For example, there are no women in BBC reading news, so we decided we would try and persuade Lord Hill, head of BBC, to employ women for this position. In essence he said that women interfered with the process of understanding the news and he also inferred that the public had a prejudice against women as serious commentators on current and national affairs.

— We answered and said surely the BBC should be setting an example in breaking this so called prejudice and not pandering to it. —

After much effort the Media Women found fifteen candidates as newsreaders. All these women had experience in the regions.

— Lord Hill replied that he was surprised to have such a formidable reply. But he said that most of the women were already employed by BBC. We said that was beside the point. We wanted somebody for national TV.

— In the BBC it's difficult to be a spokeswoman for women's liberation. The movement is connected in people's minds with a political situation such as Maoists, the Women's Liberation Front and Socialist Women. I deal with topics but not with the words women's liberation. People would be more sympathetic if the term seemed apolitical. Personally I would like to change the image. All people who criticize the movement use the word negatively, so the image never changes. —

Not long ago Joan Shenton carefully researched a program on women's liberation. She especially wanted three articulate women; one middle of the road, one extremist and one homemaker as a representative group. Before the program went on the air Joan was told she couldn't chair the interview. When she asked who would, she heard a man would do it. Several things hit home. One was that a man was moderating a show on feminism. Two, he hadn't even done any of the research. To complete this negative picture, they added two more women to the agenda, even though the entire segment was only six minutes long. That meant six minutes for five women to discuss the four main points of women's liberation. Joan turns to me, — By inviting so many women we had a monstrous program. It was an appalling example. —

She had assured the three women originally invited that they would be taken seriously. Although this was not the case, Ms. Shenton was obviously not responsible for what happened. Yet the feminists feel she sold them short. Now they won't allow her or any other TV personality to cover conferences in Oxford.

She discusses her work on BBC. — I can select what I want and do. I can be sent in the morning to do the current hot story of the day. But if I want to do something on contraception, abortion or VD which I consider very important, I'm not allowed to do it, because *Nationwide* is at six o'clock and basically a family program. —

Joan Shenton considers herself a serious reporter and states that she writes every word she says on the air. — I am often tempted not to dress up because I feel the image in the past has always been to use an actress as a front woman, to dress her up. In the fifties they were used for their pretty faces but it didn't work out. I try to look as nice as I can, but always have mastery over my material.

— In the office I'm respected for my work. But I'm often left out of discussions on an item I've been working on. I see this as disapproval. Yet I know exactly what I want when it's connected with my work. —

THE FOLLOWING day I took the Central Line to Shepards Bush, walked past stalls where clothing hung on racks. Food was piled high on other stands. People picked at the merchandise. Turning the corner I went from a general hubub to a quiet residential area and on to the BBC Lime Grove Studios.

Joan Shenton and Roz MacArthur, film editor for BBC, met me in the lobby and ushered me into an elevator. Then to a room where the filmed program of Wimpy Houses was ready for showing. This restaurant chain refuses to serve unaccompanied women after midnight. This is the result of a 1959 law to take prostitution off the streets. Joan finds it preposterous to assume women going into Wimpy Houses at a certain hour are prostitutes.

The film started and I saw Joan who was incognito. She whispered she'd carefully placed three hair pieces on her head, had a concealed microphone on her. The camera unit waited outside.

Joan had already entered the first restaurant, was sitting at a table waiting to be served. The waiter told her he couldn't serve her. Her *why* appeared to be magical because from nowhere the manager appeared and within minutes Joan was politely but definitely ushered outside.

In the second restaurant the waiter was thrilled to see a TV personality at his table but not thrilled enough to serve Joan a cup of coffee. She shrugged, — This sequence was ruined when I was recognized. —

She entered the third Wimpy House, asked for coffee and again was refused. And again she asked why. Because she was told, women couldn't be served after 12:00 pm, if they're alone. Joan persisted with why. This time she was told it was the law. Her next question was, could she return with a woman friend. She received a no and an escort to the door and out.

The film ends with Joan standing outside the third restaurant telling her audience it looked like she wasn't going to get her cup of coffee after all. Roz turned the film off and turned on the lights.

Joan looked at me disgustedly. — It's absolutely ridiculous. Three times I went and three times I got kicked out. All because of a law that goes something like this . . . if you knowingly harbor a prostitute you can be penalized.

— Afterwards I tangled with the managing director of Empire Catering (owners of Wimpy Houses) and he said he couldn't do anything about it because it's the law. I told him, in fact, you're interpreting the law to suit your own aims. —

Roz MacArthur didn't have to say anything. Her expression told me how she felt. We left the viewing room and went down to the BBC restaurant. We ate hurriedly at the counter since all three of us had appointments. Joan Shenton was cornered by some of the *Current Affairs* team. They discussed a future program. Roz MacArthur arranged a time for an interview. Within fifteen minutes all three of us said goodbye and rushed off in different directions.

JEAN MADDEN AND FRIEND

A contrast

MY FRIEND Jean Zaleski suggested I look up Jean Madden, who owns a successful art gallery in London. Originally from South Africa, Jean Madden and her husband came to London in 1961 because they didn't like the politics of their country.

Jean Madden studied business, shorthand, typing in school. Before opening the gallery she worked in the showroom of a jewelry house. She never used her business and secretarial education as she didn't like it. She went into the gallery business with her husband not because she was interested in art, but because she was interested in her husband, who happened to be an artist.

— In 1962 we started the gallery. We didn't know anybody, didn't know any artists, didn't have customers. For six months we almost starved. After a year the business began to go well, but not my marriage. Suddenly overnight my husband went mad. He couldn't stand me, threatened to kill me. —

Jean and her husband broke up in 1970, after seventeen years of marriage. — I thought the end of my world had come. I never thought of life without him. I paid him for the business. I thought I'd leaned on him but I hadn't. I'd been doing the buying and selling, everything, but I didn't realize I'd done all of this.

— Everybody thought I could make it. I had my fears, of course, but in my heart of hearts I knew I could make it. — Jean beamed, — I've had the most marvellous time having the freedom to be in business, to choose the paintings I want. I realize I found my forte. I love art. I learned by listening and working and studying. I'm doing what I like to do. —

Ms. Madden lives alone. She is certain she would never marry again but says if the circumstances were right she would live with a man.

Jean Madden's friend agreed to talk with me if I wouldn't use her name. — We're friends but psychologically we're completely different. My childhood is very vague. Whether I'm trying to forget it or not, I don't know but there was a lot of love in the family. My father said, 'only a stone can live alone.'

— When you come to a flat, to empty walls it isn't good. If you don't have money, you don't have any friends. I spent two months in New York and I was accepted because my husband was a doctor. I'm sure if I was alone and couldn't boast of a university education or a profession I would have been alone. My first question was, 'And what does your husband do?'

— As people we're all different . . . introverts and extroverts, some like cabbages. Experience affects one don't you think? I had all sorts of dreams as a child. I wanted to be a teacher, a doctor, a ballet dancer, and to be married and have children. I spent hours in the library doing nothing, just opening and closing books. —

I asked her if she was ever encouraged to do anything. She paused. — I don't understand. —

— As a child were you encouraged to work, to do anything? — She looked at me, a bitter expression dominating her face. — I was encouraged to get married and to have children.

— I was always little and I was treated as if I were a little feminine thing, but I really wasn't a feminine thing. I just looked it. I wanted to do things, learn things. Maybe I would have been stronger psychologically had I been educated to be independent. I panic when I'm alone. I can be alone in a room as long as I know there's somebody. Men are afraid to be called not a man so they wear a face to show independence.

— My husband would never give me any sympathy if I were sick but if he cut his finger he acted as if the world had ended. —

Jean's friend tells me she wasn't trained to be independent, yet she has worked since she was fifteen, and until she married was independent. — Everything went wrong when I got married. My fears started. He worked on them. I have a fear of death and he never let me forget it.

— I worked for my husband only I never got paid. Yet when I travelled with him I had to get my fare from my family. Whenever I went shopping or anywhere he'd say I don't have my check book. Pay it and I'll give it back. He said we should share and share alike. Yet we never did.

— He told me what to do, not to read in bed, not to smoke. He told me how to wear my hair. And I never had any money. —

Her divorce took three years. She never received a penny because her husband, a medical doctor, pleaded poverty and whatever money she might have received went to the solicitors in England and South Africa.

She lit a cigarette, pondered and then said, — A woman gives up much more in a marriage because she always tries to hold a man. She pleases a man because that's what she's taught. A woman has to worry when she gets older because then it's harder for her to meet a man. A man can go with a younger woman and it's accepted but an older woman can't go with a younger man. Outwardly she may look older but inwardly she's really younger. She lives longer. They call us the weaker sex but physically we're surely not. —

HOLE IN THE WALL

I GOT off at the Camden Tube station, walked to Rochester Road to a place called Hole in the Wall. There I met over thirty women representing the various workshop groups. And one man. The man who insists on being anonymous is presently meeting with five other men for consciousness raising.

I told him I'd heard he was the founder of the Men's Liberation Movement and he retorted, — You can hardly call five men a movement. —

I didn't tell him that a number of reporters claimed he was hostile, refused interviews and called him a male chauvinist. He wasn't exactly hostile but he wasn't friendly either. He didn't refuse an interview but he wasn't exactly thrilled. As for male chauvinism (which I believe all males have to some extent) his was definitely in the low percentile.

He explained his group was not in opposition to feminism but was an attempt to raise the consciousness of men. The men in this group are trying to change their values, share their experiences and not be ashamed of their feelings. According to him, men tend to hide in the world of abstraction and ideas. He believes women are in a good position because they haven't been programmed to speak in the abstract and that social changes would basically come from changes within the individual. — Revolution should come out of a gut impetus. Without it, revolution is abstract and remote from the human experience. —

He believed the radical feminists' strategy of separatism was the only way and he was in complete accord with it. Apparently the feminists were in accord with him, as he was the only man allowed at the meeting.

The representative women all agreed that autonomous groups must continue, but they realized they were lacking in organization and were determined to change this. The feminists acknowledged the Workshop Center was chaotic and that it was virtually impossible for visiting feminists and British feminists to find out what was going on in the local groups. In rejecting a bureaucracy because of its fixed rules and hierarchy of authority, they had inadvertently dismissed organization as well.

Aware that systematic planning and a combined effort are imperative, they decided that representatives from each workshop would meet once a month. These women would report back to their respective groups as well as inform the workshop headquarters of the activities. Written reports of their meetings would be distributed.

A lively dialogue on CR followed. This time I was the one being interviewed.

QUEST: Bonnie, were you ever in CR?

ME: Yes. For eight months.

QUEST: Do you think you're more of a feminist than non CR women?

ME: I can't answer for anybody else but I know it's made a tremendous difference in me, in the way I see things. The way I see everything. It's one thing to say I'm oppressed, which I always knew, and another to examine the society that encourages this oppression. It was only in group that I began to realize what my expected role did to me. No, not to me, but to every woman in the group. I don't believe you can do this out of group.

QUEST: I don't need to join CR to know I'm oppressed.

ME: But you're not the only one who's oppressed. All women are.

QUEST: That's basic. We all know that.

QUEST: We're sick of all this psychoanalysis. America's hung up on shrinks. We're not.

ME: CR is not group therapy. Group therapy examines the individual person and tries to make changes in that person. CR examines the society through the women.

QUEST: Can you tell us specifically how you changed?

ME: First of all I feel less guilt. Secondly, I accept and respect my feelings. I don't have to quote from an authority in a book. But what's most important to me is I've learned what sisterhood is. I feel a bond with all women, whether they're feminists or not.

QUEST: And you don't think others feel that?

ME: Look I can only speak for me. I couldn't. I always got along with women. I always felt closer to women than men but I didn't feel the solidarity I do now.

QUEST: How about the feminists who are only in action?

ME: You need action, but I must tell you seven of the women in my CR group worked in action first.

QUEST: Could you tell us why you joined CR?

ME: I read a lot about it and I formed the group because I thought I'd gain something from it. See there it is . . . I would gain. I don't think that way anymore. Well that's a lie. Yes I do, but not when it comes to women. I think in terms of *we*.

QUEST: I still don't see what individual changes can mean to the movement.

QUEST: I think it's a waste of time.

ME: Then for you it would be a waste of time. For me it was a very valuable experience.

QUEST: Don't you think women can do it alone?
ME: No. To recognize oppression alone further isolates and excludes women from one another.
QUEST: Don't you honestly believe that a revolution is only possible with action?
ME: Yes of course, but I want that action to come out of a united strength.

I'm not quite sure if I actually got the last word in but I gave it to myself anyhow. Before the meeting ended, three women from a CR group asked me if I would join them before I left London. They said they'd been meeting for some time and found it difficult to speak. Since CR is leaderless I gladly accepted.

JANE MARTIN, M.D.

Sex for instance is unsatisfactory

DR. JANE MARTIN* and I talked long before the actual interview. She asked me if I would like to interview a woman who was going to have a child without a husband. Sure I said. Who? She smiled. Me.

Jane met me at the train station near where she lives. She was holding a bouquet of flowers. — Sorry Bonnie but we'll have to walk. My car broke down and it won't be ready for hours. It's an uphill walk. I hope you won't mind. —

— I love walking. Even uphill. —

Jane Martin stopped taking the pill months before she became pregnant so she knew there was a possibility of her becoming pregnant.

JANE: I thought about my reaction to pregnancy long before it actually happened.
B: Why did you stop taking the pill?
JANE: It made me feel like a sterile sex machine. And there is danger in taking the pill and using the intrauterine device.
B: Comeon Jane. There are other contraceptives.
JANE: [we smile at each other and then she turns serious] If I were really honest with myself, I didn't set out to become pregnant but I thought it would be nice to have a baby. I was using the rhythm

method and was surprised that I became pregnant because we'd been careful.

B: Do you know what they call people who practice rhythm?

JANE: No, what?

B: Mommies and Daddies ... Don't tell me, I know it's corny.... Quick, give me your immediate reaction when you found out you were pregnant.

JANE: [smiling] I was quite pleased actually. I accepted that I didn't want a termination of the pregnancy but I did wonder how people would react.

The man who will be the father of her child is also a professional and according to Dr. Martin very conventional. — He became aggressive when I told him I was going to have the child. It never occurred to him that I would. He said to me, 'but I don't want to marry you. You and I are not at all suitable. Nothing is right. Not even our sex is right.'

— I wasn't surprised at his reaction. I rather expected it. I like him. We had a lot of fun together. If he was willing, I would have lived with him, but not married him. —

In the beginning she worried about the child not having a father present and wondered if it would feel deprived. She questioned if she was justified in having a baby. Then she thought about children who don't have fathers, or come from unhappy homes. She told me, — Why shouldn't a child be happy in a one parent home when she is wanted and loved? Above everything the child is most important. It must be loved and be able to relate to somebody. —

Jane Martin points out that she wouldn't stop this man from having a relationship with the child but feels from his attitude he wouldn't want it.

— I hope to have other male relationships so the child won't be deprived of male companionship. A man who thought I'd been wrong or promiscuous or one who wouldn't accept an unwed mother wouldn't be the one I'd want a relationship with.

— I hate the thought of being married, of being put in a domestic role, somebody expecting a meal at night, not having my own bank account. If I were married and worked and got a nanny, I would still feel it expected that I be a clever woman who has a profession and works and keeps a house. That this is my role. I don't know of any marriage where the woman doesn't think playing wife and mother is most important, work second. And I'm disillusioned by so many married men having affairs. All of this would eventually drag me down.

— I have a hangup about men because of my relationships. If I exert my opinion or feelings about things I get put down. Sex for instance is unsatisfactory. I find it difficult to express this to a man. Then I feel resentful because he won't listen. It's unsatisfactory because the man is in a position where he can move himself to his own stimulation. It almost seems that the woman has to satisfy him.

— Most men think or have to think they're the greatest lovers in bed and if you say they aren't it's a great big blow. Having to actually say I want something sexually takes away from the spontaneity and makes me cold. I think men who are more sensitive are better sexually and also as people we can relate to.

— If a woman could get up and walk out and say this is no damned good. Maybe not as nasty as that. Then women have the idea that they shouldn't have many lovers, just one. And the awful thing is that women have to feel a little in love with a man before she enjoys the sex. Whereas a man can just enjoy it. I think it's rubbish. A woman can enjoy it the same without love. —

— If a man will let her, — I said.

— I don't understand. —

— He wants a virgin and a prostitute in the same woman. And of course we can enjoy sex without love but men don't want to face this because it makes them sex objects as well. —

— Men are constantly being sexually stimulated, — she said. — All around the commercial world, the ads, all the media is geared toward women being sexy for men. Men's bodies can be beautiful too but we don't think in those terms.

— When I was in medical school I was the only girl amongst fourteen chaps at one stage and that was uncomfortable. I couldn't talk to them as I could to the girls. I relate better to women. I can say what I feel to them because of the emotional thing. With a chap you make an advance and you think he's thinking of you as a person but he isn't.

— Before women's liberation I would sit down and think, why am I so frustrated? Why can he do things and *he can do it,* like going to a pub and not looking like a pickup object? Why should I always be in competition at a party with another woman? I wanted liberation for women long before groups existed. I couldn't accept things as they were. —

Jane joined the CR group over a year ago and discovered other women felt the same as she. — So ok, I'm a doctor and have money and other things that they don't have but the frustration and pent-up feelings are the same.

— I got it shoved down my neck when the man I was living with found out I was pregnant. He said, 'women's liberation, women's liberation. Of course you wouldn't want a man anyway. You would want to have a baby on your own. It's your women's lib thing isn't it? You don't need a man at all.'

— And I thought it funny and sad that he didn't understand women's liberation at all. And not many men do. —

LILIANA AND PAULA

I feel my conditioning

AT THE Workshop I met Liliana and Paula, two students from the University of Trento, a social science university. They are spending the summer in London studying the British feminist movement and improving their English. We began speaking at the Workshop but it became so hectic we moved on to a restaurant.

I asked how women's liberation in Trento began and was told that four women students formed a study group, wrote a paper on feminism which was read by other students. This was the impetus for other study groups and the inevitable forming of women's liberation at the University of Trento. The feminist students read Marx, Wilhelm Reich, Simone DeBeauvoir, Evelyne Sullerot, Betty Friedan. They study sexuality, children, family, abortion, economy, biology and other related subjects. All groups write papers that are read by everyone.

Liliana spoke about her childhood in Italy. — I feel my conditioning. When I was a little girl all my education was different from my brothers. Everything was different. It was important that a woman be beautiful so she could find a man. I couldn't see myself as beautiful and I was very sad. This is very important because you see this *beautiful conditioning* affected my life. A child has to feel accepted and since I wasn't told I was beautiful I felt I wasn't accepted.

— I tried to find something else. I studied harder to learn to do something because I felt it was my only way to be accepted. I wanted to live as a man without thinking about my face, my body and the way I dress.

— When I began to study about feminism at Trento I began to know that what I felt was a thing other women felt. Before I always thought I was different from other women. —

Although Paula, Liliana and I had a tremendous language problem from the very beginning as my Italian is almost nonexistent and their English still leaves much to be desired, we had no problem relating as women.

Paula caught the meaning in my expression. — It isn't important if Liliana is beautiful or not. It's how she felt that is important, not how she looked. We know now that beauty is something inside. —

L: What Paula is saying I understand now but then it was hard because the inside affects the outside.
P: In Trento there is a beauty contest and the feminists object because we say all women are beautiful.
L: We also have a contest for the most wonderful mother. The mother is exploited 364 days a year and one day a year they give her a party ... I don't believe in marriage. In Italy the woman is supposed to be interested only in the house. I don't like the relationship. Families are together because of the economy and this is at the price of the woman and the children. They are both under the authority of the man.
P: We are told all women are inferior, that if we are not married we are not a complete woman, only half a woman. For the woman the marriage should be the only reason of her life. I wouldn't marry. Maybe someday I will have a baby but it will be because I choose to have a baby. I want a human relationship and if the man wants to be a friend he can. But when the relationship ends, it ends.
L: You know in Italy you can change the law if you get 50,000 signatures. And now that we finally got divorce there is a group that wants to do away with the divorce.
B: Liliana, do you ever discuss women's liberation with your parents?
L: No. If I spoke about it they would be afraid for me because they are Catholic and have the Catholic mentality. It is better if I speak to them about other things. I tell them how I feel as a woman but not about the movement.
P: I think to understand the real conditioning of women we have to

understand capitalism.
B: Do you believe women are more equal in a socialistic system?
P: No. Women are exploited everywhere. In socialism it is one kind of exploitation, in capitalism another.
B: How would you define liberation?
P: Where nobody in the society is exploited.
L: In Trento we understand our exploitation by studying woman's history. This is important but we must also speak of ourselves and our feelings.
P: Yes and it is very important that we listen and understand one another.
L: In Trento we go to homes and speak with other women about ourselves and they talk, and then we tell them about our study and education.

Both Liliana and Paula plan to work with feminist groups when they graduate. They are not only interested in equal rights for women but in a revolution that will change the total society.

ROZ MacARTHUR

I argued, forget that I'm a woman

ANYBODY WHO has studied feminism is aware that it is necessary to study many subjects in order to have some understanding of the feminist movement. Such subjects as biology, sociology, history, psychology, politics, economy, religion, education and so forth are essential since sexism is founded in roots.

Roz MacArthur is particularly interested in male history. She says,
— In the past period of history one's eventual station and responsibility in life were preordained by circumstances at birth. Therefore a man was educated for his leisure or pleasure, as opposed to his eventual gain.

Although we have gone forward, it doesn't matter into which class strata of society you were born, you can still make material success. But man has made the most terrible backward step in that he no longer knows his eventual station and is therefore struggling all the time.

— Because these barriers have broken, the competition between men is so fierce that they can't bear the competition of women as well. So that although the position of women in Victorian times was that of a chattel, a possession, nowadays the position is hardly any better. To maintain his position in society, a male with any pretentions towards success in his field must perpetuate a system of female discrimination.

— When men think of those millions of dissatisfied women who are waiting for their jobs, imagine how they feel. —

Roz MacArthur is the assistant film editor on *Current Affairs.* Originally she wanted to be an actress but decided to study filming instead. At Fenestra she studied all phases of film making. Finding employment was difficult for her, since it was accepted that women start as secretaries in hopes of going on from there. Roz refused to take secretarial courses, knew nothing about shorthand and typing. — Women's liberation wasn't around then. I argued, forget that I'm a woman. —

She wanted to start in vacancies that were only open to men. Work such as studio running (running messages), trainee assistant floor manager, which involves blocking the set with chalk; trainee assistant film editor, which really means carrying all the canned film to the cutting room and making coffee.

— They said we don't employ women in those positions and one said and I quote, 'We are a small organization and cannot afford fat in the organization. You must work for us in a capacity which will repay the training we will give you.' —

According to Roz, through pulling strings and chicanery, she eventually got a job in an advertising agency that made commercials. This was the end of 1965. From there on, she worked in many studios in various capacities until she got her present job.

— In the BBC there are less barriers than any other film or TV organization. I should like to be producer and director, and I think women's liberation will make it easier for me. I'm expected to be aggressive and punchy. I can now compete with men on their own terms and nobody's surprised. I don't feel I could have done this five years ago. I would have been unemployed by virtue of my demands. Things have gone much faster in the last two years careerwise. Women's liberation really has opened doors. It's not what we're saying because most people don't know, but at least they're no longer surprised that women are making demands.

— It's known at BBC that I don't wish to be assistant film director. I've always been a women's liberationist. I started to work because of economic necessity. I still work for economic reasons. —

I asked Roz if she would work if she were economically independent and she quickly answered that if she were she would start her own film company. — I need the money but I would be much better paid in other professions. Therefore, it's not just the money. To me, the position in women's liberation in modern day society is that we are striving toward a richness of life.

— I've never thought of myself as a woman in quotes, but always first as a person. I've never identified with any particular role. I don't believe in feminine or masculine attributes. Woman has been educated by man to perpetuate his concept of his own image. —

Roz MacArthur discusses unemployment which she feels is crucial. — There aren't enough jobs to go around. Since men are in these jobs, they're not going to legislate them to women. And a woman, as we know, has to be more talented than a man to be regarded his equal. —

As I left the flat, Roz turned to me and smiled. — Nowadays, even if a man is born with a silver spoon stuck up his nostril, it's not going to make any difference in his eventual competition with working class men. —

CONSCIOUSNESS RAISING AND ME

BEFORE SETTING out for the CR group I sat alone in my room and did some private consciousness raising.

When I was born the doctor announced, 'It's a girl.' When I reached the age of three I was still a girl, but my behavior led my parents to say, 'She should have been a boy.' From three to fifteen I carried the label *tomboy*. The dictionary defines this as a girl with boyish behavior. I define it as a girl who likes sports.

From fifteen to nineteen I received another label *boy crazy*. Actually I was going crazy because of boys. Insisting on expressing my opinions, my ideas, my feelings, I was told I was illogical. Logic I learned was innate in the male, and something a female didn't have. What's more she couldn't even acquire it. Because I was argumentative I was constantly being dropped by one boy and found by another, or vice versa. Expecting me to keep my mouth shut and smile at some pimply boy in unadulterated admiration was like asking a seal to sing an aria from *La Boheme*.

At nineteen, when parents were pushing their daughters to the highest bidder, I emphatically stated I wasn't getting married. But I did, because I met a man who not only liked my mind but encouraged discussions.

The first five-and-a-half years of marriage I worked, which was considered perfectly normal, since my husband attended college and we needed the money. After that the general opinion on my childless state was that I just didn't have the hatching egg instinct.

In California, seven-and-a-half years after my marriage, I gave birth to Craig. We owned a home, I had my own car, my husband was successful. This is what little girls grow up for. Used to searching for my own answers I would ask myself questions. What would happen if you left him, if he left you, if he lost his job? Where would all that leave you and I kept coming up with the same answer. Nowhere.

Periodically I worked. I went back to college. I constantly read and consistently was dissatisfied. I had Kenn, then in Connecticut I gave birth to Brian. I now had a new car every two years, a housekeeper, a beautiful home. From Connecticut we moved to New Jersey, then Philadelphia.

During this period I studied sensitivity methods, zen, yoga, religion, philosophy, Hebrew. I applied for a divorce and was told I was destructive by well meaning friends and relatives. My husband said he would only agree to a divorce if I agreed to psychoanalysis. He insisted this be stipulated in the divorce suit. 'No shrink, no divorce.'

When my lawyer flatly rejected this my husband was hurt. He was doing it for my good. He didn't like to see me unhappy. That my unhappiness related to the lack of control I had over my own life was irrelevant. I dropped the charges and went to a marriage counsellor.

The third session I was told I was competitive, aggressive, my thinking was male. I was advised to stay home like a good wife and count my blessings. After all, how many women could boast of a faithful husband who was successful, and healthy happy children. The marriage counsellor promised to help me adjust to a very adjustable situation. When she began explaining the *division of labor,* which I'd already learned when I studied marriage counselling I left.

I studied psychology again, leaving Freud fur Jung and Horney. I went into card reading, gypsy fortune tellers who read my tea leaves. I sat in full lotus position meditating. I studied health foods. I ate organically grown foods, macrobiotic foods, I took vitamins in hopes something would effect a change in me. Did I have too much yin in me or was it yang?

I had my astrological forecast drawn. It read one half of me was an emotional female. The other half was an intellectual male. This was responsible for my fucked up life.

I worked as a dancing teacher, taught creative drama, received a grant as a playwright with the New Dramatists, worked with the Lincoln Repertory Theatre, had a few plays produced. I directed an art gallery, organized and ran art openings. Although I was constantly busy, my body and mind seemed to be whirling independent of me.

Determined to put all the loose parts together I again applied for a divorce. Now came the anvil chorus, — She'll never make it. You just wait. Within a year she'll be back with him. — This time my husband decided I couldn't move from Philadelphia as long as he worked there, unless I received his permission. My lawyer was flabbergasted. — What is she, your prisoner? She's over twenty-one and can decide for herself where she'll live. —

My mother resigned herself to my decision. My brother was concerned. — Once you see how hard it is out there, you'll get married again, — and when he realized I had no intention of remarrying he yelled angrily, — You're nothing. What are you? You don't even have a husband. —

Everybody, without exception was concerned for our sons, except me. I was positive that children don't thrive in unhappy homes. And I was right.

When I examine the society in terms of myself I see a father and his father and his father's father. I see a husband and his father and so on down the line. And rabbis and ministers and priests and pulpits that are so holy, women can't participate fully. We're given the privilege of producing the males who do. I see books through the centuries, and radio, television, magazines, newspapers written mostly by men. I see politicians and governments and judges and lawyers and laws that are different for men and women. I see buildings and roads, bridges, tunnels, homes . . . male designed and built. I see household appliances rarely used by men but designed by them. And I see mountains of books and articles defining and advising women.

And I hear, 'Enjoy your children while they're young. These are the best years of your life. When they're older they won't even know you're alive.' I question why a woman should devote her best years to children who won't give a damn later on. Would any person work for over twenty years at a job when they know they're going to be fired?

WOMAN: Sometimes I wish I never got married.
GUILT: How can you when he's so good to you?
WOMAN: Sometimes I wish I never had kids.
GUILT: They're healthy and wonderful. God will punish you for that!
WOMAN: Sometimes sex brings on nausea and murderous feelings.
GUILT: What's wrong with me? Am I frigid?
MORE GUILT: Why do I holler so much? Why can't I be nice like the ladies on the TV commercials? Why don't I take better care of my appearance?
ANSWERS: I holler because nobody listens when I talk softly, and I'm damned mad because my definition of a nothing is somebody who lives in the shadow of others. And I can't be nice like those TV ladies because I'm not paid to be nice. They're hired for five minutes with residuals yet and I'm hired for life without so much as green stamps.

And I don't take better care of my appearance because the last time I did, it got me this glorified maid's job.

EIGHT OF us sat in the living room. It was the first time in two months that I was participating in a CR group, and my first experience with open CR.

Before participating in this group I thought that closed groups were best. My reasons: One built up rapport within the group, we grew together; new women not only could distract the older members but would not be on our advanced level of understanding; and those who didn't come every week would have to be filled in on what happened the week or weeks she missed.

In London the faces were different, the accents different, the culture different but that's where the differences ended. If I shut my eyes, didn't look at the faces and pretended they weren't speaking in the clipped British accent, I could have been back in the States with the CR group I knew so well. Knew because we'd known each other intimately not only for eight months of CR but many of us worked closely together in action. These seven women could be considered strangers only if I considered myself a stranger.

We all spoke about our feelings as women in the society. We had much to say except for Jennie* who kept insisting she was very happy she'd gotten married, was happy she had her small children. These were her good years and she was willing to wait until her children were older before she worked. — I'm only twenty-three, — she said. Her expression was peaceful. Betty* discussed love, her husband's love for her and I smiling said, — My former husband also adored the ground I walked on, providing I walked the ground he chose for me. —

From nowhere Jennie, the smile still on her face whispered, — Once I was carrying the baby. We started to go down the stairs. My little girl was standing by my side, holding on to my dress and suddenly I thought I'm going to throw the baby down the stairs and then I'll push my girl after her. — Her smile turned into a bewildered expression. She sat for a few minutes, not hearing what was said. Suddenly she rose, went into another room and didn't appear for some time. When she joined us she was extremely quiet. A feminist asked her something and she blurted out quietly, — I told you I'm happy I have my children. I'm very happy. —

Nobody pressed her. In a few minutes she said almost inaudibly. — I know what I said. I know. I know. —

I was driven home by Phyllis and made arrangements to see her again. She told me I added life to the group. I realized then that any new participant adds another dimension to a group. And for the first time I sensed the value of open CR.

M.P. JOYCE BUTLER

Age labels a woman

JOYCE BUTLER was elected to the House of Commons sixteen years ago. Her Anti-Discrimination Bill has been presented three times in Parliament. Each time it was voted down.

This bill, based on the Race Relations Act, will make it illegal to discriminate against women. The Anti-Discrimination Bill states there will be no discrimination in advertising, in training or education by professional bodies, trade unions, etc. It further states that the Anti-Discrimination Board shall consider complaints of discrimination, to make inquiries as to the complaint and to assure against these discriminations when valid, to take legal action.

On the telephone Joyce Butler asked me to meet her inside the St. Stephens entrance of Parliament and to have her paged if she wasn't there. I entered and was told politely but firmly the public had to go to another entrance. I explained I had an appointment with Ms. Butler, received a nod, was ushered inside and while one guard telephoned, another guard engaged me in conversation. Not being *the public* has great advantages.

M.P. Joyce Butler showed me around, giving me a historical background. In the Parliament cafeteria she handed me a copy of the Anti-Discrimination Bill and explained: – The main thing is to get a debate. If you do have a debate and there's opposition to a part of the bill, you can amend it. –

At the end of the day, if the bill hasn't been debated, they have what is called *Going Through the Nod.* This means the bill has to be called and anybody in Parliament can say *object.* If this should happen the bill doesn't get a second reading. Even if the bill has not been debated a member can object.

Each time Joyce Butler's bill has been presented there has been a dissenting voice. She tells me, – We are working on getting it ready as soon as the ballot takes place. There are ways of getting around the dissenting voice.

The House of Commons presents its bills on Friday. The Government can provide extra time for a particular member's bill. This is important since there is limited time to debate private members' bills. Joyce Butler tells me additional time was given for the divorce bill and the hanging bill.

Ms. Butler began her political career when she worked on a local council. She was always active in politics and chose a husband who was also active politically. To her it seemed natural to stand for Parliament.

– My husband was very encouraging but I think it's the woman's decision to do what she wants. I never thought about should I or shouldn't I? I just did it. If you think about ifs or buts you never do anything. I really joined Parliament on a blind impulse. If I thought of what I might come across I might never have done it. –

Her words she might never have done it applies to the dilemma of being a mother and a professional woman as well. When Joyce joined Parliament she had a four year old son and a young daughter. Parliament begins at 2:30 pm, so she spent her mornings and early afternoons cooking lunch, leaving food for the evening.

— In Parliament we rise [leave] at 10:30 pm, if we're lucky, so I was never there when the children went to sleep. I felt guilty all the time. I think most women do. I felt I was doing the best I possibly could for the children, but one is never sure. I think the problem when one works outside of the home is one tries to work harder at being mother than when one is home. One takes less for granted. So I'm not sure about quality, but certainly one tries harder.

From my own experience I well understood what Ms. Butler was talking about, and said, — I think part of the guilt I felt had to do with the attitude that when a woman stays home she's a better mother, more devoted. But when I lived in the suburbs most of us who stayed home were frustrated. After a while, some women just tuned their children out. They got together with other women to play cards or drink coffee while their children played outside. True, they were there physically but that was the extent of it. —

Joyce Butler answered, — I think the home is a base of security for children but I also think that basically children can adapt to almost every situation if there is this basic security there. If a mother were terribly frustrated it would be bad for the children.

— I go along with women's liberation. It's given a whole new dimension to women's emancipation. The big change is not in actual numbers of women working but that now having children doesn't debar a woman from public life or from working outside of the home.

— There was a celebration of women getting the vote fifty years ago. We thought what more can be done? I went around to organizations. We had meetings as to what was achieved in fifty years. Women's liberation was coming in at the same time so there was a big leap forward. Equal pay is the result of this new atmosphere. I would like to see legislation making discrimination illegal, in employment particularly. Women are accepted up to a certain point but can't go further. — She believes discrimination in education is greatly responsible.

— My constituency consists mainly of working class people, although there are a small amount of professionals. They come to me with their problems so I am more cognizant of the growing awareness of women and their problems in employment. —

Ms. Butler turned to the restaurant counter. She looked surprised. — This is interesting. The last time I was here there were women behind the counter. Now they're all men.

— During the war we had an educational act which gave much greater opportunities to girls than they had before. Once you start that process you can't have half freedom and half slavery. Any time you give something free women benefit, particularly in education where boys always had the advantages. In this society men get preference, especially where money has to be spent. —

She explains that before National Health Insurance, unemployed women were not insured. A married woman was insured if her husband was working, and if he received some form of insurance. Now Ms. Butler is concerned about women who give up their employment to stay home as full time wives and mothers, thereby forfeiting social security and other benefits. She is working to find a solution to this problem.

— I myself was never conscious of discrimination. I'm a simple soul and never notice these things. But now I notice the attitude towards older women. They're often treated with contempt, with a certain indifference, which an older man doesn't get. Age labels a woman. It's the label that's hard to fight.

— When you're a young woman it's an asset but when you're older you come up against discrimination very often. Older women get pushed around. Perhaps they depend upon men too much.

— I'm always looking ahead to the next thing. It must be terrible not to have anything to look forward to. —

THE OLDER WOMAN

LEAVING M.P. Joyce Butler and walking along the lovely Thames River I thought of her statement, — But now I notice the attitude towards older women. — I too notice the attitude since I became one of them recently.

When a woman reaches forty to fifty where is she? Society calls her an *older woman.* If she's single she'll think back to the man or men she might have married, the children she could have had . . . her lost life. She was brought up to believe in marriage and motherhood and somehow, somewhere she missed the boat . . . She's moorless.

If she's married and doesn't have children, she may have a dog or dogs, cat or cats and devote all her time and energy to her husband and her adopted family of animals. If her husband dies at this time, she may go into mourning until her own death. Both the single woman and the childless married woman may dote on nieces, nephews or friends' children.

If the woman is one of the majority, she is married and has children. She probably has worked and may still be working but her job is either to supplement her husband's income or a job she took when her children were all in school and didn't need her full time.

She's working, but unlike her husband, she doesn't base her identity on her work. Her identity is based on others, the others being her children. And at forty to fifty, when her husband is probably at the peak of his success, she's at the bottom of hers. Her children have gone or are going shortly. Her claim to fame is gone and she is put in permanent retirement.

If she hasn't worked, where does she go? She discovers that the saying *life begins at forty* is a sad joke. Who wants to employ you when you're past forty, when you haven't worked before, have no previous experience? Very few ads ask for matured women and when they do it's usually because the job hasn't any future and the salary is futureless as well. So now what???

I haven't any answers, but I have a suggestion. I suggest all women who are young mothers ask their husbands what they [the women] should do when their children grow up. I think women in their twenties and thirties and forties should all ask their husbands what they're expected to do for the next thirty years or so.

PSYCHOTHERAPY GROUP

EVERY THURSDAY night the new Psychotherapy Group meets. They deal with the effects of psychotherapy on women, both negative and positive. They question how much psychiatry is an agent of the patriarchal system.

This group also plans to do research on the different feminist groups, to see how the small group, the larger groups, the CR groups affect the members.

The Psychotherapy Group will write an issue of *Shrew* about women analysts, their work and experience with women patients, as well as the experiences of the patients themselves.

At this meeting I discovered Dorothy Tennov, a feminist from Connecticut who is temporarily living in London. A doctor of psychology, she is writing a book on the effects of psychoanalysis on women.

I have recorded parts of this meeting.

DOROTHY: My idea for this group would not be CR but a research group to study the various methods of psychotherapy and the ways women are being treated.

JANET: Therapy in England is different from the States. If you limited it to the influence of Freud, women here are damaged less. All women are fucked over by the mental illness thing, but we go into analysis less because of the lack of money.

MARTHA:* In psychotherapy I was told I wanted a child and I said no, I'd rather have an animal.

DINAH: Prejudice comes in all sorts of insidious ways. Every woman is a woman which is inferior.

JANET: Looking back on our sex education in school I don't remember there ever being a discussion on female orgasm. They discussed male orgasm abstractly, nothing to do with enjoyment, but they did discuss it. Counter to penis envy, men are fucked up because they don't have a vagina.

DOROTHY: Patriarchy sees that the male controls the society. How sexual would women be if we hadn't had a monogamous society? They get us married so everything will be tidy. They own houses, wives, children.

MARTHA: I was with a group and I made a bad joke about being a lesbian, how I didn't have to worry about abortion or contraception. I was ostracized. I felt unaccepted. One lesbian in the group managed to get a husband and even she was more acceptable. She fit more into a slot, into the conforming society.

JANET: The analyst has this thing that women are immature when they don't have vaginal orgasms and because of his Freudian thing he fucks up the women. For some women vaginal orgasm is important, for others the clitoris is important. The article I read negates the vaginal orgasm; but you can't get away from the fact that to most women the vagina is important.

BONNIE: I think it's too frightening for women to think it isn't important because of their relationship to men. If they begin to think seriously about clitoral orgasm they're going to have to reevaluate their sexuality. In other words, what is a sexual woman and if vaginal orgasm is not so important as we were taught to believe, what then is our sexual relationship to the male?

MARTHA: I thought I was a freak because I couldn't have vaginal orgasms. I'm so persecuted because of my lesbianism that I hate it here. I feel like a Jew in Nazi Germany. I have to deny my sex. Yet on the continent I can have a sex life.

JANET: We have a tendency to equate the English movement with the one in America and it's unfair. The experiences are so different. The myth of vaginal orgasm is accepted there.

DOROTHY: We play act at liberation because we still go to the same stores. We still run to merchants that want our signatures. We could think of a better society but we still have to live within it. We must change the society.

DINAH: Our primary goal now is to get women integrated into the society and Dorothy wants the society changed.

JANET: I think feminism helps you to realize the power and freedom you have over your own life. The Russian revolution didn't work because the authoritarian thing was so built into the individual. In the final analysis the change comes from within ourselves. The revolution is complete when we're all determining our own lives without reference to any authoritarian thing at all, and that's when we're working for all people. Authority is the most crucial thing because one looks for answers outside.

Dorothy Tennov and I spoke at the end of the meeting. She told me she had a list of European feminists. I made an appointment to see her at her London flat the following day.

I have Dorothy Tennov to thank for the warm welcome I received in Holland and France, for making everything easier and mostly for some wonderful dialogues.

PHYLLIS JORDAN

The relationship is defined by the sex

PHYLLIS JORDAN* and I saw each other a number of times before we really had a chance to sit down and talk. Unfortunately the time planned was my last day in London and because of circumstances I was late. Therefore, this interview is much shorter than I would have liked.

Phyllis is a systems analyst who earns more money than most men, including the man she lived with. A university graduate, she not only has the assurance of a more than adequate income but is highly respected in her profession. The dichotomy is her self-confidence professionally and her inconsistent personal feelings as a woman.

Recently she broke up with a man she'd lived with for over a year. They knew each other quite well before they decided to set up house, since both were students at the same university. Phyllis tells me she was sure that living with him would be different from marriage but now she questions this. She feels that although people treated her differently, maintaining she was still an independent person, in her own eyes she wasn't independent. Even though she and her friend decided against definitive roles and they worked together as a team, she still felt the home was her domain in terms of cooking and cleaning.

Phyllis Jordan has been a member of the Workshop and has been participating in CR for well over a year. Women's liberation is crucial for her and she explains why. — There's too large a gulf between my emotions and my mental process. I'm not going to have a relationship again until I feel differently. You learn your emotional response from the day you're born. —

Phyllis was born to an unwed mother. Her mother, a university student, was sent away by her family. She gave birth in another city, returned home and continued on with her education. Phyllis was brought up by her grandmother. Then by an aunt. Although she knew her mother, she didn't learn who she was until she was fifteen years old. Her mother had married, had other children. Phyllis went to live with her. She points out that she and her mother have a good relationship.

Phyllis Jordan believes that the mind is more likely to function independently from the socialization process. — Society defines patterns of behavior. If a man decides to leave it's considered a failure. I felt inadequate, that if I'd been different it wouldn't have terminated. —

I told Phyllis that I had similar feelings when my marriage broke up, even though I chose to end it, — I kept thinking if I'd only been more like a wife, if I'd just swallowed *the division of labor,* if I'd tried harder to be more passive. Yet I detested all those things. And I never really believed in the marriage institution. But I was told everybody gets married. And the part of me that saw me as everybody got married, while the other part always remained single. —

Phyllis had the opposite experience. She remained single but thought of herself as married. — Even though we weren't married, the relationship is defined by the sex. Therefore, it's like marriage.

— Intellectually I feel the break-up was good. Of course you want to have the emotional responses that agree with how you think you should be. If you don't want to be possessive and you behave possessively you hate yourself. —

One of the things that disturbs her is that when she and the man she lived with had an argument she was incapable of doing anything. All her hobbies and interests meant nothing and she felt completely shattered. Yet he could dismiss any argument from his mind and continue with whatever he was doing.

I told Phyllis, — When my ex-husband and I had an argument I stayed up half the night hearing all the words over and over again. Then new words would appear, all the brilliant things I could have and should have said. His words, my words, the new scenario. And I'd say to myself, turn it off already. And there he was lying on the bed sound asleep. Oh, do I know what you're talking about. —

Phyllis Jordan feels she was too dependent during the relationship, and even after the break-up when she decided to go to Scotland by herself, couldn't enjoy it because she was alone. She doesn't feel dependence is negative but adds, — I think it's dreadful that I was debilitated by that dependence. —

Phyllis tells me that during her student days she became disgusted with many female students because although they were committed to politics, drama, journalism, etc., she began to realize their commitment wasn't the same as the males. She feels women are brought up to think of themselves primarily as wives and mothers, and that this limited view is responsible for many attitudes and a lack of confidence many women show. Men, on the other hand, have no such limitations.

— I think men are irrelevant to women's liberation. They can't feel what women feel. Men don't think about who they are, what they are. They just are. They have the identity in this society. They're so confident.

— Women relate to the world, to everything through a man and this results in a bad relationship with other women. And the way men think!! Like if I go off to the pictures with a woman. Men go off together and that's ok. But they think when women do it, it's because they don't have any boyfriends. —

Tonight Phyllis was planning to go to the movies with the man she used to live with. They still see each other. However she is more comfortable in the relationship now. And with herself. She is certain that CR is responsible for the new feeling she has about herself.

— It suddenly dawned on me last night that I could do what I want with my own life, that I'm beginning to understand why I feel and how to make the actual change in thought process from the actuality. I can be in charge of my own life and do what I want, to be myself and like and enjoy myself. To enjoy it because I'm doing it and not doing it with somebody.

— Why should the man be more important than what I'm doing? And I woke up today and thought, I feel good about myself. —

Paul Popenoe
Founder and President
The American Institute of Family Relations
Los Angeles (I believe) California

Dear Paul Popenoe:

Twenty-one years ago, in the city of Pasadena, I took a course in marriage counselling at Pasadena City College. There I learned about the *Division of Labor* which you advocated strongly. I think the *Division* is your idea but since I'm not sure, I'll let that go.

I thought you might be interested in knowing that thousands of years ago there was *The Caveman's Code*. It went like this. Caveman goes out with his club, konks some innocent animals on the head and brings home the booty to an admiring, adoring wife. She, meanwhile, is sweeping out the cave, cooking dinosaur stew and taking care of the children. *The Caveman's Code* says the man's job is to supply food and necessities for the cave. The woman's job is the care and feeding of the man and the children.

So here it is thousands of years later and you're the champion of *The Division of Labor* which is really an updated version of *The Caveman's Code*. In other words, man goes out with other equipment, knocks off a few lesser animals and brings home the booty to an admiring, adoring wife. The cave has become a modern pad with TV, radio, a vacuum cleaner, other things. He still has his job and she has hers and that's the way it is.

I realize that history can't be altered overnight, but don't you think, Dr. Popenoe and staff, that it's time for a change. As recently as last week I picked up a copy of a woman's magazine and there was the good old column *Can This Marriage Be Saved?* with advice by people who work for your institute. This column gives the wife's side, then the husband's side and then the advice.

The young woman in this case was pouring her heart out. Problem after problem came out but the worst it seemed was that her husband didn't care too much for sex. When it came his turn he had much to say but he did admit that sex was not exactly his thing. And what is the advice. He has a low sex drive. Go along with it. He's not too hot in other departments either but after all marriage is marriage. So stay home and give him more confidence in himself and let's hope for the best.

In other words, stay in the cave kid, that's the way life is and if you don't like it, why'd you get married in the first place. Because when I was a student studying marriage counselling that was the advice given to me. Look, you decided to get married, so knock off the complaining. Which is what I did for years, and essentially that was responsible for my antagonistic behavior. One can shut the mouth up but it is rather difficult to shut up one's feelings. And my feelings when I was on my hands and knees scrubbing floors were murderous. My former husband didn't seem to notice my altered position in life. So when he, my caveman came home with the booty I would say things like, — Big deal. You call that money. —

Now I'm aware, Paul Popenoe, that in twenty-one years you've altered your position slightly, but you still insist man is the head of the household. He could be a blooming idiot but if he comes equipped with a prick he's the head. I'm also well aware that *The Caveman's Code* and *The Division of Labor* were set up to keep the human species going.

However, after taking a good look at the species recently, I suggest you revise your *Division of Labor* because I have the feeling that if things keep up the way they're going, we're going to be back to *The Caveman's Code* before we know it.

I would further suggest a real *Division of Labor* Dr. Paul Popenoe and The American Institute of Family Relations, where mind meets mind in harmony, instead of prick meeting vagina in war.

PHYLLIS DROVE me to the Liverpool Station, waved goodbye as I boarded the train. Later that night I stood on deck of the Dutch boat Wilhelmina which would take me to the Hook of Holland. I watched sea gulls swoop down and pick up bits of food from the calm sea.

In the morning we docked and I took a train to Amsterdam where I would meet the Dolleminas and the members of Man Vroux Maatchappy.

HOLLAND

AMSTERDAM

MY ADVICE to anyone who wants to visit the delightful city of Amsterdam is don't go in the summer. At the tourist office directly across from the train station layers of people complained in every language that they'd been waiting two to three hours for accommodations. I waded through the multitudes and decided to try my own luck. One hour later I stood at the window of my tiny room overlooking the Nieuwe Keizergracht, one of the fifty canals in Amsterdam.

Amsterdam has vending machines where you put in a coin and out pops a contraceptive. Prostitutes line the Zeedijk district at night or sit in their rooms waiting for customers while iridescent lights play on their bodies. There are glass roofed boats that go from canal to canal, past the many bridges that light up at night. On both sides of these canals are the picturesque narrow canal houses that were built in the 17th and 18th centuries and still manage to retain their charm. Amsterdam has the Rembrandtsplein with its outdoor cafes, its nightclubs. On Thorbeckesplein is a plush nite club where strippers either strip by themselves or with the help of males in the audience. On the Nieuwe Leidseplein is the COC, the discotheque and social club for homosexuals.

Amsterdam is a day city, a night city. Whatever you want Amsterdam has it. And the city where Rembrandt was born has two feminist groups: Dollemina and Man Vroux Maatschappy.

TEN YEARS ago I had a play produced. The title *N, My Name is Nicki* is based on a girl's game that goes like this: You start with a letter such as N and every time you say a word that begins with the letter N you bounce the ball under one leg. For instance, start bouncing the ball and then N (under the leg) my name is Nicki (under the leg) and I come from Nebraska (under the leg) and I am a nurse (under the leg). Whenever I hear a man say, — Define yourself, — I think of that game and understand why it was only a girl's game. Those with definitions have no need to define themselves.

The main character in my play was an alcoholic. She was based on a friend I'd known intimately. The male was a composite of two or three men in my life. A minor female character was introduced early in the play but in the writing she began to take over. Her part became stronger and stronger because I just couldn't shut her up or maybe I was simply curious and let her go on. I began to feel funny about her. Who in hell is she? Why is she behaving that way? I was close to the end of the play when I realized, she's a lesbian. As soon as her identity became clear I said, get rid of her. You don't know anything about lesbianism. But at that point if I threw her out, I didn't have a play. I finished writing it, put it in my file where it stayed for a year. And then in one compulsive rush did the final rewrite in a twenty-four hour period. I sent it out and was thrilled when I received a telegram telling me the play was going to be produced.

The strange part is that nobody questioned my lesbian until much later. A playwright friend asked, — You've tried it haven't you? —

— No — I answered.

— Then how in hell did you get the nerve to write a character you knew nothing about? —

— I wrote her as if she were a man, — I answered. Which was my way of saying I'd swallowed the stereotype.

After our conversation, in keeping with my great hindsight I purchased two books. *Homosexuality* by the late Edmund Bergler, M.D. and *The Homosexuals As Seen by Themselves and Thirty Authorities*. Themselves were the homosexuals. The authorities were the psychiatrists, psychologists and therapists who knew all about it. And the authorities used all kinds of psychological jargon for the female homosexual such as mother fixation, neurotic displacement of the libido, comparison of the female genitals with that of the male, penis envy and so forth. I read the message I'd gotten earlier as a conditioned heterosexual. Homosexuals were sick neurotic people. In my heterosexual world I saw a lot of sickies but Dr. Bergler does explain that although heterosexuals *may* be neurotic, homosexuals were *always* neurotic. As a conditioned heterosexual I got the larger message. Homosexuals were a threat to humankind, such as it is.

This I understand. A society built on the family will hardly welcome opposition. Sex by heterosexuals has the stamp of approval even in the most puritanical countries because this may result in children. The homosexual has no such reason for being. She or he does not usually contribute progeny to the world. The sexual act of the homosexual has no byproduct. And without a byproduct sex remains in its primitive form, an act purely for pleasure. Humans are not taught to live for pleasure. They are meant to produce.

A few weeks before I left for Europe a friend asked me how I felt about homosexuality. My answer didn't satisfy her. — You admit the only emotional feedback you get is from women. Right? — Right, I answered. — But when you want sex you go to a man, right? — I nodded and thought here it comes and it did. — Why don't you sleep with a woman she asked? Why should I I answered. Eyeball to eyeball she spoke, — Why shouldn't you? —

Here in Amsterdam, before having dialogue with my homosexual sisters I hear her words but instead of hearing 'right' I hear 'why'? Looking out the window of my room at a lit up houseboat I think that instead of questioning why I'm not a lesbian my friend should have been asking me why I am a heterosexual. If man is my aggressor, my put down, my oppressor, would somebody please tell me why am I sleeping in the enemy camp?

LIZ AND ESTHER

Such good girls

I WALK down the Rembrandtsplein, down the Kalverstraat with all the modern shops, to the Dam, past the Palace until I reach the Amsterdam train station. Facing it is a network of streets. Surrounded by raw herring stands, ice cream wagons selling Italian ice cream, patches of colorful flowers, are the many trams coming and going to all sections of Amsterdam. As I board my tram I see people milling about, talking, eating, rushing for trains or trams. We pass canals, glass-sided canal boats with tourists focusing cameras. Narrow streets broaden into a wide boulevard.

Thirty minutes later I step out into one of the new ultra-modern suburban sections of Amsterdam. An old woman answers the bell. I guess I have the wrong apartment. I'm sorry. I'm looking for Esther* and Liz.* —

Her accent is thick, her smile lovely. — I will show you. — She trudges up the stairs with me. — You have to talk loud. My hearing is not so good anymore. Ach, when you're old nothing is the same. You are their friend . . . ? Such good girls. Not like the young today. — She knocks on the door. — Liz I brought you a friend. Such a good girl. — She pats Liz on the cheek and leaves.

Liz looks at me, a sad expression on her face. — She is a good woman, very kind. But she calls us good girls because we don't have boys here. She would, I think, never talk to us again if she knew. — Then, — I was hoping Esther would get home early. My English is so terrible. Maybe we should wait. —

— Did you study English in school? — I ask.

— Yes, but in the nunnery they speak only Dutch so I forget everything. —

— Were you a nun? —

She laughs. — You're surprised. Didn't Anne tell you? Yes, I lived in the convent for eleven years. — She pauses. — You must think I was very religious but no, that's not the reason. —

Liz became a novice when she was sixteen, joining her sister who'd come to the convent six months earlier. She tells me her home was one of constant fighting, that as a child she was always in trouble, at home, in school. — I had a terrible temper and wherever I went they said I was a bad girl. — She entered the nunnery because everytime she visited her sister she was impressed with the closeness of the nuns, the special attention she personally received from the Mother Superior. To her the nuns represented the family she'd never had and she was certain she'd never leave.

Five years later, after taking her final vows, she changed her mind. — I thought, everything here is so nice but I wanted more. To have contact with people, to read a newspaper, to hear a radio, read a book, watch television. I thought, what do I know of the world? All I know is the life inside. So I would sneak to the village and buy cigarettes and drink the forbidden whiskey. —

— That must have been some sight. A nun sitting at a bar drinking whiskey. —

Liz looked at me and burst out laughing. — I didn't go in the habit. When I came to the nunnery I wore slacks and sweater. You were supposed to get rid of them but I hid mine in a secret place and when I went to the village I wore them.

— Once when I told the Mother I might not stay forever she said it was a visit from Satan and not to worry. She would take the responsibility. She said it was God's will that I came and it was God's will that I stay forever. She would remind me of what I was like when I came there. You know, the troublesome child, the bad child. I think, for you to really understand you would have to know the nunnery, to know the life there. And of course the Mother. She was a very clever woman. —

Liz explained that the sisters in the convent painted, sculpted, wove cloth, rugs, made ceramics, furniture and that their only means of support was selling their handiwork. The Mother Superior felt this was not enough and encouraged the sisters to study outside. One of Liz' friends studied architecture. Not so for Liz who became the cook for the sixty nuns as soon as she entered the convent. — She was such a clever woman. She knew us all so well. She wouldn't allow me to study outside because she was afraid if I went I wouldn't come back. —

After ten years Liz asked permission to leave for a week. She was refused. Shortly afterwards she became friends with a nun who told Liz her strong sexual desire was making her miserable. When she'd confessed this to the Mother Superior she was told it was the devil. But devil or no her friend wanted to leave. This was all Liz needed. Together the two planned their escape. Their scheme was discovered and the Mother Superior who was in Italy at the time was reached by telephone. She demanded to speak to Liz, pleaded with her to come to Italy, assured Liz that together they would work things out. She refused and though her friend stayed Liz was chauffeured out of the convent.
— The Mother has never spoken to me or about me since. I went there many times but she refused to see me. Now I understand that her interest in me bordered on homosexuality. —

When I first started writing I was given advice: Make your stories bigger than life. Liz' real life story tops my imagination. One month with her mother. Then Amsterdam. Answers ad in newspaper and is hired. By day, secretary. By night, her employer's mistress. Clothes. Restaurants. Sightseeing. Theatre. Office. Home? His of course. Salary? None. Three months later he tells her they're moving to France. The morning of departure. He is arrested.

Charge 1: Molesting young girls.
Charge 2: Murder.
Members of the jury, what is your verdict?
GUILTY.

— I couldn't believe it, — she told me. — I was so frightened and bewildered. I'd trusted that man. I thought he was a gentleman. I didn't know what to do. You must understand it was as if I was still sixteen. I was the same as when I entered the nunnery. I was so naive. I even told him I'd been a nun. —

At this point Esther came home and while she changed from her nurse's uniform to slacks and sweater she asked Liz how she was doing.

— Never have I talked so much and in English. —

— It's good for you to practice. —

— My head is spinning from so much English. Esther, you speak for me. It makes work for Bonnie ... my English. Am I right? — I shook my head and Esther laughed.

— See, she understands everything. I'm sure you're doing fine. Liz, did you show Bonnie the pictures of you in the nunnery? No? — She spoke from the other room. — Did you tell her about your ex-lover, the one who is in jail? —

— Yes. —

Esther opened the album. — Here she is, Sister Angelica.* It doesn't even look like Liz. And her life! To have gone through all that. —

— I don't regret anything in my life. And I must tell you that I never thought I did bad things. I always believed God helped me because at the last moment I escaped from many difficult things. —

After her lover was arrested she returned to her mother but within a month was back in Amsterdam as a student of languages. Petrified by her experiences she never left her room except to go to school. — I was afraid to go out and I thought I'd go crazy alone all day. I did typing in my room for money and that's how I lived for three months. Then I went to the hospital to study nursing. —

— When I first saw Liz I thought, what an old woman. —

Liz laughs with Esther. — I heard and read in books that when you're a real woman you wear make-up. And I did. —

— It was so bad. She wore it like a clown and her clothes were absolutely awful. —

Both Liz and Esther lived in the student nurses quarters and both dated men.

ESTHER: In the beginning I was really happy with boyfriends but then I started thinking it's not real love they're giving me. They don't give me the love I want.
LIZ: I did see men but they were rarely friends. They would tell me they loved me but they really didn't.
ESTHER: For two weeks I would like them and then I wouldn't anymore. I was always much older than the men in my thinking so I felt like a mother with little boys.
LIZ: I wanted human contact but they always wanted to go to bed.
ESTHER: At the time I met Liz my sexual life was always when I was drunk a little. I was looking for sex but I couldn't get any satisfaction. So many boyfriends and never satisfaction. I thought, I'm not doing what I like. I can only do it when I drink. That's not real.
LIZ: Esther and I are the same. In this world a man is like this. *[her right hand moved above her head]* A woman is like this. *[she places her left hand below the right one]* But two women are like this. *[she puts both hands side by side]*
ESTHER: Liz and I came to the hospital the same year. We talked a lot. Then she became ill and I thought she's really alone. She hasn't anyone. I took care of her, comforted her. I wasn't brought up with any religion so I was fascinated when she talked about the convent. We became friends, began to understand each other.
LIZ: I always had homosexual feelings as a child. But even now I think it is not important whether you're with a woman or a man but there should be love between two people.
ESTHER: After a while we went to the seaside overnight. We both love the sea. It was summer so we slept outside in sleeping bags. In the morning we went back to Amsterdam and I felt there was a change in me. I had never loved a woman before. I'd had girlfriends but no one I loved.
LIZ: Before you tell her about our first kiss can we eat. I'm starved.

We sat on the floor eating bread, cheese, fruit and wine. Esther turned to Liz: – Your English is excellent. I told you it would come back with practice. – Then, – Where was I Liz? –

LIZ: At the seaside.
ESTHER: Oh yes. Well after many weeks we had a sexual relationship and it was really satisfactory.
LIZ: I don't understand the distance between woman and man and

those who go from person to person.

ESTHER: For me the human contact is first, then the sexual relationship. For many it's usual just to have the sexual contact.

LIZ: Esther and I are happy together. We are not using one another.

ESTHER: We are not together just because of sex. I don't care if it's once a week or once a month.

LIZ: I would like to know why women feel they have to do it every night. I don't understand.

BONNIE: Because it's easier than facing the anger of a rejected male. Because it's easier than hearing him scream you're frigid. Because the next day you won't have to see his look of hurt or look of fury or look of rejection. Because in the long run you believe it will make your life easier.

LIZ: But that's not liberation.

BONNIE: Who said it was.

LIZ: Bonnie, do you regret your life, your marriage?

BONNIE: As a person yes because I negated too much of me for too long. As a writer no. I have enough life experiences to write for the next hundred years.

A note for the authorities who claim female homosexuals overidentify with the mother, fear the father, are looking for their cut-off sex organs and so forth and so forth and so forth. Esther comes from a happy home where both parents related well to one another and to their children. I quote: — I know what a happy home is. I've been luckier than most girls. My parents are good people and they love each other. I've always wanted to help others so being a nurse is very satisfying to me. —

Esther and Liz told me they would not consider joining gay liberation simply because they don't believe homosexuals should be isolated from the larger society. Their friends and families know they are homosexuals. — We are concerned with a humanity that reaches out toward one another, accepting each other and all the different life styles. —

WOMEN IN HOLLAND

WOMEN IN Holland are considered amongst the most liberated in the western world. Divorce, contraception and abortion are legal. Abortion however is only legal for medical reasons. As a result there are special planes that go to England for abortion. The cost: 1,000 guilder. (approximately $270.00) A new development which is distressing to feminists is the government's insistence that all abortions be registered.

Day Care Centers: There is a shortage of day care centers and since the fee is high, only those with well above average incomes can afford them. They are also available for those on welfare. Mothers whose incomes are inbetween are just out of luck.

Education: The law requires all children go to school until the age of sixteen. This does not apply to housekeeping students (exclusively girls) who may leave at the age of fourteen. In the senior high school only 25% of the graduates are girls. This percentage has been consistent since 1930.

In Holland, once you enter the university you continue until you receive your doctorate. Women receiving their doctorates in 1960: 18%. The figure for 1970: 17%. Divide the 17% in half and you get 8.5%, the actual number of women working after graduation.

Women students in the teaching faculty number 51%; 23.5% are in the law faculty; 12.6% in the social sciences; 12.6% in science; 19.4% in medicine and 12.9% in agriculture. The lowest figure is in engineering where the percentage for men students is an unreal 98.7%.

Working Women: In this liberal atmosphere 22% of the working force are women. The figure for the unliberated Spanish women is 23%.

Another contradiction. Statistics show that the number of women working in the western world has been on the increase since 1950. The only exception is Holland where the number has decreased. Due to the longer lifespan of women and the relatively young age of mothers when their children leave home, the work force of women over forty-five in Europe has steadily been on the increase. Again, not so for Holland, where the figure has gone from 16.9% to 13.4%. However, employment for women 14 to 19 has increased. This has gone from 48.7% to 49.8%, hardly an earthshaking change. The married percentage (no age recorded) has risen from 7.1% in 1955 to 18.4% in 1964, a sizable change. More recent figures are not available.

Parliament: There are 150 representatives in the House of Commons. Of these 12 are women. In the House of Lords where there are 75 members, 1 is a woman.

One percent of the judges in Holland are women.

Marriage: Sexual freedom is basically accepted. Legally it is nonexistent. Therefore unmarried couples can live together, but since common law marriages are not recognized, these couples are unprotected by the law.

Homosexuality: Until recently two consenting adults twenty-one or over were protected by the law. Those younger were subject to arrest. Now the legal age for homosexuals is eighteen. No such age limit for heterosexuals where you can have sex at any age providing you're a she and he's a he or vice versa.

M.P. GERDA BRAUTIGAM

Is a man who works in a factory liberated?

— I AM NOT a feminist. I have never been a feminist. I don't understand why you want to talk with me. —

At the Red Lion Cafe I listened to Gerda Brautigam. — I have to laugh when you talk about women's liberation. Like you've found a new religion. Is a man who works in a factory liberated? Liberation because you've seen the holy light? — But when she spoke of feminist groups and insisted groups were another form of slavery, adding that it was unnecessary to have a movement I interrupted, — Could you be a socialist without a movement? —

— No — she answered. — That's the strength, making power out of the numbers of people. — Then, — My father was a socialist. He said once socialism was in the world all our problems would be through. Now we know it isn't so. You can't make a paradise of the world. Vietnam, India, the Middle East. Our problems are children compared to those of the world. In Holland our housing shortage is acute but go to India and you see problems and comparatively we are happy. It's a luxury fighting for women's rights. Look at Israel, how they fight for that piece of land and with less sympathy from the world. The woman I admire the most is Golda Meir. What she has to put up with, the problems of her country at her age. We are all children compared to her. —

Eight years ago she gave up journalism to become a member of Parliament. — That was luck. Who gets the chance to start a new life. It was a big challenge but I'm glad I did it. — Five years ago Gerda Brautigam married the man she'd been living with for over twenty years, so both would be protected financially in case of death.

— We don't recognize common law marriages in Holland. I think it relates to our Calvinistic nature. We allow everyone to live as they want, but not to have the government legislate. I was fifty-three, my husband sixty-three and it seemed ridiculous to marry, the 'do you take your lawful husband'. I asked them please don't make speeches. After the ceremony they make a speech about building a house, setting up a family, and the importance of education for your children. When you're older they make a speech about the loneliness of old people. I said please, that would be too ridiculous. —

M.P. Gerda Brautigam travels forty-five minutes daily to The Hague, works sixty hours a week. Her father, a self-made man, was also a member of Parliament. He insisted that his children have the opportunities he never had. Opportunities differed depending on whether you were a boy or girl. The boys went to the university, the girls to the gymnasium. — Nowadays a girl would feel it unfair but I never did since my parents were limited financially. —

Immediately after graduation and for the next six years she worked for a small newspaper. — I wanted to be a journalist from the time I can remember. — During that period she married for the first time. Both she and her husband were in the Socialist Youth Movement. — Those days it was idealism. You must love. Nowadays I would have an affair with him for three or six months and it would be all right. We live more or less in our surroundings. I was the kind of girl who couldn't stick to one man in the beginning. I separated from my husband after two years and then I had the affairs I should have had before. —

She met her present husband in 1940 when both were in the Resistance movement. After he was arrested and taken to a concentration camp, Ms. Brautigam was forced to leave Rotterdam since she was being watched. In Amsterdam she continued her Resistance work. In 1945, after a three-and-a-half year separation they began life together again.

She was one of the journalists who covered the Eichmann trial. — People my age, because of the war, are cynical, wary of people. You have to have a sense of history to understand what happened. Most people don't have a sense of history. Why didn't the Jews resist they ask? You must have an army, weapons, something to fight with. —

On the women's movement: — There is nothing to keep a woman from doing what she wants. She could be a sea-faring captain, anything except maybe a rabbi or a priest. Women's liberation says we are discriminated against, but I think it's nonsense, untrue. What they object to is the pattern of life. Women stay home. Men work. It's true but if you don't want to live in that pattern you don't have to. Maybe it's a fault of my character but nothing would stop me. If women want something they can get it. They blame it on others, a husband or the government or there not being enough nurseries. You have to pay for everything in life. I chose a career. When my husband came back we did talk about whether we should have children or not. I thought I would miss something by not bearing a child. Bearing the child was more important to me than having it. Then I thought it ridiculous to bring a child into the world that you didn't want. I don't think it's a natural instinct to want a child. But if a woman makes a decision to have children she shouldn't cry about it. You have a very good expression in the United States: 'You can't have your cake and eat it.' —

— Men manage to have their cake and eat it. —

— Bonnie, when a man gets married he gives up things. He must work. He can't sit in the Dam Square. —

— You're right. But he also gains free household help, a free nursemaid for his children, free sex because when he gets paid it's his salary. And as a mother I can tell you that when you're walking around with that belly you haven't the vaguest idea of what being a mother means. Gerda, you're obviously a strong-willed, motivated woman. Don't you think you should try to encourage other women to make choices? —

She answered my question with a question. — Don't you think educating women is important? But if they're happy at home having children let them have it. —

— Don't you think women are conditioned to feel motherhood is the ultimate happiness? —

— I agree women are conditioned and they should have the opportunity to study again after their children are grown. The mother is unsatisfied and wants to work but her experience is limited. She should be able to work with people, in nursery schools and with old people. —

— You're relegating women to the same supportive roles. —

Gerda Brautigam chose to ignore my statement. — My sympathy is not with those women who have a university education. It is with the uneducated women who don't have the opportunities. They feel they could be useful to the community, to help sick people and old people. They could be helpers but they lack knowledge. —

— You seem to think that women are suited for one thing. I wouldn't want to be a helper. Would you? —

— No, I couldn't do it. — She looked at me, smiled, and then continued. — My mother wanted her girls to get a good education. My grandfather, an old fashioned Catholic said when he talked about me, 'What nonsense! What if she gets to be a lawyer and can't mend her own stockings.' My mother said, 'If she's a lawyer she can pay somebody to mend her stockings.' And that's what I did all my life, paid somebody to do it. —

When Ms. Brautigam was asked to give a speech on her twenty-fifth anniversary with the newspaper she said, — The main thing is my parents' belief that a girl has the right to a good education. —

— Do you think your life would have been different if your parents had been different? —

She reflected. — I don't know if I would have had the strength to lead the life I did if it weren't for my parents. I owe them a lot. We should convince parents to give girls the same opportunities as boys. Even if the girl decided to stay home her education would not be wasted because she would give her daughter the same opportunity. —

— You're telling me two different things. That a woman can do what she wants. Yet you tell me your parents are responsible for your strength. —

— I don't know about strength but I do owe the most to my mother. Her viewpoint was strong that boys and girls should be equal. I agree with Dollemina when they say men like to have a woman at home. He has to be head of the household. I realize the base, especially with working class people. During the depression women had to work. Now men want to feel they're able to support their families. I agree that the wife has the right to work. —

— If the husband objects what happens to the wife? —

— She blames it on him and rightly. —

— Before you said women blame their condition on the husband or government and you seemed to feel this unfair. —

She laughed. — It wasn't an absolute. — Then, — Older women do charity work and it isn't much of a satisfaction but the husband doesn't give them much of a choice. —

— You know Gerda I'm deliberately trying to pin you down. —

— That's fine. When I was a journalist I did that to many people. — She was silent for a minute. — Bonnie, I'm a bit of a cynic. Can you really change fifty years of attitudes, a different mentality? —

— Yes I think so. —

— In the past five years you have the emergence of free sex. Previously sex was only allowed in marriage. Then if you loved each other you could live together. Always love. Then came the idea that you could enjoy sex without love. I think the decision to make love should be a woman's. A man on TV said love is nonsense. Just jump on them and do it. I don't want to be jumped on. I want to make the decision, not them. I think the resistance is they don't want to be jumped on. The woman doesn't want to be the thing with the hole that is to be used. In this respect I agree completely with the feminists. Women shouldn't be used for the fun of it. It could be for pleasure or love and it is up to the people to decide. This has been a problem for centuries. A man could do what he wanted and women had to be the object for men. It's quite another concept now because we have choices. My sympathy is with the older woman rather than the young because the young have their whole lives before them. —

She agrees with the philosophy of the youth movement that there is more to life than working and has decided that this will be her last term in Parliament. — After forty years of working it will be heavenly to write, to study, to do all the things I've always wanted to do. As the young people say there's more to life. —

Walking along the Dam Square Gerda Brautigam told me, — I'm certainly not against the women's movement. Basically we agree. I like working with women in a party set-up. They're practical and level headed, more than men. —

As we parted she said, — Liberation is liberating yourself from people, leading your own life and not giving a damn what people say. As soon as the criticisms of other people don't touch you anymore you're liberated. —

MAN VROUX MAATSCHAPPY

MAN VROUX MAATSCHAPPY, which is a rough equivalent of the National Organization for Women has approximately two thousand members. Over five hundred live in Amsterdam. This first feminist group in Holland was formed by two women and one man.

In 1968 three isolated incidents occurred. In the magazine *De Gids,* an article appeared by Joke Kool Smit entitled *The Unpleasant Feelings of Women.* [this is a loose translation.] At the same time Professor Hank Misset was writing articles for *Vry Nederland* on labor, specifically on the inferior status of working women. And on television Hedy d'Ancona, social geographist, discussed the general dissatisfaction of women.

Although Ms. Smit, Professor Misset and Ms. d'Ancona were aware of each other professionally they did not know one another personally. When all three received numerous letters and phone calls in response to their works they decided to meet. Letters were answered, phone calls were returned and in September 1968 they met for the first time. Other meetings followed and in December 1968 a feminist organization with the official name of Man Vroux Maatschappy was formed.

The purpose: An action group that would fight for equal rights for women.

Their committees: Equal pay, abortion, education, day care centers, part time workers.

Each group has its own speakers. On the regional level each group is coordinated by six people. On the functional level the groups are represented by one person. MVM maintains internal communications within the movement and is super organized.

ANNAMARIE DE SWAAN ARONS

Men don't ever listen when you talk

— TAKE THE number 2 tram to P.C. Hoofstraat. I have to pick up my children but I'll be back at 4:00. — Annamarie de Swaan Arons, former secretary of Man Vroux Maatschappy talked while her children played in the yard. She said she became interested in feminism when a thirteen year old girl was sent to her as part of a school program. The girl worked in the de Swaan Arons household during the morning and went to school in the afternoon. At age fourteen she would graduate and receive a certificate which would qualify her as housekeeper-nursemaid.

Annamarie explains, — Actually when the girl completes the working and school course she is put on the Labor Department list of unskilled labor. I called the school to discuss this and heard remarks such as, 'They're not intelligent and we have to keep them busy until they finish school. And in a few years they'll be married anyhow.' I thought it was terrible and I tried to talk the girl into getting more education but she was so conditioned she wouldn't listen. When I spoke with her family they said they wanted her to be a housekeeper. —

Conditioning is something she well understands. She believes that although she was given the same educational opportunities as her three brothers she was always under the impression that to her parents marriage came first. After a year of medical school she quit to get married. Married for seven years, the mother of three children, she is returning to school this year. Her parents are disturbed that her children will be cared for by somebody else. This does not bother Annamarie or her husband. Her participation in the feminist movement, particularly the van Baalen CR group is responsible for this decision.

— When we started CR, we said there's so much inequality between men and women and we only thought women should have the same chances. We couldn't define what we wanted changed. Now it goes much deeper than being disappointed, having less chances, not having the same piece of cake. We want a different world. —

In the spring of 1971 Annamarie and her husband travelled to the U.S.; he on a business trip, she to speak with women's liberation groups. — In Berkeley the women were so well educated. They handled themselves so well in terms of speaking. Yet the public was blasé. — In New York she met with many feminist groups, attended a press conference on abortion. — I came back with the feeling you should not spend that much time on changing laws when the mentality hasn't changed. Of course the laws have to change but when you have more strength it's easier. —

Jakob de Swaan Arons came home from work. While Annamarie went into another part of the house to take care of the children, he cooked. He told me they both joined MVM in April 1969. He became a member because he believed the movement had validity but admits it was mainly supportive for Annamarie. — In general we share things that move us. My consciousness wasn't too raised at that time but I had sympathy for the movement. Now my sixth sense has been developed. I see documentation all the time and I try to do something about it. —

Jakob is a chemical engineer. In the laboratories where he works he only knows two or three women who are research chemists. — I spoke to one of them recently and she said women are treated nicely but there's much more concern about their appearance than their scientific approach. She was once told, 'Why don't you wear hot pants? You'd get more attention.' The women chemists say that although they do a good job it's difficult to get approval. — Jakob stopped stirring the food. — It would be an advantage if a woman was ugly. It's sad but true. —

Annamarie came in as he was saying this and added, — Men don't ever listen when you talk. They notice your legs, how you're looking, but not what you're saying. —

Jakob continued, — The most difficult thing for me to accept is that some women emphasize that men should leave the meetings. I had difficulty accepting it but I have more understanding now. Most men have their own worlds and are now learning to cooperate with women. A woman is rarely your friend. She can be your wife, your lover but rarely your friend. Men have friends. Women must work on comradeship with other women. Men don't believe they can be friends and I recognize this as another form of discrimination. I never had women friends. I was attracted sexually. Their whole world seemed remote. Now I feel different. Annamarie is really my first friend. I never met a woman so behind a man.

BONNIE: Behind a man? That's a funny expression to use when we're discussing equality.
JAKOB: I know it sounds discriminating.
BONNIE: How would you feel if Annamarie achieved more than you? Would you think she was being competitive?
JAKOB: I wouldn't mind it in her own field but I would have difficulty accepting competition from her in my field. I could say something else but it wouldn't be true.
BONNIE: In other words, Annamarie is allowed to excel providing she doesn't enter your area of work.
JAKOB: My status with Annamarie has nothing to do with my work but in how I relate to her as a person and how we each relate to the children in our private lives.
BONNIE: What will happen if a child is sick? Who will stay home?
JAKOB: I'd stay home if it was important for Annamarie or we'd both put things together and decide. I feel men and women are equal intellectually. People confuse nature with culture. It may be that women have more responsibility because they think a human being is more important than a career. I feel that places her on a higher level than men.

BONNIE: I think that's a tired argument meant to place women where men want them. Because if the argument is valid then nursemaids are more important than scientists. I'd like to ask a question Jakob. Do you think women have the same sexual feelings?
JAKOB: No. I found out there are essential differences. Certain things are blocked in people.
BONNIE: How about the double standard of women and men?
JAKOB: At one time I would have been offended if a woman made the first advance but not now.

Note: I have written the de Swaan Arons, have sent them a copy of this interview and asked them to make any changes they liked. Annamarie acknowledged my letter but I haven't received any alterations. I assume they are happy with it the way it is. I personally feel that I goofed badly in the last part because I neglected to get Annamarie's comments. However, Jakob's statements are to me most revealing so I have decided to leave the interview as it is.

WHEN I WAS LITTLE

Primer — second grade

WHEN I was little my mommy would wake me up and say good morning. And daddy would say good morning my pretty girl. We ate a good breakfast so we could be strong and healthy. Daddy would go to work and I would cry. Mommy said, 'Daddy has to go to work so we can eat and have this nice house.' Aren't daddies nice?

Mommy would let me help do the dishes. And she would put on my pretty dress and we would go outside. I played with my friends and mommy would sit and talk with the other mommies. And I would see policemen helping children across the street and old ladies and other people too. I would say, 'Hello Mister Policeman.' He would say, 'Hello little girl.' Aren't policemen nice?

Mommy would take me to visit the fire station. I would see all the firemen. Mommy said they help people when there is a fire. They climb ladders and put the fire out with water from hoses. Aren't firemen brave?

One day I got sick and mommy took me to the doctor. He put a wooden stick in my mouth and told me to say aah. Then he gave mommy a piece of paper and said it would make me all better. And he gave me a lollipop. Mommy told me doctors study for a long long time so they know everything to make people better. Aren't doctors wonderful?

Mommy and I went to the drug store and the man in the white coat gave me medicine to make me feel good. He showed me all the bottles. He has to know about all of them. Isn't he smart?

We went home to our house. The postman gave mommy letters and it made mommy happy. Mommy said he always brings mail even when there is snow and rain. Aren't postmen strong?

Mommy made me soup and jello and she read me stories. Then she tucked me in. When I woke up mommy was cleaning the house. She had the radio on. I heard the president speak on the radio. Mommy told me he took care of the whole United States and he was very smart. She said he had men in Congress who helped him too. Presidents must be very very smart.

When I got bigger mommy took me to school to meet the principal. He told me all about the school and my teacher and what fun I would have. Mommy said he is the boss of the whole school. Isn't he wonderful?

I got to be five years old. Mommy said, 'Today is the first day of school.' I washed my own self and brushed my teeth and put on a very pretty dress. Daddy said, 'My little girl is so pretty.' And he kissed me. Then he went to work so we could eat and have our nice house.

Mommy took me to school. The nice policeman helped us cross the street. My teacher said, 'Good morning boys and girls.' She showed all the girls where to play. She showed all the boys where to play. The girls played with dolls and clothes and houses and carriages. Just like mommies. And we played nurse and teacher too. The boys played with cars and trucks and guns and buses. They played doctor too and fireman and policeman. Just like daddies do.

One day my teacher asked all the boys and girls, 'What do you want to be when you grow up?' All the girls said they wanted to be nurses and teachers and mommies. That was nice. All the boys said they wanted to be doctors and postmen and soldiers and firemen and policemen and engineers. And I said, 'I want to be the president.'

My teacher said, 'You can't. A girl can't be the president.'

'But I want to.'

'No,' she said.

'Yes yes yes,' I said.

My teacher got very mad and told my mommy and daddy. Mommy said, 'Girls grow up to be mommies or nurses or teachers.' Daddy said, 'My pretty girl can be a singer or act on a stage.'

'But I want to be a President.'

'No,' said mommy.

'No,' said daddy.

'Yes yes yes,' I said.

Daddy was very angry. Mommy was very sad. And I was so happy.

DIANE

As a married woman I lost my identity

SHE MET me at my canal house and we walked around Amsterdam while she pointed out the sights. At a table in an outdoor cafe on the Rembrandtsplein Diane* tells me she certainly relates to the women's movement but she's too old to join. — I'm forty-nine. —

— Diane I'm forty-five. —

— But you're so energetic for your age. —

— I'm basically a very lazy person. I push myself. —

— Are you saying it to help me or is it true? —

I laughed. — Oh it's true, believe me. —

The only survivor of her family she says, — I feel discrimination as a woman and a Jew. As a Jew I was robbed of my surroundings and my people. There are no words to describe what they did to people like me. A friend of mine who also lived through the Second World War also said to me we are all invalids. We work, we look nice but we are invalids. Genocide not only kills all the people who belong to you, but also kills your identity.

— As a married woman I again lost my identity. You don't know it. There isn't a moment where you say I've lost my identity. It goes gradually. When I was a child I couldn't live a day without playing the piano but I stopped during my marriage. My husband never took me seriously. He had the attitude that I was beautiful but inferior. I got the feeling I was some exotic being. —

Recently separated from her husband she is searching for something to do. — I don't link identity with work. For me it means economic freedom. And there's work and work. Some dull, some interesting. At my age where do I start? I haven't worked for twenty-five years. But I can't visualize another thirty years not doing something to occupy my mind. If you don't work you're not part of the society or the world. —

She looked out into the street, then at me. — I'm angry. What will I do for the rest of my life? I left law school when I married. I think I would have finished if left on my own. Now I'm sorry I didn't. Yet I thought if I succeeded my husband would have felt inferior because he didn't finish school. Now it's gone wrong anyhow and I think, what a pity that I quit school but I couldn't have known that so long ago. Then I wanted a home. I wanted children. My daughters are the only relatives I have. My family, cousins, aunts, uncles, girlfriends, boyfriends, everybody who made up my world, a world I accepted as real disappeared. I no longer had roots. And now after twenty-five years of marriage where I devoted my life to my husband and my children that too is gone. What will I do to fill the vacuum?

— A friend of mine lost her husband and she says she's no longer a person. He's not there to tell her she's pretty, to take care of her. She says she was something because of him, the way he saw her. . . . The relationships of the young are healthier. Yet I see the same dependency in young girls, that they are still trying to please men. I think Anne* and Alan have a good relationship, don't you? —

— It looks good. —

— I tried to play up to my role and now that I don't have to do that I feel free. I want to be myself now, whatever comes out of it. — But she complains, — My husband feels I'm still a possession of his because he pays for me. He feels he owns me and the home. He's the legal owner. —

She pauses, smiles listens to the colorful street organ outside the cafe. She explains that years ago when they didn't have radio or TV it was an amusement for the people and they danced on the street to the organ music.

— When I was a child I remember the organ grinders and their little monkeys all dressed up in doll clothes. We used to put pennies in their hands. — I said.

— My age, it isn't such a bad age. And I've known marriage and children. A long summer of a woman comes at my age. Didn't an American writer say that? But a second thought is it won't last that long so I think maybe the ten years from fifty to sixty where you're still relatively young is good. Maybe when I'm sixty I'll feel differently.

— I'm not a person of this time. Yet some of the new ideas become a part of me because I'm living in this time. You read the paper, you see TV, you talk to people so some of these ideas become a part of you without your knowing it. I don't know how I'll feel in five years but I'm still attracted to the strong male. And I hope by the time I'm sixty I won't think the way I look is so important. I can't creep out of my skin all at once. I must live through my own experiences. —

Note: Diane is the mother of Anne, whose interview appears later in this section.

DOLLEMINA

ONE MONTH after MVM was formed a second group sprung up. In January 1969 twenty men and women got together and formed Dollemina. In February their number grew to 4,000. Within six months they had over 8,000 members. Dollemina drew many of its members from the Socialist Party and was conceived as a socialist movement.

Action groups were formed immediately: abortion, unmarried mothers, equal pay, speakers' group, day care centers, education, media. Every Tuesday in Amsterdam the coordinating council meets to plan activities for the following week. There is also an open speakers' meeting for new members.

Although Dollemina is the largest feminist group in the Netherlands a number of women have dropped out. The reason: A few knowledgeable women and men took over the meetings, became authoritarian figures and isolated many members and potential members. Then there was the socialist ideology that had to be accepted by all members.

On November 9, 1970 a TV program co-hosted by Dollemina and MVM called *Op de Vroun* (Straight On to the Women) was aired. It dealt specifically with women's problems. The program was well organized. Therefore it came as a surprise when an uninvited woman ran to the microphone, gave the number to call for abortion and left. As a result Dollemina received over one hundred seventy calls in thirty-six hours. Previously only MVM was doing abortion referrals. Now Dollemina has four abortion clinics as well.

TWO EX-DOLLEMINAS AND A FEMINIST RAP

THE RED light district around the Zeedijk canal is filled with sailors' bars, blaring juke boxes, restaurants, sex shops. The books are familiar, the paraphernalia too. Even Zelda is for sale. During the late afternoon, men can be seen leaning against store windows eyeing every female. Their bored sexy expressions make them look like retards. Tourists walk alongside pimps, prostitutes, workers on their way home.

I climb the stairs to an apartment where I meet with Rita Hendriks, Elizabeth and Lizbeth. — Isn't this area fascinating? — Elizabeth says. — What a place for a feminist! —

Rita who was with Dollemina from its inception talks about this feminist group. — We thought we had to start with social problems before women could see the whole picture. I thought the special thing in Dollemina was that we were men and women working together for women. And we had so many good looking women which I thought a good thing because people identified with them. Many of us would go to schools to speak to the boys and girls there. — But she believes the Dollemina women lost out when the men began taking over the meetings. A number of women left in protest. Rita was one of them. Elizabeth, who'd been with Dollemina for a year also refused to stay. Both Rita and Elizabeth went to the Redstocking camp in Denmark.

Rita tells me — In Denmark I understood what feminism was all about. Dollemina wanted everybody to get the idea of socialism. If you had the idea of feminism as well they said you were not a socialist but an MVM. If you didn't agree you remained an outsider. I myself had trouble integrating and finally gave up. —

Rita claims that Dollemina couldn't accept that all women are oppressed regardless of their economic situation. — We are not hungry, we don't need a place to live so how can they understand. When you have to struggle for your own life it is important to have a feminist group with just women. In the beginning you think change depends on the big things. Then you realize it's the little things that keep women in their place. Still you can't divorce yourself from the politics of the country. I started the woman's group after my experience at Redstocking. I knew we lost many women because of the structure of Dollemina and I felt we must reach them again. And I wanted to contact the women who were not in groups. —

At Redstocking Rita Hendriks had second thoughts about the good looking women in Dollemina and wondered why she thought this important. — I never thought about looks in Denmark. Then I realized women are sex objects only in a male world. We are sex objects no matter what we do or think. When I came back to Amsterdam I saw this in everything, even in myself. I used to say I'm wearing make-up for myself but I realized it wasn't true. I built my idea of myself through others. You had to be a good looking girl to catch a man. Everything about me was an obsession, even the hair on my body. Now everything is growing but the hair on my head. —

The three burst out laughing while Elizabeth took me by the hand and showed me a framed picture of Rita taken before her stay at Redstocking. Her perfectly made-up face, long mascarad lashes were framed with long flowing hair. Rita's hair is now close cropped. Her face is absent of make-up. She no longer shaves her body. Elizabeth laughed. — You know the advertisements for cosmetic houses where they say before and after... — Lizbeth finished the sentence. — ... Rita has done it in reverse. —

Rita Hendriks teaches kindergarten. She admits she once had a boys' corner, a girls' corner. Although this has changed she is disturbed that five year olds are already conditioned when they come to her. Speaking of herself she says, — You know I always thought I was very emancipated. I was never pushed into a corner by men. My personality is strong and in my work I never was the underdog. Now I say yes I have these things but still to others I am a sex object. —

Elizabeth who joined Rita's group at the beginning is an interpreter. Actually she came to Rita's as her interpreter but Rita discovered her English was not bad. Talking about men Elizabeth tells me, — It's not as simple as saying I'm going to be liberated and you must cooperate. You're my oppressor and everything you do is wrong. Everything you do is shit. As a girl you learn to be afraid to be left out of the social life. You want to be popular.

— My protest began in my sexual experiences. I was free. Free? I didn't dare refuse a boy. This chap kept saying I need you, I want you and you don't care for me so I slept with him even though the sex wasn't good. I thought I had to do anything to keep him. Being alone was worse for me than being with this chap. I needed a boyfriend so badly I'd pick up with any type. I've been swallowing my anger for years and even now I can't cry out and say to men, you shitty lot, you shitty lot. —

Like Rita, Elizabeth explains she functions well in her professional life but she adds, — In my emotional life, and sex is a part of it, I have great troubles. —

Lizbeth is a student of social anthropology. She studies the various cultures, how one culture overlaps another. She discusses religion, economy, work habits, sex, the family and how dependent they are on women. — I can relate my studies to my personal life and recognize that women are part of a sub-culture. —

Her exposure to the women's movement came one month ago when she joined Rita's group. — I'm impressed with the closeness I see. But when I'm with women outside of the movement I feel the competition. When Elizabeth and Rita told me about the camp in Denmark I connected it with a holiday I took with two girlfriends and we are good friends. Still we have competition. And I compared it with Elizabeth's experience at the Danish camp where they were free of it. —

Elizabeth commented, — I had this feeling of love for my sisters in Denmark and now I have it more. All these feelings of repression and oppression, fears, jealousy, inhibitions I view as mechanisms of keeping you in your place. I don't have a special boyfriend now and my old feelings make me fear that. I want to express myself and my ideas but the boys I'm with never think about that. But sometimes you just feel like sex so you do it. —

Lizbeth's voice was barely a whisper. — Sometimes you do anything to get a man. Outside in Yugoslavia I felt exactly like the grass on the ground around me, cold, when this man came over me. —

MY DOLL

I AM so lucky. I have a new doll. My doll pees. And she cries mommy. And she has pretty blond hair with curls. She has blue eyes and long long lashes and her eyes close and open.

I am so lucky. My doll has a blue dress and a pink dress and a yellow one too. And my mommy knitted her a sweater. In the morning when it's all bright and shiny outside I take her for a walk in the doll carriage my daddy got for me. She lies there in her carriage and sleeps. If I sit her up she opens her eyes. Her name is Helen.

My brother goes out too. While I take Helen for a walk, my brother plays baseball or football and he fights and yells and does other things. His name is Joey.

One day I pressed my nose against the cold window and I watched the snow falling down. The whole world was white. I told Helen it was snowing and she looked at me with her eyes and said — Mommy. — I told Joey and he yelled — Yippie! — I dressed Helen very warm in her sweater and I tucked her in her carriage. Then I took her out.

Joey was throwing snowballs with his friends. My friends were walking with their carriages. I looked at Helen and said — Helen do something. — She said — Mommy — and she peed. I got mad and said — No do something. — She said mommy and she peed. And I yelled — That's nothing. Do something. — Helen closed her eyes and I said — That's nothing. —

I took Helen and smashed her against the wall. Then I made a snow ball with my hand, a big one, and I threw it at Joey.

EXCERPTS — ELLIE AND MARYAN

I don't like the word lesbian

ELLIE* IS employed full time, is married, has two children. She is a bisexual who belongs to MVM and Gay Liberation and Anneke van Baalen's CR group. Maryan is a homosexual who was formerly with MVM but is now with Gay Liberation. She is a psychology major at the University of Amsterdam.

B: Maryan, why did you quit MVM?
M: It's not really a feminist group yet. Most all the members are married. I couldn't speak about homosexuals. I wanted to put something in the paper; addresses of people here who are homosexuals for those in South America because the situation for homosexuals is very bad there. The members said what has that to do with us?
B: Do you think it's easier for a lesbian today?
M: I don't like the word lesbian. It's an insult to me. The word is homosexual and it should be the same for both women and men.
B: Do all homosexuals feel the same about the word lesbian?
M: I don't know but that's how I feel. You asked me do I think it easier for a homosexual today. No. It's still against the law and when you have to tell your parents it's the same. Most students say they

don't know any homosexuals. Everybody knows homosexuals but they don't know they're homosexuals. Once we are more in the open and others realize we're here they'll have to change.

E: I don't think that will change things. You think it's the same but when I'm on the street with you and we're kissing each other I feel the pressure. In the beginning it was me loving a woman and being able to love men but once I stepped out and felt I had to be open and honest it changed me. I felt it as dirty. The women I met questioned me. They said you think you are a bisexual but you are a homosexual.

M: Women don't want to get rid of their heterosexuality, being passive, not talking. Perhaps you can't put away all the conditioning.

E: I honestly never felt the difference, whether it was a man or woman.

M: I never loved a man.

E: Then I thought perhaps it's true what they're saying. Maybe I don't realize it. Now I correspond with a woman who's also married and has homosexual relationships and I realize it's natural for me.

M: Before, if I couldn't find a woman, I'd go to bed with a man. I don't do that anymore. Actually I knew I was a homosexual when I was thirteen.

E: I didn't even know about sex until I was seventeen.

M: Women often don't discover they're homosexuals until they're thirty-five. *[grins over at me]*

B: I'll never see thirty-five again.

M: *[still grinning]* Some women don't mature until they're older.

B: How much older?

M: Stop joking clown. You're joking because you don't know what to say. I'm going to take you to the COC Club.

B: Good. But before we go would you tell me how you felt when you discovered you were a homosexual.

M: It was terrible for me. I have a mother, a father, a brother, a sister. It's not just what I am but what they are. My parents still don't know. But they're disappointed in me. When I told my sister she just said, 'so.' She accepted it. My brother didn't even know what a homosexual was. He studied about Greece and Rome and still he didn't know.

B: Ellie?

E: For me it was good. I knew I was a bisexual over a year ago but I did nothing because the woman I loved was in love with somebody

else so it was impossible with her.
B: Ellie, does your husband know?
E: Yes and for some reason he doesn't mind other women. Maybe it's because he can't compete. He heard me telling my children there are men and men and women and women who form a kind of marriage. He didn't like my saying that.
M: I think in all relationships roles are changing because of feelings and knowledge. Most men don't choose women who are as bright as they, but there are some who like bright women and older women because they can learn more.
E: I feel the oppression when I have sex with a man. There are difficulties in both relationships but with a woman there is the possibility of equality.
M: When you're a homosexual you have nothing at all. Everything is against you. Homosexuals often stay together for two years. Nothing ties you together like children or approval of family and the larger society.

Maryan made a date to meet me at the COC. The next morning when I woke up I found a piece of paper on the floor and discovered it was a note from Maryan, but couldn't figure how it got under the chair. She called later on and asked if I found her message. Yes I found it but how did you get it in my room. — I was riding by on my bike and figured you must be sleeping so I tossed it in the window. Where did it land? — Under the chair by the door I told her.

She laughed. — What power. —

FOUR MVM WOMEN AND A MAN

LESA* INVITED me to her home so we could discuss feminism in America, in Holland and to share my experiences in Ireland and England. They were appalled at the Irish women's situation. — Don't Irish men realize how backward their country is? Why don't they do something as well? —

The women in MVM consider it perfectly natural that men are part of the woman's movement. Although they feel that men are often responsible for woman's situation, this does not apply to those in MVM who according to them are different.

In the middle of discussing Lesa's two abortions after having four children, her decision to return to the university, Joyce's* insistence that she is not much of a feminist and cannot see man as the enemy ... Mary* telling us that she cannot have orgasms with men, only with women ... Sue* telling us she had sex with a woman but didn't like it, that she too is back at the university because marriage and children weren't enough for her ... Joyce telling us she was not oppressed, never felt oppressed and thoroughly enjoys watching her children grow up and Mary disagreeing, arguing that most women she knew were not so happy and when you keep saying that, they will cling to your ideas because those ideas are considered normal and acceptable. In the middle of discussing orgasms, why women fake them, why men were such poor sex partners and was it natural for women to stay with one man or with any man ... In the middle of all this an MVM man walked in. From an active dialogue where words rushed into other words, the room became conspicuously silent. The man shook my hand, welcomed me to Holland. He looked from woman to woman. And stood in the midst of our silence. Turning to Lesa he asked, — Isn't this the night for the MVM meeting? —

She answered, — I thought everybody was notified we'd decided to cancel the meeting so we could talk with Bonnie. —

Oh he said and remained, sitting himself in the middle of the room. We were the circle and he was the focal point. Lesa tells him, — We are discussing things that concern women. — He reacts by not reacting. Suddenly sounds come and go. All talk at once. All stop at once and on and on. I look at this man. He appears uncomfortable, embarrassed but stubbornly determined to stay.

ME: You must be aware that your presence is intimidating.
HE: As a feminist I feel I have the right to be here.
LESA: I told you this is not a meeting of MVM. We are women talking.
HE: [to me] I can leave because you don't have the opportunity to speak with Dutch women every day or I can challenge you and fight what you say.
ME: You can't challenge me because I am only interested in what women say.
HE: There are limitations when the dialogue is between women.
ME: Why what can you contribute? Can you discuss your abortions? Can you discuss your clitoral orgasms? What female experiences have

you had?
HE: I gave up a lot of things to give my wife opportunities.
MARY: The only way you can help us is not to talk with us but to talk with other men.
HE: Oh! I've observed the power play in MVM.
MARY: Yes but it was all male controlled.

End of group dialogue. After a few individual attempts to continue, in spite of the man who was still sitting in the middle of our circle, Mary shrugged and talked directly to the women. — I went alone to the Redstocking Camp. Anneke and Rita and Hilly had gone before and there was a group that followed. But I went alone. In the camp I could see that in each country things were different for the woman but in feelings it was the same. I asked myself was this a movement for women in my position, middle class with children. But there were unmarried women in the camp and they felt the oppression as well. —

At this point the man rose, said goodnight to everyone, including me. Although his mouth smiled his eyes were furious. I've seen this look before. It follows the 'I am liberal. I'm with you. Now you accept me, never question my motives and I will help you.' When you don't follow the rules of *his* game you receive *The Look*.

As the door closed behind him there was a rush of comments. He was a true feminist, he was a misfit with other men, he was empathetic, which made it worse for him, he was a hard worker for feminism, he did make things easier for his wife. So why did he behave that way after we explained the purpose of our getting together? Oh for God's sake said Joyce, he had every right to be here. I simply don't understand why we couldn't speak in front of him. Well wait a minute Joyce maybe it was just me. Am I the only one who felt intimidated? It turned out everybody felt the same, everybody but Joyce who thought the whole scene ridiculous. I told you I wasn't much of a feminist. Yes I believe in equal pay and schooling. I'm even going back to school myself but I can't see where any of that has to do with men. I like men. I am not oppressed. I never felt oppressed and I never will. She sat for a few more minutes and left.

We continued talking for another hour and then I left.

EXCLUDING MEN

ANNEKE TOLD me about the meeting. — Come if you're free. —

I climb the narrow staircase of the canal house. The minute I walk in the door I realize this isn't just another meeting. My stomach is knotted. The air is tensionfilled and womenfilled. Fifty women representing both Dollemina and MVM are having a joint meeting for the first time. Excluding men.

Anneke explains the meeting was called to see if both groups can work together to eliminate the manipulation of women in groups by men. — The women are going to speak in Dutch because it's easier. We'll translate as we can. —

Feminists from both sides speak. They each look to their own group for support. And get it. Both groups insisting theirs is the ideology. And to prove solidarity they draw physical lines as well. Dollemina sits on one side of the room. 'Society is the enemy.' MVM on the other side. 'Man is the enemy.'

One of the women from MVM begins discussing a personal experience she's had with a man. In MVM. Another woman talks. And another. Women begin to smile. Then laugh. A small contingent from Dollemina remain firm in their Marxist belief. They don't speak. Two of the older women bend from the sides of their chairs and whisper to one another. They start to laugh. Suddenly one breaks in and talks about her encounter with a man in Dollemina. Everybody roars with laughter.

The tension is broken. One after another they speak. Sometimes two, three women are rushing in to talk at the same time. Seriousness, anger, more often than not turns into laughter. Experiences are shared that are too close for comfort. And as they share they begin going to the other side of the room. The dividing line is gone. They are now woman to woman, rather than group to group.

Mary whispers, — This is marvellous. Hilly . . . the woman from Dollemina, the one who spoke first . . . you know I never heard her talk about herself. Always before when I ask her something she tells about socialism. She is not really a leader but like a leader. You know, the women respect her. So when she spoke it freed others. —

Now the question: Should they continue to meet without men? Without exception, all the women from MVM say yes. Some from Dollemina agree but Hilly and her contingent cannot see where this will accomplish anything.

Jonni looks at me. — They are saying we can talk until we're blue in the face. Talk is nothing. We have to change laws and the system. —

The two CR groups were started by Anneke van Baalen of MVM and Rita Hendriks of Dollemina. The women from both groups are at this meeting. Rita and Anneke talk about the CR experience.

Mary translates, — What they say is, if we are oppressed we should at least have the right to examine what we feel and not be crushed by the men in our groups. —

— Crushed? —

— You know. When they make the decisions and don't let you speak or else they do but don't listen. — She stops when Hilly talks and then says, — She just said the society holds women down. —

There is a very long interchange without any translation. Ellen sees my expression and smiles, then scoots over from the other side of the room. — Jonni told Hilly that in CR we discuss our feelings only in relation to the society. That we do agree with her. Society is guilty but there are many men in that society. And for a change we want to talk about it without their help. —

I hear Hilly speak. Mary is excited. — Hilly agrees. She says we're right. —

A vote is taken. The decision is unanimous. CR groups will be formed immediately.

And for women only.

Mary walked me back to my canal house. She explained that the women were very happy about the decision. Happy they were finally getting together. She stopped walking. Looked over at a lit bridge and then said excitedly. — I'm having a birthday soon. Will you come? I consider myself a year old because that's how long I am with the women's movement. — And then, — Remember last night I told you my father loved me because he thought I was like him and Lesa answered he loved an illusion? She was right. So many people love people that aren't there. You have no right to make people into what you want ... Come to my birthday party. It will be fun. —

She said goodbye, promised to see me again.

THE COC CLUB

THE NEW Merriam-Webster paperback dictionary (my travelling dictionary) defines stereotype as: 'repeated without variation, lacking originality or individuality.' Society has always been more comfortable with its stereotypes than with its individuals. It's important to know who's who and what's what. In the 20th Century one must stand up and identify oneself. And to keep us in our stereotypes we are given traits, characteristics, features and mannerisms.

When they tell a woman she's so feminine she can be certain she's gone into her assigned slot. This remark is usually a compliment. But let's face it, how can a man be sure he's masculine unless she's feminine or better yet how can he remain on top unless she agrees to stay on the bottom. Of course this can backfire and the 'you're so feminine' may be an accusation or a challenge. — Women are so feminine. Could you do plumbing, could you do heavy construction work, could you be a moving man? — Invariably the man who asks this can't do these things either but that doesn't stop him from saying — you can't do it because it ain't a woman's job. —

You're right. It ain't a woman's job and you've seen to it by keeping us away from all those 'men's jobs.' While you were learning to use your muscles, I was killing my eyes trying to thread a needle for the sewing class I flunked.

If you've read the above you can see I started out with stereotype and sort of went round which means I digressed, an assigned feminine trait which I've gotten to like tremendously. For years I heard, for God's sake, you're a bright woman. Why can't you stick to the point? I now find those who fervently stick to the point quite dull. The female mind has been encouraged to go in every direction which keeps the mind sharp and flexible. It seems to me that men have rigid minds that go in one direction and if another mind turns the corner, they are totally lost.

And for those who are lost, we are now entering the COC Club where the rock music is heading straight for me, forcing my body and ears into immediate shock. The club is packed to capacity as Maryan, Anne and I search for a table with available seats. I could tell Maryan was saying something but what? Again she yelled but this time I heard. — What do you think? —

— Think? Here? You've got to be joking. —

— Clown. What do you think of the club? —

— Beautiful. —

Anne leaned over. — Are you two talking? I think I've gone deaf. —

Maryan shouted, — What will you have to drink? —

We ordered and between numbers another shout, — Do you like to dance? —

I answered, — Yes I love to dance. —

— Would one of you like to dance? —

Anne said she'd rather watch so Maryan and I joined the dancers on the crowded floor. The blasting music made conversation impossible. Arms, legs, bodies moved in exaggerated slow motion as hysterical strobe lights blinked on and off. My eyes joined my body in shock. Maryan leaned over me, — You're not bad. —

— I used to teach dancing. —

— I'm not such a good dancer, huh? — Then laughing, — Clown, stop mimicking me. —

Finally the person in the control booth decided to give us a break. The music and lights dimmed as couples held each other in a fox trot. Maryan explained that the COC Club was conceived over twenty-five years ago and at that time it was called The Shakespeare Club. Until 1970 it was strictly a social organization. Now action is taken to instigate legal reforms as well as change the image of the homosexual. The members are forcing confrontations, working politically and demanding an active part in the society. They are hoping that in the future when two homosexuals buy property the mortgage will contain both names to protect them in case of separation or death. This problem applies to unmarried heterosexuals as well but they can marry if they choose. As for Maryan, a heterosexual male friend has asked her to marry him claiming he enjoys her company. — He says we can both lead our own lives. I don't want that now but maybe someday I will. —

Maryan told me that the COC was good because it gave her a chance to meet other homosexuals but she wasn't too crazy about dancing, drinking or the noise. She prefers conversation. — Most homosexuals don't know other people. They're just living in their own world. — From serious she turned playful and gave my arm a sock. — Anne's talking to a woman. What do you say? You really should try it once. You might even like it. — I burst out laughing which I realized immediately was a mistake. — Go ahead laugh. You know what laughter is don't you? —

— Oh shutup Maryan. I know what it is. —

She stopped dancing, hugged me and we both laughed. The music blasted once more, the lights went insane as we joined Anne at the table. Drinking our drinks, watching the couples on the dance floor, we resorted to sign language with a few words thrown in. At 1:00 am we said goodnight to Maryan. Anne and I walked to the canal house she and Alan shared.

ANNE

I know what a woman likes

ANNE PUT up coffee. She told me that while Maryan and I danced a woman came over to her, offered her a cigarette — which I accepted reluctantly because I didn't want to encourage her. — The woman asked Anne if this was her first time at the COC. She then asked if Anne had a special friend. When she answered yes she had a boyfriend she was living with, the woman became angry and told her she had a boyfriend too.

Anne told me she asked her what she thought about the club and the woman said it didn't help the people much, that they are drugged with the noise and forced to face each other sexually. — They're obliged to communicate in music and dancing but not really communicate. It doesn't change anybody's attitudes but only confirms attitudes that already exist. And when it's closing time they still have to face the real world. —

Anne has her own ideas. — I don't think we are all heterosexual or homosexual. People can have a little bit of both in them, but today they're forced to be accepted by one group and in that way hide a part of their personality. There are more shades of being. The COC puts people in a place with others just like them. They're only seemingly happy. They're allowed to be themselves only for as long as the club is opened.

— I never had sex with a woman but once I was with a woman who said she'd never had an orgasm and I thought, I could give you twenty-five orgasms a night. I never said it or did it because maybe I wouldn't like it myself but I know how. I'm not sexually attracted to women but if there weren't any men around I would be with a woman. —

Anne tells me that when she and Alan decided to share an apartment two years ago they were determined to have an egalitarian household. — We didn't say this is what you should do and this is what I should do. We said we should both do as much as we can. Alan did the shopping but since he didn't know the difference between pork and liver, he bought the wrong things. So now I shop and cook and Alan does the housework which is fine because I hate housework. In my home my mother did everything. She tried in every way to please my father but my father was authoritarian and very difficult to please. Alan's father is more polite but the situation is the same. Now and then Alan is like his father. You can't escape your background. Once when we had a row he became angry and said, 'get out.' I said, you're the one who's angry. You get out. —

Nobody left but Anne claims that at that moment he behaved as if the apartment they shared (originally his) was his property and Anne was also his property. She tells me that although they behave very much like a married couple she wouldn't consider marriage. — It's to make other people happy, to satisfy parents, friends, neighbors but it has no meaning for me. People don't like people who attack their ideas. If I show I'm different and they even allow themselves to think I'm right, it's frightening because they think they have the only moral way, the only right way. They build their lives on one set of values and if they think they're wrong then maybe their whole life is wrong. —

When it comes to children she says she doesn't want them. — I like working. My work is very important to me and I don't want to have to stop at 4:30 because the children are coming home. I don't want to spend all those years caring and worrying. One man takes enough of your emotions. —

Even though she doesn't want her own children she would like to live in a commune and help care for children. She says she is upset because her paternal grandmother lives in a home for the aged. — If I lived in a commune I would have my grandmother with me. I think it's horrible for her to be in an old people's home where she only sees old people dying. In a commune you could have your own life but also be responsible for others. It isn't fair to put old people away when they can't earn any more money. Divorce too is painful. But if you lived in a community like that you would be with other people, get comfort from them. It's artificial today. Even to see your friends you have to make appointments. —

Anne asked me how the interview went with her mother. — Isn't she a wonderful person? — She explains that two years ago she phoned Diane and told her she wasn't coming home that night. Two nights later when she finally appeared Diane was distraught, claimed Anne would ruin her name. — Now she's happy because she likes Alan. —

As she said it I remembered Diane's words. — Both my daughters are living with men. Neither one wants to get married. — I had asked her if that bothered her. — No, she answered. Why should they get married? As long as they're happy. Isn't Anne a lovely girl? And I think Alan's a darling man. Both my daughters are encouraging me to work. They think it's bad for me to stay home but I don't stay home. I go to concerts with friends, to the theatre, to restaurants and I am studying Spanish. They say it's not enough and I suppose they're right. It isn't. —

Anne interrupted my thoughts. — A woman who has a husband can live totally without thinking. She doesn't have to use her brains at all. My mother looked towards her mother and father who were very happy. She thought if she pleased her husband everything would be fine but it wasn't. Now that she's separated from my father I would like her to find a job, to work at something she likes. —

At 5:30 am when I finally put my writing pad down Alan entered the kitchen and fixed hot soup and bread. At 6:30 they walked me to the Niewe Keizersgracht. The air was sweet with morning. Our shoes clicked against the deserted cobblestone streets. Nothing moved in the canals, the bridges were no longer lit, the water was still. I listened to the echo of their goodbyes and opened the door to my room in the canal house. I pulled down my shade and tried to sleep while I listened to the sounds of Amsterdam waking up.

JOKE KOOL SMIT

To say no alimony is scandalous

THERE ARE forty-five members of the Town Council of Amsterdam. Only three are women. Joke (pronounced Yoka) Kool Smit is the sole woman in a thirty member delegation of socialists. When I entered her office she was busy preparing her farewell speech. She explains that it is a feminist speech and will be backed both by Dollemina and MVM. Joke is leaving the Town Council temporarily in order to help build a stronger feminist movement. Then she and other feminists plan to come back to politics but they will no longer play what she calls 'the male pecking order game.'

Some time ago Ms. Smit was asked to deliver a speech on women to working class people. According to her the speech was a failure because she was insistent that women have the right to work even though their husbands work. The women listening thought, what does she want us to do, go back to the factory? They told her that since she had a degree it was easy for her to find challenging work. They didn't want to go back to the factory.

Joke claims that she didn't take into consideration that in the late nineteenth and early twentieth century all women whose husbands didn't earn enough money were forced to work. It had been a victory for women of this class not to work, a liberation for them to stay home and care for their family. She says that when she spoke the women must have thought, what does she want to do, put us back in time?

As a result of the way this speech was received she wrote a rebellious article stating that as women we have one duty, to look at what's good for ourselves rather than what is good for our husbands and children. This time the response was tremendous. She received many phone calls and letters from women who shared her feelings. This article and others previously mentioned were directly responsible for MVM.

Joke Kool Smit is interested in the minority group phenomenon called the *Professional Woman's Syndrome.* Many women who are very bright and have established a name tend to underrate discrimination. She talks about Mary McCarthy as a case in point. When Ms. McCarthy was interviewed for the French newspaper *Le Monde,* she said in essence that of course equal pay is right but the real liberated women are not in the movement. Joke's answer was, – My dear Mary McCarthy, you wrote *The Group* and what did these women do with their lives? You've written all the details, described their lives without realizing what's wrong. –

Joke is very interested in the books by Evelyne Sullerot, particularly *History and Sociology of Women's Work,* a historical analysis and survey of how things were in 1968-9. Ms. Sullerot states that when a profession goes up in status men come in and take over. When it goes down, the men leave and women enter the profession. For example in the United States this happened in social work and teaching. When Joke spoke to Evelyne Sullerot, she brought her attention to a book published in Scandinavia in 1964, edited by Professor Dahlstrom titled *Changing Roles of Men and Women.* In this book they question men as part of the scene, challenging the old concepts and stating that men would have to change if equality was to become a reality. Ms. Smit describes the books written by Evelyne Sullerot and Betty Friedan as dealing exclusively with women, the dual roles of women. They do not bring men into the scene.

She admires Ms. Friedan and says, — It's easy when you're talented to write a book but to start a movement is another thing. To do the dirty work as well, to do mimeographs, make phone calls rather than to just sit there. — This is a dilemma for Joke Kool Smit because she prefers to write too. Yet she feels that writing books is not enough. — Too many talk of women as me, not as they. They're not reading or writing or talking about women as sisters. —

In the beginning, she tells me, most feminists in Holland were young married women with children who wanted to work. They couldn't see the problems of divorced women, disapproved of alimony and felt somehow the State should help these women so they wouldn't have to be degraded by their former husbands. They wanted training so they would be self sufficient and able to support themselves and their children. — Now when so few women have professions, to say no alimony is scandalous. When husband and wife are both working and sharing, alimony shouldn't be given. Child support yes because the man is responsible for the children too. You're making more victims when you say no alimony. —

In Holland where everybody gets a pension at sixty-five, there is a group of women asking for pensions at sixty. They're unmarried, secretaries or low salaried workers. They want to create a special situation for the older unmarried woman. — Before MVM, politicians and women's groups opposed this. They said we should have equal rights and if this one group gets it they will be privileged. In high principles they were right but they forgot something. They forgot that these low skilled office workers were doing stupid work for forty years and often had to care for parents because the single woman generally has the responsibility. It's a ridiculous situation when you say at sixty-five you have to retire when some are ready to quit before and others want to continue working. There's also a big difference between the man who's taken care of by his wife and the wife who works and takes care of the home too. In general the women in this group are underdogs economically and socially. Then too, the problems of women are different. There's the unmarried woman, the married, with children, without children. You don't have the right, if you're better off yourself, to not recognize special problems of other women.

Joke Kool Smit, an assistant professor of French, writes for magazines and newspapers and has collaborated on two books. When she was a literary critic, she says she constantly wrote for the same in-group. Now that she's writing for the women's pages she finds she's fallen down from the hierarchy and is not taken as seriously. She equates this with politicians who don't put women's rights first. — They think when they do this they're doing marginal things, they're representing a sub-culture. Yet when they're busy with foreign affairs or social affairs, general human problems, they're doing serious things, part of the general culture. —

She points out that in every society people do bright intellectual things that are useless. She no longer wants to write literary criticism and feels she can spend her time more usefully. For her the feminist movement is the most important. Aware of the many ideologies, she states that women must join forces if the movement is to live. — Agreement on every point doesn't matter. We should be allowed our differences and avoid witch hunting at all costs. —

Ms. Smit was brought up as a Calvinist which in her words is a — rigid ridiculous education with a strong emphasis on obedience. You should believe in God or there's no redemption. All others who don't believe will never make it. — During her youth she quarrelled with the ministers and finally at eighteen left the church. But she claims her background has influenced her. I still have a Luther complex. He said, 'Here I'm staying. I can't do otherwise, God help me. Amen.' So you can say once a Calvinist always a Calvinist. Once a puritan, always a puritan. —

Joke discusses leadership. — If leaders have a task it's to show that things are possible that are not yet possible. Leaders should help others reach their potential so they too can become leaders. Yet that attitude is paternal and I don't like it. It's a problem I haven't resolved. — But she insists that women in the movement should be responsible for their fields of knowledge. They should not be looked up to as authorities but rather as women who can give other women information. She believes they should be responsible for a year and then other women should take their places.

Because of Joke Kool Smit's commitment to the feminist movement and her work and her husband and two children she has little time to write. She feels she's entitled to time but never seems to have that luxury. She laughs, — My wish is to be in prison for three months. I ask my friends, don't you have a decent crime for me, but nobody does. —

ANNEKE VAN BAALEN

Loose parts again

BY THE time I met Anneke van Baalen I'd already talked with many homosexuals and bisexuals. Driving from my canal hotel to her home in the country we discussed heterosexuality, homosexuality. She told me, — I distrust the homosexual as well as the heterosexual relationships as they are today because the patterns are the same. Must there always be the oppressed and the oppressor? We must question our own sexuality, and discover what we are as women. Women can relate either with men or women or we can simulate sexual relationships with machines.

— Sex in itself is a simple basic thing. I don't think it is the important force. That you have a sexual need is true but you could have these contacts simply. It wouldn't have to be an obsession. I'm not certain what sexuality is when all our emotional needs of touching, of being loved, of loving are channeled into heterosexual genital contact. I think this chains us to the social situation. It happens in education. Boys are forbidden to cry, to feel emotions, even to love people so that only sexuality is left.

— Sexuality can't supply the food for all our emotional needs. When you go to the zoo and look at the apes with their arms around each other it has nothing to do with sexuality. If you disconnect all the powers that have to do with sex it isn't that important. In *The Human Zoo* by Desmond Morris he says that certain primate tribes have the same kind of power relationships we use in our society. Baboons use erections to intimidate enemies. I think the male animal has to use his power because sexually he is weak. —

There are three generations of judges in Anneke's family. She is a lawyer, assistant professor. She tells me it was expected of all the children in her family to study and succeed.

She explains that as a child she identified with her father because she didn't want to be oppressed. At the same time she identified with her mother because she was a girl. This contradiction carried over into her married life where she dominated her husband in her thinking and organizing things. Sexually she played a passive role. — You should get strong and active for sex but I always felt tired, lost my strength in it. In sexuality I lost all the self I had in my other relationships. Real equality isn't built into relationships as we know them. You have to experience it in order to use it. It shouldn't be an abstraction but a reality. The oppressed has to change things. The oppressor can't because the structure won't allow him to see things as they are. Like a master can't know his servant. —

She tells me her relationship with her husband has changed since her stay at the Redstocking Camp and her participation in the CR group which she started. — For instance, I feel warmth towards my husband and it doesn't always lead to sex. He can now accept the warmth and loving whether it leads to sex or not. —

Ms. van Baalen believes that inequality in the female-male relationship is responsible for much of the hostility couples experience. Rather than deal with the cause, people make patterns of their hostility. This inequality is also apparent in the distinct class differences in Holland.

— In Amsterdam people stay in their class for generations. Therefore children in the lower strata are not encouraged to go into higher education. Class differences are so real here. People know which layer of society they're from. They carry their social background with them. You can climb but people do remember you were poor. You haven't the right accent or manners. Even the way you eat distinguishes you. The upper class women have elements in them of being elite. They have to recognize this and get it out of their systems and the lower classes have to fight this. —

The summer of 1971 Anneke van Baalen was ill, depressed. She'd formed a CR group in April when she realized MVM was not getting to the real causes of women's oppression. She felt political action was necessary but the men in MVM were inhibiting feelings of sisterhood. She tells me she was exhausted from work and the tremendous amount of time she was devoting to the women's movement. Rita and Hilly of Dollemina called her, told her they were leaving for the Redstocking Camp the following day. Go with us they said. — Suddenly I realized it was important for me to go and see if the Danish women had succeeded.

— The camp was open to women, those with children and those alone. Women came and went. I always thought about feminism and the women's movement and here it was. I became aware of how we compete with other women, how this competition is taught from the time you're a little girl. It was an experience being in a society without men. Even the concept of beauty and ugly changed. The weather was so lovely so some wore clothes, others didn't. At first I looked to see what was ugly and beautiful and then I couldn't tell. They were just women because there were no men about. I was there three days and for the first time I felt like myself. —

Anneke points out that before joining the movement, her life never had a center but consisted of loose parts. She says she worked but didn't identify with her work. She had sex but didn't identify with it. She was a mother but couldn't connect with her motherhood. — Now I'm trying to be the same person doing different things. —

She picked me up at two in the afternoon and dropped me at the hotel after 11:00 pm. We talked in the car, in her backyard, inside her home. We ate and talked. At one point she sat down exhausted, said she couldn't speak anymore and then talked about individualism and her belief that feminists would have to lose their individuality in order to gain something more important. She discussed groups and why some people were always attacked in group. — Groups need a victim because of our competitive social structure and it's always the intelligent one with a strong voice who becomes the victim. —

I talked about philosophers and she interrupted. — All philosophy is male oriented. Female philosophy has yet to be written. — End of that discussion.

And then, — I can't talk anymore. I'm lying here on the sofa, my eyes burning from weariness, my body and mind so tired they must belong to somebody else. — She burst out laughing. — Loose parts again. —

Anneke van Baalen lying there, complaining that this wasn't an interview but an endurance contest. And my mind racing to all my loose parts, together once I thought and now scattered in Ireland, England and Amsterdam with all the feminists I've spoken with.

FRANCE

PARIS

THE TRAIN stops at Gare du Nord. At dawn. Suddenly I find myself in this enormous station. The ceiling has to be one hundred feet from where I'm standing. Looking up I see striped rays of morning sun make their way through the arched roof. The light shoots out, mingling with the soft dawning Parisian air. The air is different. The feeling is different. This is Paris.

I am in the Paris of Anais Nin and Simone DeBeauvoir, Gertrude Stein, Colette, Djuna Barnes. The Paris of the twenties. While Parisians of the seventies rush all around me. In business clothes. Overalls. With attaché cases. And lunch pails.

Small shops in the station open their doors. Shopkeepers sweep the entrances while yellow pieces of sun play on the straw brooms. Voices over loud speakers tell about the coming and going of trains. I think. I don't actually know because my French consists of hello, how are you, I am fine, thankyou, goodbye, I am tired and coffee with milk please.

I scream into the busy station. I AM IN PARIS. Nobody notices. I am in Paris. The Paris of books and paintings and sculpture and songs. The Paris of Gershwin and Rodin, Ravel and Offenbach and Edith Piaf.

I move to a phone. I call a recommended hotel in Montmartre. I dream myself into a small cafe when I hear *allo, allo.* Reading from my Berlitz book I ask for a *chambre.* Staccato words rush for my ears. They speed by. Finally I am forced to admit I don't speak French. The other voice tells me it doesn't speak English. I am holding a dead phone.

I move into the station. The crowds of people have grown. Everyone is rushing somewhere. Porters quickly transport baggage. I don't know a soul here. I don't recognize the language. I get a panicky feeling. How will I communicate with the feminists? I don't speak French. I make three attempts to ask where the tourist bureau is. The fourth person stops, listens, shrugs and moves on. Finally a couple who have backpacks with Canadian flags on them take me to the office. Outside I wait with other tourists for the doors to open. I am trying to devour the French dictionary. How can I learn French in a couple of weeks?

In ten minutes I have been reduced to a lost child.

From the minute you enter Paris until the second you leave, you have a persistent feeling you've personally invaded the city and the Parisians wish to hell you'd leave. The French consider France the world. And anybody who can't speak their language is little more than a peasant. So call me peasant.

At the tourist office I ask for a room in either Montmartre, Montparnasse, St. Michel or St. Germain. I specify what I can afford. The woman at the desk, her sensibilities shocked beyond recovery, as she listens to my French, finds me a room near the station for more money than I can afford. When I politely ask again for the same areas at a lower price, her annoyance is so apparent and so vocal, I immediately forget what little French I know and begin my own vocal performance in English. For a half-hour I sit. Finally I am informed by this good will ambassador that she has a hotel for me in Montparnasse, that my room will be held for exactly a half-hour. When I ask how long it takes to get there she sneers, then smiles broadly, – a half-hour. –

My life seems to be in half-hour slots.

While I struggle up and down stairs with my luggage and typewriter on wheels, these lover boys watch. No help from these sweethearts. In the metro, trying to get out at St. Placid and not understanding how the doors open, I miss the stop. At Montparnasse which is next, I almost get cut in half by the door. No sweat for the French men who are too busy eyeing my boobs to help. Thinking with the brain is apparently a luxury for these Neanderthal men.

Chivalry for the French lover means helping you onto the bed before he mounts you. While he eyes every female in sight, from the top of her head to her toenails, if she has any sense of smell, she's holding her nose at the same time. French men find absolutely no need to bathe. Every woman, from fourteen to eighty, is a slab of meat for the taking. If she happens to be a foreigner she's champing at the bit, foaming at the mouth, literally dying for sex. If she's middle aged they're giving her a last chance. Welcome to Paris Bonnie.

I DON'T know how many times I went to the Frenchwomen's Liberation Headquarters at 13 rue de Canette before I learned they are often open only from 6:00 pm to 9:00 pm. Finding the office itself was a feat. On the street is a restaurant. Next to it is an alleyway. You go through the alleyway and find yourself in a large courtyard. Narrow staircases lead to the top of buildings.

The hall lights, as in so many of the Mediterranean countries, are timed to stay on for a certain length of time. Then starts the fun of finding yourself on a dark staircase without the vaguest idea of where the light switch is. That is after you crawl up the rest of the stairs on your hands and knees.

Eventually I found the office. A note was pinned to the door. I copied the French. Translated it said there would be a meeting at Montsouris Villa that evening. Rather than go back to the office again I decided on the meeting.

I took the metro to Gare D'Orleans and discovered I should have gone to Porte D'Orleans, which was another direction. It took forever to find a person who would tolerate my French and point me in the right direction. A half-hour later I arrived at Port D'Orleans. Out on the street, I was greeted with shrugs and disgusted expressions when I asked how to get there. I landed at Villa du Parc Montsouris, which isn't even a loose translation. It's another place altogether. Walking through the grounds I saw only one sign of life. I knocked on this door and was told that Monsouris Villa was a ten minute drive. In controlled hysteria (it was now 10:30) I asked if anybody spoke English and was told yes. Ingeborg Rawolle who opened the door is Professora d'Education Musicale, Chef d'Orchestre of Cite Universitaire in Paris. She offered to drive me and then suggested she wait in case I was too late. The villa had no sign of life. Disgustedly I entered the car and was driven back to my hotel.

Ingeborge Rawelle was completely unaware that women's liberation was in Paris. Where are they she asked? I would like to join. She had much to say about the injustices she suffered as a woman, a musician, a conductor. Yes, she would like a dialogue with me but when? She worked seven days a week. Determined to reveal her story she agreed to give up her Sunday afternoon.

MOUVEMENT DE LIBERATION DES FEMMES

THE FOLLOWING night I went to the Frenchwomen's Liberation office. There I met with six feminists who explained that they refused all interviews with writers and the media. In the beginning they agreed to dialogues but since the press distorted all their statements, labelled them lesbians, silly girls, they distrusted all writers. As far as they were concerned I was a sister and as a sister they would not only speak freely but assured me they would contact other feminists and give me all the help I needed.

The women from the Mouvement de Liberation des Femmes discuss the 1968 French Revolution and when I interrupt, they explain it is important for me to understand what happened.

On March 22, a group of students from the Maoist Movement began a strike against the capitalist system. Accusing the government of maintaining this system in order to exploit the French people, these students demanded a complete change in the society. In the universities they wanted to control their curriculum. Marxists, Leninists, Free Communists and other leftist organizations joined the strike. Workers demanded self-administration in the factories, as well as fair wages. Eventually the strike reached the masses and suddenly out of fifty million French people, ten million were on strike. All transportation came to a halt. Shops were closed. With no work, people suddenly had time on their hands. They strolled along the streets. Strangers began talking to one another. Although there were demonstrations, constant clashes between the police and the people, the feminists claim it was a marvellous period. Something unheard of was happening in France. People from all classes were communicating, exchanging ideas and listening.

As a result of this revolution, a small group of women got together and started to realize their own oppression. They understood that the Revolution was the result of the masses' dissatisfaction with the capitalist system. But if the society changed how would that alter the status of women? The revolutionists discussed the people's oppression, but never considered the oppression of women. The women became aware that the oldest class/caste system was based on sex and that the revolutionists would not eliminate the autocracy of the biological family. Determined that action was necessary, these women formed the Frenchwomen's Liberation Movement.

By June, twenty-five women were meeting in small groups. In September 1971 they had well over two thousand members. The feminist headquarters at rue de Canette has been opened for a year. A feminist gave them the use of the office, so there isn't any rent to be paid. All workers are volunteers. MLF produces a monthly newspaper titled *Menstruel,* which is a joint effort of all the groups.

There are approximately twenty autonomous groups in Paris. The general assembly meets every Wednesday night. The four main platforms of MLF are: abortion on demand, free contraception, equal pay and child care centers.

Abortion: In March 1971, the Abortion Committee collected 352 signatures of famous women who had aborted. Entitled the *352 Abortion Manifesto* this paper was published in *La Nouvelle Observateur.*

The same month Law #1373 was debated in Parliament. It proposed the legalization of abortion with the following conditions:

A: If the pregnancy is the consequence of a criminal act of violence.

B: If the life of the mother is in immediate danger or she has had previous medical complications.

C: If the doctor is certain the child will be born with a grave mental or physical deficiency.

Law #1373 never got past the debating stage, but even if it had, the feminists would have fought it. Their figures show that one-and-a-half million French women have clandestine abortions every year, at the risk of their lives. Sixty-six percent of these women are already mothers. The majority are being aborted for economic or personal reasons. Therefore, MLF considers this proposed law a hoax. They point out that in drafting this law, scientific, sociological and ethnic experts were consulted, but not the women who abort or give birth and have children.

One of the MLF pamphlets asks:

Who decides the number of children we have?

1. The Pope, who doesn't have any.

2. The President, who hasn't money to educate the children.

3. The Doctor who respects the fetus more than the mother.

4. The husband who makes *guili-guili* [a French expression that means he or she tickled me] in the evening when he comes home from work.

Contraception: The French feminists are trying to educate women on this subject, but contraceptive advertising is illegal. Contraception, however, is legal but only available through a doctor's prescription. The idiocy of the situation becomes apparent when one realizes that eighteen to twenty-one year old girls can get pills at the pharmacy without a doctor's prescription. Providing they have authorization from their parents. But women over twenty-one are dependent upon doctors who are often ignorant of all methods of contraception or refuse to give information to them.

In 1970 only 5% of French women were taking the pill. MLF blames this on the intensive propaganda against contraception. The feminists claim the economically deprived women have the most children, since they're the least informed.

The Frenchwomen's Liberation Movement has made the following demands: Propaganda against the pill must be stopped. Doctors must be taught about contraception in medical Schools. Contraception information must be given in schools before the students reach puberty. There should be a contraceptive pill for men. (I feel compelled to comment on this last demand. As for me, unless I was with the man when he got the prescription from the doctor, went to the pharmacy with him, looked down his throat as he swallowed it and examined his mouth carefully afterward . . . forget it.)

Equal Pay: France has the highest number of professional women in Europe, second only to Russia. However, they are not accorded equality in status or money. The MLF figures show that the average man earns 33% more than the average woman. The government claims this difference is only 7%.

Child Care Centers: Feminists have opened two day care centers. Both are run as cooperatives. The education, obviously is egalitarian.

Some Actions: In August 1970, when MLF read that the Women's Liberation Movement in America was having a Woman's Rights Day March, they decided to have their own action to show solidarity with their sisters in America. On August 26, they went to Place d'Etoile, under the Arc de Triomphe, to the Tomb of the Unknown Soldier. There they placed flowers and chanted, – There is somebody more unknown than the unknown soldier. That's your wife, mister. –

At the beginning of 1971, the well known magazine *Elle* organized an assembly for women. MLF came to this congress uninvited, to challenge the concept of women by this panel of male experts. The feminists stated that the patriarchal society defined women as objects, mothers and consumers in order to keep them in their place, and maintain the authoritative position of the patriarchy. The feminists accused the congress of pontificating about marriage, femininity, maternal instinct, the household, while they failed to realize the real problem. MLF stated that they not only refuse to accept their reactionary concepts of the family and sexuality, but also any system that feeds on the life of women. — These are the causes of our oppression. That's what we have to fight. — The feminists gave their arguments and rejected any dialogue. They said they were through discussing these conditions with men who persistently set themselves up as experts on women. As far as the Frenchwomen's Liberation Movement was concerned, the time had come for women to define themselves and other women. The male experts definition was for the sole purpose of keeping the society as it had been for thousands of years. And this they would no longer tolerate.

At the office at 13 rue de Canette I met Mijo, who'd been to the International Feminist Congress in Stockholm, run by the feminist Group 8. She suggested I contact Nicole Baylac who'd also been to Stockholm.

NICOLE BAYLAC

They make the women feel guilty about their bodies

TO REACH Nicole Baylac's apartment from Montparnasse, you walk through the beautiful Luxumbourg Gardens and on to St. Michel, the students' quarters on the Left Bank.

Nicole Baylac spent the Spring of 1971 in Berkeley, California. One month of that time was spent in a collective, where singles, couples, married and unmarried, between the ages of twenty-three and thirty-five lived. The collective was nonprofit. They sold organic foods.

Before her experience in Berkeley, Nicole identified women's oppression with a class struggle. Coming from a working class family, she felt certain she could only feel close to women with similar backgrounds. In the collective, the women (mostly feminists) got together once a week for CR. Nicole said she not only saw women getting in touch with their feelings for the first time, but she began to recognize that sexism thrives in all classes, all cultures.

She returned to France in May 1971. — I remember when I arrived here there was such a gap in my relationships with men in the U.S. and here. In France the man who is not a sexist is considered effeminate. Why? Because he's not a male in the sense of the culture. Most men are brought up to be nonfeeling. They don't care about a woman's feelings. This is considered weak. You can't find an equal relationship here and I do understand why women get together. —

In the movement, a lot of women become lesbians because they become more sensitive to their real relationships with men. They see they can have good relationships with women and they say why not? I think, for example, that two women from two different countries have more in common than a man and woman from the same country. —

She claims that women are brought up to give men pleasure. Now they are beginning to think of their own pleasure. — I think it's a Mediterranean idea. It's the same in Italy and Spain. Here the relationship between the woman and man is medieval.

— France has always had its leftist groups who were intent on freeing the proletarian people. The feminists don't want a political platform but it is difficult for French women to think in a new way. Feelings are not acceptable here. We don't really have CR. When a new woman comes into the group we teach in an intellectual way. We say we have a project. —

Nicole Baylac majored in psychology. After graduating she worked for close to four years in marketing research. — I wanted all women to be free from their sexual roles but in my job I was obliged to link them with these roles. — She asserts that in marketing research they reinforce traditional roles, playing on the guilt of women if they don't conform to these ideals. — For example, women should be good mothers. To sell a product they say, you want to be a good mother. You should get this for your child. Or for example, they make the women feel guilty about their bodies saying you smell and this is not good. You must change it. Men won't look at you if you smell, so use this. — She quit when she realized she had the choice to liberate women or alienate them.

Nicole is now a freelance writer. She's planning to return to the U.S. and write a book about the movements, particularly the woman's movement and the youth movement. She also plans to cover collectives, free clinics. To write about all people who are trying to free themselves and find a new way of life. — In France we are not aware of what's going on in the U.S. The French speak about drugs and crime but not about all the exciting new movements. —

Nicole Baylac went to Group 8's International Congress for Feminists in Stockholm to learn about other feminist movements and to meet sisters. She believes the European women were particularly interested in the American feminists, and were affected by the warmth they had. — I think the American movement is the strongest in the world. I felt closer to the Americans because they had already developed sisterhood. —

Feminists went to Stockholm from the U.S., France, England, Italy, Holland and the Scandinavian countries. They were totally unprepared when Dollemina arrived with a male feminist. The American sisters were adamant that if he stayed they would leave. Dollemina insisted they would leave if he couldn't stay. The following day the American women put a note on the door, 'Feminist Congress. No men allowed.' For two days the women met without the man, to the dismay of Dollemina. As a result, Dollemina and part of Group 8 met separately. On the third day the man left and Dollemina and Group 8 then joined the other feminists. Nicole believes this dissention forced the Dollemina women to think in another way. — In the beginning when Dollemina discussed their political ideology it was one thing, but when they spoke of themselves there was a contradiction. I felt that the women in Dollemina began to change their ideas.

— Stockholm was a good experience. I feel stronger. It's difficult to explain. Maybe you feel isolated when you don't know where you're going. It's good to know there's strength in other countries, and it gives you ideas. I feel that my fight is right when I know other countries are going the same way. —

TODAY MLF is translating feminist material from other countries into French. They are emphasizing CR, since they believe this is essential for all feminists. One of the papers I notice is the American feminist paper *Rat Manifesto*. Mijo and Danielle take the photocopy of *Guidelines for CR* drawn by the Women's Collective of Stratford, Connecticut which I brought with me. An American who's living in Paris enters and begins working. A feminist from Chile, who's been studying in Paris and plans to return to her country is talking with a Mexican feminist. How do you start a feminist movement in your country?

French women are on the phone, telling others about actions, meetings. There's to be a demonstration on Friday. I'm advised not to come. The police are bound to be there and there are always feminists who get arrested. Another group talks about how they go to the food markets and rap with women shoppers about feminism, hoping to form autonomous groups in the areas. I'm told — See Catherine Bernheim. She's translating *Abortion Rap*. . . . Call Renee. She was with Gay Liberation and is now with us. . . . Take these papers with you and you can study them in your spare time. Mijo, did you tell Bonnie about the Mother's Day demonstration? Mijo turns to me, asks if I have a list of American books. She's planning to go to Amsterdam to purchase books, visit feminists. She asks if I have names of any Dutch feminists to add to her list. Are feminist books in English available there? I tell her yes. From time to time women turn to me, speak in French, and then realizing I don't understand, communicate with gestures.

The office is packed with feminists. Periodically I hear questions. — Did you see the Dolleminas . . . ? Did you hear about Stockholm? You know they brought a man to the Congress. — I tell them I was present at the first joint meeting of Dollemina and MVM, where only women were allowed. They stop working when they hear this and talk excitedly about this new development. They ask about feminism in Ireland. Many have been to England and are in constant touch. One feminist asks, — You're writing a book about feminism in Spain? Good. I know two women who want to do something there. I'll give you their addresses. And call Doreen. She has a friend in Madrid, although you know it's absolutely impossible to do anything in the open there. Mijo pipes in, — Add this address to the list. She speaks English so you'll be fine. — Please don't insult me, I grin. I speak Spanish. I'm good for at least a fifteen minute conversation.

— Where do you go from here, — they ask and when I tell them Italy they give me addresses and phone numbers. — Tell them to keep the lines open and we'll contact them when there's an international action. — Mijo adds, — Call Julienne in Rome. She was with us in Stockholm. — She stops working, joins me in the front room.

MIJO

Be beautiful and shutup

— AS A GIRL you are economically dependent and don't want to hurt your parents. It's a false sense of love. Your parents give you the life but they create you for their needs.

— My mother was a slave of love. My mother's mother tried to show her that the only life was that of a wife and mother. She felt it was her duty to spend her whole life taking care of her family. My mother was destroyed before she got married and my father completed the job. —

Mijo claims she was so repressed as a child that her revolt was in not speaking but only in answering yes or no. She always felt sex must be dirty, by the attitude at home. — More than dirty. It was something not to be discussed. — She believes the Catholic influence is responsible and claims all the girls in her school were in the same situation. Some, she says, are married now and living like her mother. — They're objects. Be beautiful and shutup. That's what a man wants to do for a woman. I think it's incredible. Men can have pleasure sexually but it's not for a woman, so if a woman has pleasure she feels guilt. My mother told me, 'You think it gives you pleasure to sleep with your husband. It doesn't.'—

Five years ago, when Mijo expressed the desire for higher education she was told, 'If you want to go to the university, we can afford to pay, but it's not for you because you are unable to learn, and then you will only get married. ' Deciding not to heed the advice, she went to the university, majored in Law.

When the revolution broke out in May of 1968 it was a shock to her. The system in which she lived was being completely destroyed, and although she tells me she understood nothing, she demonstrated, worked on committees, went to factories to observe. — It seemed that conditions everywhere were unfair. Workers didn't only want an increase in wages but to change everything in their lives. — And for the first time she consciously realized how destructive the family structure was for her, and tried to make a break but couldn't.

In 1969, her third year at the university, she thought about joining the leftist movement but according to Mijo, she went as a stranger to observe.

In 1970 she moved away from home, shared an apartment with another girl. Her family refused to give her any more money, so she found a night job as an usher in a cinema and continued her studies during the day. — In France, if you have parents who can afford to pay for your education, you can't have a scholarship. — Although it was very difficult for Mijo, she learned she could function independently.

Last year she went to the University Vincennes, an experimental school created by the government after the revolution. This university is free, open to everybody, young and old. She points out that it was a failure for the government because it became a school for revolutionaries.

Once more determined to act in a socialist movement she went from group to group. She began to argue loudly because wherever she was she saw women in the leftist movement doing secretarial work and other shitwork, while the men made the decisions. She claims people listened to her but when she was finished it was as if she'd said nothing.

She joined *Vive La Revolution.* In April 1970 they decided to disband, maintaining if you want to have a revolution you have to change the mentality of the people, that the structure is always oppressive. They added that if you are not able to make your own sexual, cultural and economic revolution, then there is no revolution.

When *Vive La Revolution* dispersed, the women from the group went over to MLF, and Mijo went with them. — In France, for me, it's a contradiction between the women who are coming from the leftist movements who want a revolution and still keep the male concept, which is intellectual, and the feminist women. In July 1971 we began to realize there is a feminine analysis. It's a beginning.

— In Stockholm, I felt what sisterhood was. The most important feminists were the Americans. They were really together as sisters, although they didn't know each other. None of us had that warmth. Even I held back. They really led the way and it was incredible. In eight days, we had created a community. Before Stockholm, sisterhood is powerful was just an intellectual idea, not a reality. We were all sorry to leave because we realized something wonderful had happened. —

Mijo feels the American feminists were different because all had been in CR groups. — Here we're afraid of our feelings. We think it's childish. — She believes this is mainly due to the male concept that feelings are a woman's thing. But she is certain that CR is not only possible in France, but will work. She also feels that most French women haven't read the main feminist literature. This is why those who read English plan to devote much time to translating material.

As we talked, one of the women came in and asked in French if open CR was feasible. Mijo acted as interpreter and we discussed the open CR concept.

Mijo continued, — Just by yourself, you cannot create something. You need women together. You cannot say I will speak about feelings. You must feel first, become aware. In France, it is so deeply imbedded that the woman must be the most beautiful, the most admired, that they still regard themselves as rivals of other women. —

She tells me about the Mother's Day Demonstration this year. A group of women from MLF went into a park, to a monument created by General Petain. This monument, dedicated to mothers, shows a woman surrounded by children. The feminists draped this statue with dirty diapers and all the real symbols of motherhood. They cut all the flowers around the monument and started to leave. Mijo said they were absolutely terrified when they suddenly noticed policemen had surrounded the park. Hundreds of policemen and approximately twenty-five women. The feminists continued walking, carrying the newly cut flowers, wondering where they were going from there. The police detained them for ten minutes, then let them leave.

I spent four separate occasions with Mijo. She mentioned that the Frenchwomen's Liberation Headquarters had been bugged. She told me that every time they had a demonstration, plainclothes policemen were always there. This was substantiated by other feminists. — They know what we're doing before we do it. —

Twice when Mijo came to my hotel, I noticed two men outside. Once I remarked to her that I'd seen them before, that I felt they were watching me. She said they were there when she came to see me. We walked to a travel bureau, as I wanted to check on some reservations. When we walked out, they were there. We went to a restaurant. They entered, had coffee at the next table. Back to the hotel, and sure enough our buddies were there when we left. As Mijo said goodbye she burst out laughing. — The police wanted to find the president of the women's liberation. They couldn't understand why we didn't have one. — She shrugged. — They can follow me. It doesn't matter. Now I recognize them. —

INGEBORG RAWOLLE

I will be married in 200 years

INGEBORG RAWOLLE is a refugee from East Berlin. She was one of many who participated in the June 17, 1953 revolution in East Germany. Forced to leave because of her actions, she came to France to study for her Doctorate of Musicology. Since she chose to write about the 16th century composer Jean Maillard, France was the logical place to go. After doing research for five years, she had to quit as she was financially strapped. And by then she had become very involved in the orchestra at Cite Universitaire.

Cite Universitaire has students from eighty countries. When Ms. Rawolle first came here the orchestra consisted of seven students. At that time she conducted a choir that gave performances during holidays and special occasions. She decided to create a full orchestra and choir. There are one hundred members in the orchestra now; fifty in the choir. They give concerts throughout France, in Spain, Belgium, Italy and Germany. When they play in East Germany, Ms. Rawolle is forced to stay in West Germany until they return.

In 1958 she gave a concert dedicated to peace. Nine years later, she decided to give three concerts for peace, on the anniversary of the first concert. Ingeborg Rawolle rehearsed the orchestra and choir for one year in preparation for these concerts. She arranged for three separate halls, for posters, advertising, publicity, all the countless details that make up a concert. The first performance was to be given on June 17, 1968. In May the French Revolution took place which automatically cancelled all engagements.

Convinced that the concerts must be given she accepted Monday, October 28 for the premiere, as this was the first available time. Many of her sponsors were unable to attend the second series because of the postponement. The cost of the concerts doubled as well.

There were new posters to be printed, new tickets, advertising, publicity and so on. Although the concerts received critical acclaim, Ingeborg Rawolle found herself with a deficit of 34,000 francs. She is certain the concerts would have been a financial success had it not been for the cancellation of the scheduled performances. Since she signed all the contracts, made all the arrangements, she feels responsible. She knows she could declare bankruptcy, but this would finish the Cite Universitaire orchestra and choir. To her, this is out of the question.

So far, she had paid back 23,000 francs. Friends, students, former students both in Germany and France, aware that the deficit is a direct result of the French Revolution and not the fault of Ms. Rawolle, have contributed sums of money. One couple took their savings and bought her a much needed car. Her lawyer works without remuneration. Ingeborg is certain that if she were a man she wouldn't have to pay the debt.

— I was told the concerts were too big an undertaking. I was warned that it was a mistake, but I had strong convictions. A man with strong convictions would be accepted. He wouldn't be held responsible for the circumstances which postponed the concerts. A strong woman is not accepted. If I were softer, spoke as they would like a woman to speak, lied and said you were right and I was wrong, it would be easier for me. —

To pay the debt, she works from 6:00 am until 11:00 pm, teaching at the university, in private schools of music, giving added private lessons in violin, piano, guitar, flute, zither and drums. At 11:00 pm she drives to Montparnasse where she lives with friends. Lives with them because she cannot afford her own place now that she is paying the concert debt. She is not allowed to use her room in the university for sleeping.

We walked to the cafeteria to have lunch. It was jammed and we had to stand in line for some time, talking above the deafening cacophony of voices. Over lunch and wine, unusually good for a university, I asked Ingeborg where she had her beautiful bookcases and cabinets made and was told she not only made them herself, but designed them, cut them to size, did all the construction. She also made her drapes. She designs and sews all her clothing, including her concert wardrobe. As we were leaving the cafeteria, two male students blocked our way, eyed us up and down, making remarks. Ingeborg glared at them. I didn't understand what she said but it was quite obvious she was infuriated.

Back in her room, we discussed women's liberation in France. She said, — It's strange to meet you the way I did and then to find you're a feminist. I'm seeking women's liberation, to participate. The law is made by men, for the advantage of men. If I were a man I would be very successful. Last year I worked fifty-four hours a week in lessons alone. —

She talks about her experiences as a woman conductor. Not long ago, a friend of hers, a professor in Strassbourg informed her that he planned to leave, and he thought it a good idea that she go there and lead the choir, take his place. A few days later, he contacted her and told her he'd hired a man, that he felt a man was better suited for the work. — For me it was one lesson more. —

Another time she was asked to play the violin for a group at Christmastime. She readily accepted but told the professor that since her time was limited, she wouldn't be able to dress or wear make-up. — I told him I'd come as I am. — He answered, 'No, you cannot do that. When I'm in my office and a woman comes to ask for something and she's negligent about her appearance I am not ready to help her. But if her appearance is attractive I am more open to her problems and consent to whatever she asks. A woman must be attractive.' — Ingeborg Rawolle, convinced that her performance was the most important thing, came as she was. — For a man it's easy to conduct a professional orchestra, but a woman conductor must be attractive. The appearance is important for a woman.

— Prejudice for a woman begins when she has something to say. If I played the male game, I would get more but I refuse to do this. When I demand my rights a wall goes up. A man has the right to make demands for his work, but not a woman.

— I will be married in two hundred years when things change but not now. I would like to say once to a man, take off your trousers. I want to see if your legs are good enough for me to marry you. Men have all the rights to disturb you. Look at those men that interrupted us to stare.

And then *Madame* has the good connotation. She is worthwhile because she has a man behind her. Very often in the newspapers, when and if they speak of a woman somewhere, they give her status by saying she is a mother. They consider a *Madame* much more important than a *Mademoiselle*.

— A man resents it when the woman is motivated. They think music is fine as a hobby but not to be taken seriously. You can do it on the side. But a man can work all the time at whatever he likes and at night you must be home for him and all must be ready. There are many intelligent men who choose very simple women when they marry because they can't stand the competition. A woman can say I'll give up all for you. I cannot. I wouldn't. If a man is a violinist in an orchestra and his wife is too, that's fine. It's the same with professors. In music there is only one conductor. —

She mentions her many married friends who say they are happy but when she spends time with them she realizes in most cases it is all surface happiness. — The couples get used to one another and stay together out of habit. When a young woman gets married she has children and gives up her work. They say they will do it later when the children are older, but they cannot. When you're older, it's not with the same spirit or strength. A woman must have much courage to devote her life to her work and profession. I think even courage is not enough. —

Ingeborg Rawolle points out that it takes a week to work on a

Beethoven symphony. — When I'm finished, I'm empty inside. I have nothing left for a husband. I must know the music by heart, when the french horn comes in, the violins. — When she is depressed she takes a Beethoven or Schubert symphony, works on the score and this gives her all she needs. When I ask why she chose these two composers she answers, — They were alone in their life and I can feel it in their music. I gain courage from them. I'm very thankful for this.

— I would like all the governments of the world to be half women, in administration, in industry, in all walks of life. Even when a man is stupid he can get ahead. A man can be an executive with a female secretary but where are the women executives with the man as secretary?

— I am looking for a movement of women who are struggling for themselves, for a different way of life. For women to find pleasure in their work, in their lives. The education is all wrong. You hear all the time a girl is weak, not so strong, not so capable. It's a pity women believe that. In life you have problems all the time. If I were married I would have other problems but I couldn't have the pleasure with a man that I have with music. They say what a woman needs is a man. — She laughs. — I say not at all. I could use sleep. —

THE FRENCH men are incredible. Working on my notes at 2:00 am I hear a knock on my door. — Bonnie, it's Pierre. — I open the door and a mouth speaks. — I just came back from the south of France. I had to see you. Will you have a coffee with me? How are you? You're tired, no. You worked hard today. I can see it on your face. You work too hard. — He has concern for me.

— Yes I'm tired. I worked fourteen hours today. —
— You won't have a coffee? —
— No Pierre I won't. I'm going to sleep. —

He has concern for him. — I'm tired too. I just had a big trip and I came straight here because I wanted to see you. I don't even have a room. It's very late you know. Can I stay here? —

His face has gone down to his knees. I don't answer. Just look at him hoping something that resembles a brain will suddenly emerge. It doesn't. My hand points to the door. He's found his voice once again. — I'll call you tomorrow. —

— I'm working tomorrow. —

Dejection is replaced rapidly with anger. — I said I'll call you. — Exit

Pierre, whom I had a few drinks with five nights ago, who talked and talked until I was bleary eyed, in hopes our conversation would end up in the coziest of places, the bed. Whose mouth never stopped until infuriated I said, — Don't you ever listen? — and his amazed expression, — Oh, did you want to say something? — Who in two hours professed undying love, swore he would show me every minute corner of Paris and France as well, who mentioned all the places we would dine and gave me menus in advance. Gastronomical delights: *Pate de fois gras, huitres, caneton a l'orange, fondue bourguignonne.* Realizing I wasn't going to be his dessert, he promptly vanished. Two nights later, sitting in a cafe in St. Michel with a feminist, who should come walking by but Gorgeous Pierre. — Hello Bonnie. What are you doing? — Any idiot can see we're drinking coffee but not Pierre. Exit an unloved Latin lover.

GISELLE VAGUELSEY

There are no strong men

GISELLE VAGUELSEY heard through Jeanine that I would be at the rue de Canette office. She dropped by on her lunch time and invited me to her home for dinner.

I was late when I left the office. Then did my daily act of getting lost in the metro, then searched for sweets for her children. I could sense Giselle was annoyed when I arrived so late. Before I finished apologizing she told me it wasn't that. She had to be honest. She was sorry she'd invited me.

— I have nothing to say. I don't feel the need to talk. I've turned things round in my head and talking doesn't help. I often feel like I'm batting my head against the wall. I want to get to the point where I know myself well enough to live easily, to live happily without problems. —

Giselle meant what she said. After dinner we sat in her living room. She only talked to tell me she didn't want to talk. I spoke of my life. She seemed interested but expressed no desire to communicate. I told her I'd joined the feminist movement after going to a lecture by a Jungian analyst.

— He was talking about creativity, differentiating between the sexes. He said that men were naturally creative. That creativity in women was taken care of when she had children. Listen to this one Giselle. Women in the arts were generally lesbians. I mean, if you didn't have babies, all that creativity was left in the air. And I looked around at the audience and at this pompous authority on me and I thought, what does all this bullshit mean. It means nothing to me. —

Giselle laughed. — I once belonged to a psychodrama group. It was in fact therapeutic but very impersonal. I didn't know anything about the other people there, even their names. In psychodrama we had two analysts, a woman and a man. They spoke after every session, drawing conclusions. It was exactly like the mother and father. —

Women's liberation gave her a very different experience. In CR, feminists met once a week, sometimes through the night until 5:00 am, but they were sharing common experiences. There was a nucleus of ten women with other women joining them periodically. For one year they spoke of their feelings, relating them to the society, of their oppression as women. One night the homosexuals in the group claimed they felt oppressed and decided to form their own CR group. The heterosexuals tried to convince them to stay, determined that they should be together. But the homosexuals refused. However, they remained with MLF.

The feminists in Giselle's group spoke of the family structure. — Some hated their fathers, were afraid of them, had dreadful childhoods. Even if it was exaggerated in the facts, they had lived it like that and the picture they kept was a dreadful one. —

She says her parents adhered to traditional roles. — The funny thing is when I speak of it with my father . . . I can't resist . . . he doesn't seem hurt at all. He says women have no luck in society. Although he did do things like help with the dishes he was very repressive, and my mother who had a keen mind, didn't develop half her possibilities. She wanted my father to be head of the house, the man, the power.

The strong father who is protective doesn't exist. There are no strong men. And you shouldn't need protection but even though you know that, you are still looking for it.

— I live hostility strongly, especially when I relate it to my childhood. You remain a traditional being in your heart and body, but your head won't accept it. I feel the most attracted to the most oppressive men, but I can't accept it at the same time. You dream about being a submissive person, and you can't accept that either. —

Giselle claims that before she joined MLF, she was alienated from women, thought they were only interested in trifles. Now she understands women and herself, and feels a closeness, a sense of sisterhood. She's very disappointed in men, in relationships women have with them. — The best one I have, which is still imperfect, is with my husband. Though I feel repressed with him. Sometimes we're glad to be together and sometimes we're fed up. Now I feel I shouldn't get married again. But when you're alone, it's not the same, even if you have friends. You don't exist in the same way. Yet, there's a contradiction because when I'm alone or with my friends I feel much more free. But then suddenly I get fed up. At the beginning of my life with my husband I went to Germany and England alone, to study languages and to be by myself.

Giselle Vaguelsey received what is considered more than a Bachelors Degree but not quite a Masters. She was married at age twenty-one, continued at the Sorbonne. She spent two years studying at *Ecole Superieure d'Interpretes et Traducteurs,* a school for interpreters and translators. She's worked as a teacher, translator, in the public relations section of a computer firm. She remained in public relations for more than a year and quit because — I was exploited more than I could bear. — She worked for an employer who was always ill, gave her full responsibility but not the salary or acknowledgment. On September 1, she obtained her present position in a private college. There she screens potential students. The college is specifically for workers who wish to improve their knowledge and thereby improve their positions. There are courses in public relations, marketing, economy, administration. All courses are directly related to the companies in France, with a view of the European common market. They run from two to four years, are given at night.

Ms. Vaguelsey must keep busy or she feels useless. Although she's aware she's more than useful for her children, this is not sufficient for her. — Yet in my most depressed periods it is always my children who keep me alive. Why? Because I feel they really need me so it's expressed very simply. They need a bath, they need a meal, so you have to pull yourself together. I do what I have to and life is simple. When I had children I didn't think about why. I just had them. And now when I think of the life they will lead afterwards and the society they'll have to live in, which I don't like, I think I wouldn't have children. —

— Intellectually to live alone is the best solution, but when you're educated in a so-called privileged relationship, where you are not used to living alone, you can't be happy alone. I try to educate my children differently, so they may be more independent, but I think they will look for a special relationship and this will tie them. —

Last year Giselle took part in a number of feminist actions. She and others contested UNESCO's stand that nothing was better than married life. The feminists stated that the couple today is a hypocrisy and that women should take responsibility for their own lives.

Another time the feminists were invited to Drewx, an hour-and-a-half from Paris, to speak about women's liberation at a political meeting between a leftist organization P.S.U. and the Communist Party. They spoke and showed a film about a women's strike in a factory. The film reveals how the women factory workers stood together, took care of each other, had genuine concern for one another. [More about this later]

She also took part in the second edition of MLF's paper *Menstruel.* Giselle wrote the front cover, edited articles by feminists, worked with others to produce this newspaper. – It was a wonderful experience. We discovered each other. We trusted each other's judgment. –

She looked at me and smiled. – I'm glad I spoke with you. My contradiction is always to want to be with people, with the movement, as strongly as I want to be alone. People are always dropping in at any time of the day or night and in a way I love it. I want my home to be open as strongly as I want to be by myself, to read a book. Sometimes I feel I am wasting my time. The contradictions get stronger as I get older. I dislike the social system. Yet I work in it. I know what could be freedom for a couple and I can't get it just the same. –

As I stood at her door saying goodbye she tells me she had to force herself to speak in the beginning but suddenly the conversation became easy. – Bonnie, can you really relate to all the women you talk to? Don't you ever get bored with us? –

– Bored? Never. When I started this book it was impulsive. I didn't think about what would happen. I thought, I'll interview feminists, I'll write it down. But each dialogue, because it was an interchange has forced me to come face to face with myself, face to face with all the parts of women. Each dialogue opens a door. I realize now the doors are endless and will continue for the rest of my life. In the beginning I thought in terms of the book. Now I think in terms of women. And for me that is the most gigantic step I've ever taken. –

JANET SMITH

I've never felt so much an object in my life

THE FIRST time Janet Smith*, an American who graduated from a university in California, came to rue de Canette, a French feminist, learning she didn't have a room, offered her one free. — She didn't know anything about me. There was this immediate open trust, the first time I found that in Paris. —

Janet came to Paris in 1970. In California, she found herself dissatisfied with the American society. Her goal after education was to leave, — and in a way I had to admit I was copping out because I was feeling the tensions of a polarizing society. So I found that while I was learning much about myself and changing, I was also in the process of destroying myself. —

She found Paris a difficult city to live in, the people cold, the language a problem. Ms. Smith studied French at the *Alliance Francaise* for an hour a day for four months and worked as a housekeeper in exchange for a room. The family accepted her solely as a housekeeper, so she lacked a human relationship. She worked two-and-a-half hours daily, six days a week and aside from her room received only a tiny breakfast. Janet lived off her savings and the money she earned tutoring in English.

When she learned to speak enough French she obtained a job in a restaurant as barmaid and hat check girl. After working there for a short while, she found it unsatisfactory and left for a two month holiday travelling around Europe.

Janet became interested in the feminist movement in California but didn't join. In Yugoslavia she met an American feminist from New Haven who told Janet she was coming to visit the feminists in Paris, and gave her the address and phone number of MLF.

She talks about her feelings. — Women are allowed to think to a certain degree and beyond that the man feels threatened. I guess it's one of the signs of the broader problem, but I've never felt so much an object in my life as I do on the streets of every country I've been in. I've noticed this with other women I've been with this summer. Most of us come from middle class backgrounds. Yet after you've had just enough, you surprise yourself with how suddenly violent and angry you can be. You can be very calm to begin with but after the fiftieth man bothers you,

you become completely violent. I saw one girl, after being accosted by a man, throw a rock at his car. Yet it bothers me because they are controlling. If I don't react it's because I'm forcing myself and if I do it's in a violent way that they've preconditioned. That's why I feel so helpless. —

Janet goes with men but only for short periods because she feels the relationships are incomplete. She has the feeling of an egalitarian relationship with women but hasn't had sexual relationships with them.

— If a man's a machine I'm not interested. Once in the middle of sex I realized that the man was only interested in himself so I left. A man allows you intelligence to a certain point and that's usually three degrees below what he thinks his capacity is. A man accepts you up to the level of his self-esteem and beyond that he can't.

WHY WERE YOU OPPRESSED or DON'T GIVE ME EXCUSES

I LOVE when a man says to me why were you oppressed. Damn it, you're a bright woman. Don't tell me you didn't know. Why did you stand for it? And don't give me excuses. And then he goes into a song and dance about how he feels for women, how he understands.

Listen mister, you understand nothing. You'd have to creep inside my skin to understand. Let me tell you what it feels like to be hired, to work in a responsible position and have your boss scream, get me coffee, hang up my coat. And another one hands you the key to his apartment. How about it Bonnie? Ok, so I didn't get the coffee and I didn't hang up the coat and I didn't go to the apartment. But let me tell you, the rage I felt inside is something you could never understand.

Nor will you understand that while you're screaming why did you stand for it. your very manner is just as intimidating as the animal who screams get me the coffee.

You talk about blacks being oppressed. Well I say it's easier for them, because their oppression is right out in the open. They don't have to wonder whether they're being treated like shit. They know it every time they go out into the white world. But a woman is different. Her oppression is so covert half the time she'd have to be a genius to realize it.

We're set up as patsys in the kindest way. Here darling let me take your coat, here love let me light your cigarette. Buy whatever you want my sweetheart. Nothing is too good for you. Sure nothing is too good for you except living your own life. And all the time you're reading articles about your poor overworked husband who's doing it all for you and the kids. Bullshit.

And there are psychoanalysts working on you, telling you to be feminine. And ads telling you to be pretty. And advice columns on how to be a good wife, how to save your husband from a heart attack, how to be a good hostess, and recipes; mountains of them. Yes sir, he lights your cigarette, opens the car door for you, helps you with your coat, but when you're down on your hands and knees scrubbing the floor he sits and reads the papers.

What I feel is something you couldn't understand in a million years. Column upon column of experts, analysts, marriage counsellors all saying don't withhold sexually. Of course. After he insults you hop into that bed. Your life blood isn't enough. Give him your body too. Or when he doesn't talk to you all night because your conversation is just 'woman talk' and what's that, or he's tired from work. But in the bed he sees you. Ah there you are!! Suddenly he finds you interesting. His weariness disappears. Well give sister give because isn't he proving his love.

Tell me mister, do you know that feeling?

And how about being told you're a castrating female. Well, I searched the dictionary and there's no word for a man castrating a woman. Why, when it's done from the day she's born.

And how about all the authorities who tell us how our minds work? You think like a woman. How do you know how we think? You can't imagine how we think or feel. But one thing I'll tell you. The oppressed may be angry, infuriated, intimidated but we never feel guilt or shame because we weren't the oppressors.

And since I've been told countless times what you think of me, I'll tell you what I think of you. You're weak because only the weak oppress. And you're scared because fearful people need a scapegoat. And you're insecure because you fight too hard to maintain your position of power. And you're not the virile male because your great marvellous organ has one orgasm and it's finished. Then look at how glorious it is, lying there limp, which is what it is most of the time. It's not a weapon. You've made it one but I don't buy that crap.

As for the world you created, look around and tell me how proud you are. Your great technological advances have advanced us to the stage where we can be totally obliterated by one button. You've thrived on war, built your economies on war. You've exploited, killed, murdered every minority race and religion and one majority, us. You feed off the swear of the poor, off the sweat of your women and you call that progress.

So mister here's some advice. Now that your job of defining us is finished, try defining yourself for a change. And then I'll talk with you.

RENE RICHELIEU

I am first a woman and then a lesbian

RENE RICHELIEU* was in a CR group for homosexuals and a member of Gay Liberation. She also went to MLF once a month. In the summer of '71 at the MLF office she met Diane Schulder and Florynce Kennedy who wrote *Abortion Rap.* They discussed their book, their wish to have it translated into French and their desire to speak with the French feminists about abortion. Rene spent a week with Ms. Schulder and Ms. Kennedy. During this time, a press conference was arranged at the *Beaux Arts,* a publisher was obtained partly through the efforts of Rene, and Rene tells me she gained two friends. Because of this chance meeting Rene had the opportunity to meet the Parisian feminists who are working on abortion. She found this group — very together, very close, — and decided she would devote her time to working with them.

— In the gay group it was not like this because there's much possessiveness and jealousy. There are about one thousand members, only one hundred women, so most of the time is spent on male homosexual problems. In women's liberation there are more than two thousand feminists, only one hundred lesbians. — Yet she claims it's difficult to speak because the lesbians are such a minority.

She is criticized by the homosexuals because she works for abortion. — They said what do you have to do with it. My problem is I am first a woman and then a lesbian. I support all feminist causes. — She knows many other lesbians who work with MLF and refuse to turn their backs on the oppression of women.

Rene believes the feminists form an aristocracy, stressing their oppression intellectually, rather than trying to change themselves. One evening they discussed writing books about the feminine history in

France and they decided they would begin with Marxist philosophy. — I said they were fools. You can't write an intellectual piece. You have to understand all people. The women argued that Marxism was one of the realities. I said yes, but there are women who don't know about it, who aren't ready for it.

— For me, when I joined women's liberation, I wondered about the women in the group who were lesbians, who led two lives; their life with other lesbians, their life with their parents, teachers, friends. The first time I loved a woman my parents knew. They accepted it. Everybody knows I'm a lesbian. But I know many women who hide their lesbian life from their parents. I cannot understand this contradiction. If we're in women's liberation it is because we want a revolution, but if we don't make the revolution in ourselves it is really stupid. —

In Stockholm she felt most of the women were Marxists and Leninists who spoke about politics rather than their own personal problems as women in the society. The American feminists claimed lesbians became lesbians because of sexual politics but not through feeling. She understands what they mean when she relates it to her life. — When a man makes love with a woman he loves a certain idea of a woman but not the person. His education dictates what a woman should be and the woman conforms to this idea. Their idea of a woman is rigid. She's this and this and this but more than that they cannot recognize. My first experience with a woman was when I was twenty-two and it was the first time I felt completely loved. For example, a man tells you you can't do this, you can't make this. A woman must do this because she's a woman. Love is defined between men and women but there is no definition for homosexual love so you can create your own definition. — She adds, — Perhaps it was political but I say I became a lesbian because I loved a woman. —

Loving a woman and making love has the same meaning for Rene. — For me, the sexual feeling is not separate. To love is to love the entire person. It is important for me to engage my entire being in a relationship. — She states that a woman is not a sexual object to her, nor her possession. — Everybody is free. If someone is with me and wants to make love to another woman, it's all right with me. Why should we give such importance to love making. — Sex to her is just one facet of a relationship and she cannot comprehend why all the other facets are permitted but not this one.

At one time she lived with a heterosexual woman, enjoyed the relationship, which did not include sex. She's had similar experiences and says, — Why am I obliged to make love with a woman who is sleeping in the same bed with me, even if she is a homosexual? It is not one who decides. It's a decision both make. I went to Stockholm with a bisexual who at the same time was in love with a man. We shared the same bed but nothing else. She always spoke of this man so I understood. It was not a problem. —

Rene Richelieu is presently writing a novel about homosexuality. Briefly it is about two women living together, fighting the society and one of their families who uses repressive means to separate them.

— People understand little about homosexuality. When two women live together, they don't want to become like men. For me, it's difficult to work in a society that refuses to recognize homosexuality. When I say society doesn't recognize me, it's not because I want to marry a woman or be integrated into this society. The society tries to integrate women into it, but their way forces the woman to lose all her identity. —

She tells me she knows many homosexuals who are in psychiatric institutions and visits them regularly. — Homosexuality is considered a sickness and we are constantly harassed by the police, the law, the government. I went with a woman for years and her parents insisted she go to a psychoanalyst. He told her I was bad for her, that she was sick, that he would cure her. —

Rene was a philosophy major who quit six months before she was to graduate. Her leaving directly related to the harassment she had to withstand as a homosexual. And then her relationship with the woman she loved became traumatic. This woman became confused as a result of her psychoanalytical sessions and was eventually taken out of the school by her parents. She reveals that the male students took great pleasure in fighting both Rene and the woman. When I asked, do you mean verbally or physically, her answer was — physically. —

TONIGHT I decided to take a walk along the Champs Elysees. A number of feminists warned me not to walk there at night. Why? I learned why. You are constantly propositioned by men of every description. Octopus hands grab at you. Drooping eyes stare at you. I well understood the fury of the woman who threw the rock in the car window.

These birdbrains all have the same line but I have to admit that one was ingenious, if not an outright con man. Following me from the Arc de Triomphe to the park which leads to the Louvre, he kept pleading in English that he was lonely, he needed company. Wouldn't I please join him for dinner. When he saw I was completely uninterested, he offered to pay me for his pleasure. Twenty-two hundred francs was his offer. How he came to this odd number I'll never know. He did have a problem though. In his wallet he only had a five thousand franc note. He wanted to give me the money in advance to prove his sincerity if I would give him twenty-eight hundred francs change. This conversation took place while I zigzagged from one side of this beautiful boulevard to the other side and this con man rushed along behind me. Finally I turned around and threatened to call a *gendarme*. This cooled his ardor and cured his loneliness and he walked off with his five thousand franc note intact.

So much for the Champs Elysees at night.

EVELYNE SULLEROT

I think of my mother. I always say, — We have done this! —

WRITER OF seven books on women, all widely read by the European feminists, Evelyne Sullerot spoke with me on the telephone. — Of course I'll see you. Who have you seen, how long are you staying? — When I told her my departure date she replied, — What a pity! I'm leaving Paris in two days and I won't be back in time. — She was committed to write an article, appear on television, had luncheon engagements and would barely have time to pack her clothes. She suggested I read her article in the current issue of *Realite* and use that for my book. When I explained that the book contained personal dialogues, she agreed to see me on Friday for one hour, which she felt was hardly enough time but the best she could do.

Sitting in the living room of Ms. Sullerot's home I turned on the tape and she spoke. — Very briefly I will tell you what my interests are. Fifteen years ago I founded the French Movement for Family Planning. I discovered I was not able to discuss many things with all the specialists so I started my studies again . . . to know scientifically speaking, to answer all the opponents and so on. Then I was very interested in some studies I could make for the National Center of Scientific Research on the attitudes of women, on sexual education, abortion, contraception and so on. I was impressed by the impact of feminine magazines. —

Evelyne Sullerot earned her doctorate when she was thirty-four. She studied mass communications for women, and published a book on the subject which was a great success. — I must say that at that time my boss, if I can call him my boss, was a very famous sociologist. I asked him to do a thesis on the feminine press and he said it was so light and frivolous. So I published it without his patronage. —

She thought she would find that women's magazines had existed only since the nineteenth century, but when she searched she found them as far back as the sixteenth century. Ms. Sullerot studied more than one thousand magazines. Her first book, *La Press Feminine,* analyzed the contents of the magazines of the nineteenth and twentiety centuries; the journalists, the morals, themes and failures dictated to the woman. To Ms. Sullerot this study is interesting because — it was the whole story of sexual moral pedagogies that were dictated to women through the press. To simplify I would say there were two kinds of magazines; the magazines written by men for women, and magazines written by women for women.

— Most of the time the women's magazines were fashion magazines. How to dress yourself and how to behave. Advice, always advice. This is how to be a woman, an elegant woman, this is the way to be a good wife, and this is the way to be a good society woman and so on. These magazines were rather frivolous and full of moralism at the time. It is very interesting because I made some studies of vocabulary and I could find the evolution of the word woman. First it was lady (dame), then it was the sex (la sex), and then it came to be a woman (la femme). It was very interesting to see the connotations of this word. —

The second category of these magazines was written by women who were feminists. — I found more than fifty books in the sixteenth century on the equality of women and men, long before the suffragists. Of course, at that time, there were so few women and men who were able to read and write that of course there wasn't a large impact. —

According to Ms. Sullerot adultery is accepted in France. — In France the families are closer, but it's not at all puritanical. You do not divorce when your husband has a mistress or your wife has a lover. The big thing is to be able to speak to one another, to have the same ideas, to be able to exchange ideas, to have the same feelings. I'll give you an example. My mother told me when I was fifteen . . . she died when I was seventeen . . . before you marry please look at that man and ask yourself, do I think I'm able to speak with that man for forty years. I've been married twenty-five years and I'm not afraid to finish my life with my husband because I know we're always going to have things to tell each other. —

I ask her why adultery is acceptable in France and not in the U.S.A., and I'm told, — Americans are more sentimental than the French. You want passion and a stable marriage and the two things are divided. I shock women when I say you may even have different lovers at the same time. You may have very rich and deep relationships with two or three people, completely different. When you are yourself a person it is possible. And I think that tenderness and courtesy is more important for a long married life than illusions like having to do everything together. Togetherness is something I hate. —

Although adultery is accepted, it is not so acceptable for a woman. As a result she admits women are hiding their dual lives. To add to this dichotomy, when both husband and wife work, it is expected that during the two hour lunch period the woman will shop, cook and serve lunch.

— So even though you have the second highest number of professional women, — I say, — you are still expected to play the female role, and this extends to the woman's sexual life. Is adultery really acceptable here? —

— I think it's very difficult to bear at a certain time but I really think it's impossible to imagine that a woman and a man can be faithful to each other for thirty-five years. —

— What I'm saying Evelyne is that although it may be accepted intellectually, when people are in danger of losing their possessions they are just as vulnerable here as elsewhere. —

— Yes but in the advice columns for women, when women write that their husbands have mistresses the advice is always, you are deceived as anybody so act as anybody. Act as if you do not know anything. It is always, this happens to anybody so you are anybody now. You are going to be strong. Do not express anything because if it is serious you'll have time to know and if it is not serious you have not expressed anything and you have saved your marriage. So cheer up and pull yourself together and be the winner. I have tried to make an analysis of all these advices, not to judge, but just to know what kind of art of living it expresses. And it expresses a certain way of living which says do not complain, do not weep, do not shout and you will be the one who is mistress of herse f

BONNIE: In other words, have control over your emotions.
EVELYNE: Yes and it is not so terrible.
BONNIE: When a woman has that kind of control she's denying her humanity.
EVELYNE: It depends on what you call humanity. For me, the respect I have for myself is my humanity and to cry and make reproaches is something I do not call human.
BONNIE: Then you're denying feelings. You're saying feelings are not natural.
EVELYNE: No, no, no. I mean that in each set of circumstances I try to have a scale of values.
BONNIE: But where did that scale of values come from?
EVELYNE: The most important thing for me in marriage, I speak for me, is to always have what I call tenderness and courtesy and confidence.
BONNIE: And for me the most important thing is for women to stop playing games, stop perpetuating all the myths which have been shoved down our throats by men.
EVELYNE: I agree. That's what I wrote in one of my books, that the one freedom we can gain is the freedom of speaking, not only of doing things, because we know women can do things, but to speak of these things, to write of our experiences. But let's make a difference between speaking of your own life and speaking in general.

— Evelyne, the impact is completely different when you speak in generalities or from personal experience. For instance, a group of women can argue that abortion is a woman's right, we should have control over our bodies. But if one woman talks about her abortion and says yes, I had an abortion, I did not want the child. I made my choice and it did not destroy me, this one woman's impact is far greater than the group of women who speak intellectually and collectively. —

Evelyne Sullerot, pressed for time, having given me over three hours instead of one, says she realizes this is the main discussion in women's liberation, but she can't talk about it in a few minutes. She does insist, however, that the *352 Abortion Manifesto* had a very bad impact. She believes the list would have been more effective had it been an open list, rather than a list of very famous women who had abortions. Her opinion is that it is better to fight to change the law, change the facts, rather than publish private papers with names. She is now writing an anthology of love. — I'm writing on the sexual amorous life of women, of adultery. I prefer to write in general and to change the state of mind, rather than to make confession. —

Aside from her many feminist books Evelyne has written two unpublished novels, a side of her she claims people do not know, but something she felt she must do. One novel is about her mother, her sufferings, the way she was squashed down. — She was a charming, cultured, intelligent woman living in a time when she couldn't reach her potential. My mother was my inspiration. Every day of my life, when I am happy, when my work is recognized, I think of my mother. I always say, 'We have done this.' —

Her mother died tragically and she thinks of her life and death daily. Her brother was a political prisoner and her mother, forty-two years old and very ill, died waiting on line to give him a parcel. — She died at the worst moment, when we were both starving. She died without hope. —

Both Evelyne and her brother were in the underground movement during the Second World War. Evelyne, at age sixteen, was a political prisoner. She laughs and tells me her virginity was saved by the war. She explains that in prison there was a German guard who had an eye on her and kept trying to get her into the infirmary. A woman prisoner told her 'Don't go into the infirmary or you'll go into the frying pan because he wants you.' The woman, who Evelyne claims was very maternal, advised her to 'bite your tongue or your cheek and when he takes you spit some blood into your handkerchief and keep coughing. And he'll leave you alone.'

— And that's what I did. For years and years afterwards I sent postcards to this woman. The story is funny because the prisoner, who was a prostitute, saved my virtue. —

DEAR ABBY, DORIS, MARY, DR. ROSE FRANZBLAU:

I KNOW I should be grateful that my husband doesn't beat me physically, is good to the children, is not an alcoholic or drug addict. I realize that his running around with other women will pass, his having difficulty remembering my name is just a phase. After reading ads I am aware that he keeps away from me because I haven't been spraying my organs. The real me smells of woman and I know how offensive that can be. I am waiting for licorice spray to come out because that is his favorite.

Dear Abby, Doris, Mary, Dr. Rose Franzblau and the rest of you advice givers, yould you please send me your serial number, patent number, price, etc.? I would like to buy one of you. I understand the antique market is going up.

JEANINE RICHETTE

I always felt guilty about my children

— I'VE BEEN to England quite often and I can see the difference between men there and in France. Even as a young girl I wanted to be appreciated for something else. If boys found me attractive before I spoke, I couldn't understand it. I refused to dress in what was considered a fashionable or feminine way, and I was very unhappy because I was completely different from other girls. —

Jeanine Richette* belonged to the same consciousness raising group as Giselle but for her it didn't work. — I often had the feeling a level of honesty would begin and then stop. It doesn't work here. I don't know why. — But she admits to many changes in her attitude. — I didn't think of myself as a woman before. A woman to me was like the second rung, unimportant, so I never thought of myself as a woman. — Now she does.

Jeanine, a math professor in a university, works for the satisfaction, independence, to be free and have her own life. — I have a friend, a very typical story. Whenever I talk to her, she gets the desire to work. My friend's husband gets angry and says I'm not good for his wife, because of the way I am, my independence. —

She is interested in the Gauchists who want a different society, who assert there should be no hierarchy. They claim the mathematician is no better than the factory worker, that it takes many people to make a product and all should have equal say. Jeanine claims that because she lives in a large apartment, has a husband and children, has money, works in the system, she can't be called a Gauchist. — But between living in poverty and working constantly for more power there should be something else.

— When you try to imagine a new society, there is man inside so you have to think of a revolution for everybody. Some women say that women should have the same rights as men in our society. I agree of course, but it's not the thing I want. I want the society to change. —

She points out that MLF has worked hard to effect changes. — Our office is open at night and a member, any member will refer a pregnant woman to a doctor. The doctors were doing abortions in their homes because it's illegal and cannot be done in a hospital but many doctors are now afraid of prosecution so we send the woman to England quite often. —

MLF also has a group of advocates who work with them. When there is a judgment against a doctor or a pregnant woman, they are defended by these lawyers. Six months ago the so-called offenders went to jail immediately, but now that the feminists are so vocal, they are not imprisoned so quickly.

Four years ago a friend of Jeanine's received a two year sentence for having an abortion. She is certain that people are more aware and sympathetic since the inception of the MLF Abortion Committee.

Two years ago a good friend of Jeanine's became pregnant. She tried unsuccessfully to locate a doctor for her friend and in desperation stole stationary from a doctor she knew. She then wrote a letter stating that this woman had had German measles and signed the doctor's name. Her friend flew to London with the forged letter and had her abortion.

Jeanine joined MLF in November 1970, after going to classes on feminism at the University of Vincennes. This class was permitted because it was given by a teacher, rather than a member of women's liberation. In February, after much discussion and debating, the university accepted the demands of the feminists who wanted to produce a film on women. They asked for camera equipment, a class to make the film, etc. But tragedy struck when one of the feminists involved was paralyzed in a serious automobile accident. Everybody was so crushed. They temporarily stopped production. Now they go constantly to the hospital to visit their sister, the only family this feminist has.

Jeanine is one of the women who goes to the markets to speak to women shoppers about women's liberation. Since it is illegal to speak before a group, they come to the market with written material. — There are policemen around who are ordered not to let us speak. Not just MLF but anybody. Even when a group gets together and speaks loudly, within a few minutes there are policemen who break it up. — Feminists work in their own areas and have been relatively successful in forming autonomous groups.

She talks about her childhood. — When I was a child, I refused to act like a so-called girl. I liked to camp, go on boats, loved sports and I fought. When I got older I wanted to study, to work, not to get married but have twelve children. — She laughs and says, — All of this together. — When I question why she did get married she shrugs and says, — I don't know. I liked him but yes that was the only reason and I thought for my parents I had to. —

Her six year old daughter masturbates in front of others, which disturbs people. They call her daughter dirty. It doesn't bother Jeanine but on the advice of others she went to a psychiatrist who stated it was Jeanine who was the cause of it and she should go for treatment. She refused. — I did the same thing as a child. Because I was Catholic I had to go to the priest. He told me it was the worst thing I could possibly do. It was terrible for me. —

We discussed working mothers, the guilt placed on us.

JEANINE: When I was pregnant I looked for somebody to take care of my child because I didn't want to stay home, but everybody was saying she's crazy, she's wrong, so I felt guilty. But I knew I couldn't stay home. And one year after the second child was born I heard and now will you stop working.

BONNIE: I worked in New York, lived in Jew Jersey. That was about ten years ago. Brian was two, Kenn four and Craig was seven. I commuted on the bus every day and every day I cried. I had somebody taking care of them and yet I felt so guilty. Why am I leaving them? They're wonderful children. You'll be punished. It took me a long time to get over the guilt. And now my children aren't with me and I won't see them for a year. To get to that point takes a lifetime.

JEANINE: I always felt guilty about my children. When you're pregnant with all your family falling on your back . . . Oh now you will be a mother, oh now you will have responsibility, oh what a wonderful thing. And I felt a complete stranger with those words. So I remember when I was in the hospital with my first little girl. She was two days old and I was looking at her and saying, poor child. I am completely crazy to have made you. You have no mother. I am not a mother. And I was very afraid.

CATHERINE BERNHEIM

An oppressor always has to deal with his oppression

CATHERINE BERNHEIM, freelance writer, is translating the book *Abortion Rap,* which will be published in France shortly. Sitting in my room, she told me she's been involved in women's liberation for one year. She claims that in the beginning when women had problems she had an answer for everything. — It was awful. I mean, I would say, ok what's your problem. I can do something for you. Now I understand that we don't personally have the answers for others. —

She is certain that men should not be part of the movement. — If men come in they say, ok I'll do something for you, which is not doing something for us, because they should be doing something about themselves first. An oppressor always has to deal with his oppression, so if they join they have something to gain.

— I have a brother and he's a fine Mediterranean male, very kind and very sweet with his daughter and wife. He is one of the best we can find in France. — Catherine says she speaks of his oppressiveness to him and he answers good naturedly, 'I'm oppressive. Ok, tell me when I'm oppressive.' We were playing a card game, you know and I found out that he was playing as a man, to win. And his wife and I said we don't want to win. We're playing for pleasure. He said ok, you have something in the hand. If you don't try to win, where's the pleasure? Well we said, the pleasure is in playing with other people. And he couldn't understand that.

— Another time we played ping pong. He was hitting the ball in the corners and I would hit it back but not in the corners. My play was kind of a defensive one and I was very pleased I could return the balls, and he was very pleased because he was trying to make me lose and the whole game went like that and it was awful when I understood it.

— Well let's forget about games. You can live without games. I went to my home once and a man followed me. He was very drunk, really bothering me. He wasn't strong at all because he was staggering and I was afraid, which I shouldn't have been, because I was the stronger of the two. But I climbed the stairs, two by two and rushed in my room and said why am I afraid? I can push him and get him out, but I've been brought up to be afraid. And that's the way women are living. —

Catherine Bernheim and I discussed the high percentage of professional women in France who have strength in their professional lives but still are oppressed personally. She says, – People are told that you have a professional life and a private life and maybe a lover, which is another private life and you are building walls between the lives. People see their lives as if they were in drawers. The first drawer is my private life, the second is my professional life and if I'm very strong in the professional life and I'm not in the other one, of course it's because they're not in the same drawers. And maybe one of the answers would be to have one big drawer with the whole life so you could be a real person and not the divided person you think you are. People think they're one person but you can see their lives are divided. The division should be at one time. I mean, in one minute you can divide yourself but not in one day. It's difficult to say. When you speak to somebody you're not only what you say. You've got your whole life inside you. That's what I mean by being divided. The way I speak to you is not the only way I could. You know what I mean?

BONNIE: Yes. I think I do. I hope so. I'm not sure.
 [We laughed]
CATHERINE: Well it wouldn't be too clear in French.
BONNIE: Please don't speak in French. That would cut me off completely. That would be locking me in the drawer. . . . Catherine, when did you find out you were a homosexual?
CATHERINE: I was a young girl of seventeen and I said ok, that's the end of the problem with men. So the first man who asked me to go with him I told, no I won't go with you because I'm a homosexual, which for me was clear. And he said ok, bring your girl and then we'll be three. It was such a disappointment because it was another kind of oppression I didn't know.
BONNIE: Are you saying you're a sexual object whether you're a heterosexual or homosexual?
CATHERINE: Yes but it's reversible. What I mean is when I meet a man and I know the only way he can be interested in me is to treat me as an object, I treat him like an object first. That is to say I'm making a demand.
BONNIE: Are you bisexual?
CATHERINE: I was bisexual when I was about eighteen, from eighteen to nineteen, because I thought I wouldn't be a girl anymore, so I

tried to be a so-called girl. When I spoke to them as objects they didn't like it at all. They were always asking for some love or feelings.

BONNIE: Are you comfortable as a homosexual?

CATHERINE: Yes surely.

I asked her if she found exploitation amongst women. She replied, — Exploiting is not the word. Maybe you can find mannish habits. I'm speaking of my experiences now. It wasn't the same before. As a homosexual I had a very disturbing life from seventeen to twenty-two. Then very quiet. Then I met a girl in the movement and this relationship was quite different from any I had before. There is no woman who's stronger than the other in the movement but I could have been stronger in another love story. So if we're seeing homosexuality as part of our life, in the feminist movement, I think that's the best we can do now. —

Catherine has a friend who's pregnant and she says that even though she will never have a baby, she can relate to her friend. She feels a common bond with all woman in the movement. However, when it comes to her sexual life it's a different story. — When you meet women they all say they are heterosexual. A heterosexual will say I met a very fantastic man. But a homosexual will say I met somebody. They don't say I met a girl. So the thing is all that silence, not being able to say you are in love with a woman, and you are one too. I think that's true of all homosexuals, even the men. The heterosexuals don't see that my life has the same value. They say I'm a 'poor girl'. —

I told Catherine that I'd heard that expression before but didn't understand it. After trying to define the phrase, looking up the words in a French-English dictionary, we decided the closest word was caricature. She replied, — well I'm not a caricature of a woman. My sexual life is a caricature to them. —

I asked her if she felt guilty when she discovered she was a homosexual and she replied, — Yes. No. I felt guilty but I felt what was good for me I had to live, even if I felt guilty. But when I speak to other women they don't say the same. Sometimes they don't want to live it because they say that's no good. The thing I found out about me is that everything I wanted to live I lived. —

Catherine Bernheim was one of the women who wrote the text for the *352 Abortion Manifesto*. She was also one of the nine women who demonstrated at the Tomb of the Unknown Soldier. —We went because all the papers were saying there was a big march of feminists in the U.S., saying these American women were funny but there wouldn't be a movement like that in France. And the women in the movement here felt we had to say something, that we're here, that the movement is increasing and to show we were in sisterhood with American women. So we went there and seven of us got arrested. —

They were arrested because they didn't get a permit for their action, but she adds that had they asked they wouldn't have gotten permission. She feels it's bad to have demonstrations illegally but worse not to have them at all.

Catherine worked on the film *Le Film des Tours* with Giselle Vaguelsey. It runs for eighty minutes and a dubbed version is planned for America. The feminists show this film in universities, in factories, wherever they can, with the stipulation that some of the film makers must be there to speak personally after the film is screened. The film shows that although eighty factory workers, all women, worked together for fifteen years they knew nothing about each other, until they were threatened with unemployment because their jobs were being eliminated.

When these women decided to strike they began talking to one another for the first time. And in talking they discovered they had a common bond. Catherine continues, — In the discussions with the audience they try to understand why these women found they had something in common. And we try to say we made this movie because we are women. We went to the factory when they were on strike and we said we're coming because we're women. We didn't need to say anything else. There were a lot of leftists coming and saying, tell us about the strike and so on . . . and how about the managers. They were taking facts, but they didn't care at all about the women. But when we came we asked if they needed anything, how could they manage being women. They had to go to the factory and strike, go home and take care of their families, shop, cook dinner. We understood because we are women. They saw that we were speaking the same language. And that's what we say when we show the film. —

— Are you saying they found a common bond? —

— Yes, and they found common enemies too. The women speak about the police and the managers, so they had to be together against the common oppressors. They found out the union was not so much the friend they said they were. —

Although all the women factory workers gained much from this experience, they were fired. The feminists who made the film remained friends with the women. One of the workers will undergo surgery shortly and the feminists plan to help her and her family.

Catherine discusses the feminist movement. — The difference between history and individuals is that history is a thing you can feel and know, but when you're an individual you don't feel it in your life. I expect lessening of oppression for women. When I don't know. A year, maybe ten years. For me, I hope to be less frightened by things because the most important thing is changes within the individual. What I mean is that as long as there are frightened people on earth, there will be people to frighten them. When the fear is over, you may still try to frighten somebody but you're not effective. It doesn't work. If I have something to wish it's that all the oppressors won't find anybody to oppress. They can still be oppressive but there's nothing they can do. —

Catherine Bernheim and I continued talking at a tiny restaurant in St. Michel. I told her there was no necessity to use her real name. Her immediate response was no but I asked her to think it over and let me know. The next day, when I came back from at meeting at MLF, the concierge handed me a letter. I was so touched I would like to share it in part.

Sister:

Thinking of the question of name or no-name, I guess now I really want you to write my name and this for many reasons.

The first is, as we were saying yesterday, the time is now for us (I mean lesbians) to live in the open air and stop hiding in the dark. For me it seems to be the same old problem of fear which has to be cut off us, even if it takes a little flesh with it. You know what I mean. And show other women (I mean nonlesbians) that we're not what is said in books. We're not those damned women. I think lesbianism makes a woman see herself and her sisters as values. I mean beings with whom she can measure the world, as well as men. Sees all of it with women's eyes.

I still have the same problem of being clear and understandable but I think you'll deal with me.

The time's coming when the problem of one woman becomes the problem of every woman. Then you may understand that abortion is my problem as well as the hiding of lesbianism is yours.

So that's why I'd like you to write my name as I write it at the end of this letter. If ever the word 'political' still has meaning, let's say it's political. You know I'm not thinking of myself as a lesbian first or a writer first, or anything first but all of that at the same time.

The letter is signed 'in sisterhood.' Cathy Bernheim.

MICHELE VIAN

We don't want the government. That's the point

I CALLED Michele Vian at the suggestion of Dorothy Tennov, who met her in Paris months before. Ms Vian is one of the 352 women who signed the *Abortion Manifesto*. — First Simone deBeauvoir signed and I signed and all around Sartre, and then we asked friends. If we were famous women who signed the Manifesto it was because we were afraid others would be arrested and they would think before arresting us. And we could say if you arrest the others you must arrest us too. —

— That's very strange, — I said. — Is there a law for the famous and another one for the other people? —

— It's always been that way in France. That's equality in the French Republique. —

Michele Vian is a translator. She was married to the late Boris Vian; who was a well-known composer, writer, poet, jazz trumpet player and engineer.

She explains that before the legalization of contraception in France it was possible to purchase the pill in other countries. However, if these pills were discovered at Customs, they were automatically confiscated and the woman was out of luck.

Her first two abortions were, in her words, easy but the third one left her sick with fever. None were performed by medical doctors. When I asked her how she felt about her abortions she replied, — I felt relieved of course. And I never felt anything toward the child. It wasn't a child to me. —

Michele Vian, a member of MLF, is unyielding in her belief that the movement must not infiltrate into the political system. — We don't want the government. That's the point. I've always been in politics. I am, it's no secret, Sartre's mistress. He makes politics. I make politics because I think he's right. He's the greatest for me and in whatever he's done he's never been wrong. He's good and not only do I love him but

I think what he says is true, and what I say is true, so we are both equal. — She tells me she's been with Sartre twenty years. When I ask if any of the abortions were his children, she answers yes.

Michele showed me a photograph of a young man in a park. He has a bewildered expression on his face. Surrounding him are the police.
— This is my son. He was there to play the guitar. You can see the police have broken his guitar. You can't go anywhere. Nobody can go anywhere. You can't wear long hair. You can't be young. If you're young, you're guilty. —

— Are you saying this is a police state? —
— Of course it is, — she answers. — Sartre has a process tomorrow for instance. Eight months ago they took our newspaper away so there's no liberty of press. We've got to be women and men together to take this fucking politics off. Socialism is shit, republique is shit, everything is shit. Only revolution is good. You can't do anything, you can't say anything and your friend Dorothy Tennov has seen how many police there were when we went to the Latin Quarter. As mothers, first of all as women, we must stop the violence of the police. This can't go on. —

Sometime ago Ms. Vian and others (not MLF) were arrested for political reasons. Appalled by the conditions in prison they went on a hunger strike and issued the following demands: Prisoners must be permitted to read the newspapers, have radios and talk amongst each other. — We were arrested as if we were not political and were treated like the other prisoners. We didn't mind being treated like the others but they were treated so badly. — Their hunger strike proved successful and their demands were met.

Michele Vian fervently believes that the bureaucratic governments must be abolished in order to achieve revolution. She maintains that violence is a by-product of oppression.

BONNIE: Michele, I know you believe it's necessary to change the mentality of people. How do you propose changing generations of conditioning?

MICHELE: Work has been done by all the militants, most of them quite young, through the peasants, through the workers. We're trying to inform, saying no you have the right to do that, or yes you can do that. As you said before make them have consciousness of their own selves, their own rights, and not getting pushed and crushed all the time. In France the government is the police. The police are the gov-

ernment. The Minister of the Interior is the Minister of the Police.
BONNIE: You believe this country should be run by everybody. No leaders.
MICHELE: No leaders. Something is sure. This state must change, because it's unbearable. We're in a pre-fascist state and it is frightening.

Michele Vian is certain that woman's oppression will be eliminated when the government changes. I argued that the only possibility for change was a feminist movement consisting of women only and that our main purpose would be to kill all the patriarchal institutions once and for all. She disagreed and insisted that for her a revolution had to be one in which all people participated.

BONNIE: Before when we were talking and I said raising women's consciousness I didn't mean giving the other person consciousness. I think every woman must do this for herself by examining the society in terms of her own life experience, as well as studying all the institutions that are responsible for her oppression.
MICHELE: And all the time you're doing this the police are harming your sons and daughters.

WHEN YOU purchase a *bon dimanche* ticket you pay for the furthest stop and this entitles you to get off and on the train as often as you like. A marvellous way to see the countryside of France, to exercise your legs as you run for the train, and a sure way to keel over from exhaustion. But sightseeing and exhaustion are absolute musts for the tourist.

I started my Sunday marathon at Gare de Montparnasse, by purchasing a *billette* for Chartres. My exhaustion began before I boarded the train. Just trying to figure out where I would stop, train schedules, how long I would stay in each place made me wish I'd stayed in bed. My first stop was Versailles.

One could spend the entire day in Versailles just strolling through the beautifully sculptured gardens, the enormous parks, looking at the lovely statuary. Like all tourists I immediately broke into a sprint when the train stopped. This proved to be an advantage because flowers, trees, sky, everything looked like an abstract painting.

In the palace, in one tremendous room there were paintings depicting the history of France. These paintings were in groups of threes. The first showed the commander followed by the officers, followed by soldiers, all in full regalia, on their horses entering a sleeping city. The second entitled *Siege* or *Bataille* shows the bloody battle. The third called *Victoire* is the bloody mess, the dead bodies, the victorious army proud. (Good show and all that) I was viewing history. It is impossible for me to understand why these paintings were displayed so conspicuously. If I were a man, and happily I'm not, I would hide them. If death and murder is the goal of history, then I admit they've been extremely successful.

From Versailles I missed the train for Ramboille, then caught the next train and wandered around this lovely quiet country village for an hour. Then ran for the train going to Chartres, two hours behind schedule. Standing on a very long line waiting to enter the magnificent Chartres Cathedral, I asked if the line was always this long. I was told that the Paris Symphony was giving an all Bach concert in the cathedral and I was standing on the ticket line. I promptly forgot about my marathon and was transported into the magnificent world of Bach and the glorious Paris Symphony orchestra.

THE IDEAL FEMINIST

BEFORE LEAVING Paris I called Yvette.* She warned me she was very anti-women's liberation. We planned to have lunch together.

While we ate she presented her arguments, arguments that every feminist has heard over and over and over again. Prerequisites for anti-feminists: Do not read feminist literature. At all times be sure to keep a closed mind. Always present your viewpoint based on the first two prereuuisites.

She did agree with one point. Equal pay was a fair demand. Author's note: She works. She's underpaid . . . To her all other demands were unimportant. The movement, she informed me, consisted of women burning bras, man-hating women and lesbians running wild. She waited for my statement.

— Yvette, if we want to burn our bras, let us. After all, they're our breasts and our bras. — Her answer: —That may be true but men ridicule you because of it. — My answer: — We've never demanded that they wear jock straps so why should burning bras disturb them. — Actually it doesn't disturb them. It's a cutesie tactic meant to avert the threatening issues and ideologies of feminism. And it shows the world how silly (in keeping with the feminine stereotype of course) women are. (What can you expect of them?)

Yvette asks, — Could you please tell me why the feminists picket beauty contests? It's utterly ridiculous. — I reply, — We hate to see all that waste of energy, time and money on female beauty contests, when everybody knows that women are not the most beautiful people. You realize we're incomplete don't you? We know man was created first and we're told he has the body beautiful. So in all fairness to them, we should have male beauty contests. The winner, of course, would have the best shaped and largest penis. — Yvette starts to say something, then chooses to erase my last statement.

She continues. — It's not that I'm against women's liberation. There are some very feminine women who speak about equality. What I don't understand is why you don't let these women speak for you instead of the other kind ... I don't believe women should compete with men. They shouldn't go to school or work when they have children. Children are the mother's responsibility. After all, nobody forces them to get married. Everybody's free. But the fact is it's not natural for women not to have children. And Bonnie, whether you admit it or not, women need men. —

My answers are so apparent by now, I'll go on to the next topic. Homosexuality. — So many homosexual men in Europe. And now the women too. It's embarrassing to see them, the way they look and talk. — I tell her about the lesbians I've had dialogues with. — Ah yes, — she answers, — but they sound so nice. They're different. —

As I listen to Yvette, I begin to realize that she's not really against the movement. It's our image that's disturbing her. She doesn't even object to lesbianism providing they don't look like lesbians, don't behave like the stereotype. And feminists are fine providing they look like Gloria Steinem and have the wit of Germaine Greer.

In other words Yvette you'll give us the go signal if we start behaving in a decent acceptable manner. What you want is a nice respectable ladylike movement.

Sisters, let's listen to Yvette. Let's have a real feminist revolution. We'll charm them with our demands in our cute little mini-skirts, our boobs pointing in whatever direction the bra manufacturers decide. Let's be witty and demonstrate with smiles on our faces, capped teeth first naturally. Let's be the kind of feminists we can all be proud of.

ITALY

ON THE WAY TO ITALY

DEAR JEAN:
WAS IT ten years ago that we stood at Kennedy Airport while those bagpipes played and I crying no I can't go and you pushing me forward with your pained expression while your arms hung helplessly at your side. When was it?

Sitting in P's car, driving through the magnificent Swiss Alps I see my sons and me bellywopping down the Connecticut hills. Throwing snowballs at each other. And on a bitter cold afternoon calling Louis Untermeyer, begging him to read my play. And he saying no over and over again. Days of taking care of children and nights of writing with little sleep. Please Mr. Untermeyer. Three afternoons later a call from him. I had no intention of reading your play. I was going to read two pages and say nice try girlie. And then compliments. Is he talking about my play? Come over on Saturday. Bryna and I want to talk to you. And my answer. I can't. It's my son's birthday. As you know Jean I did see them but not on my son's birthday.

How long ago was all of it? Standing in my lawyer's office stubbornly insisting no, I will not accept alimony. I can stand on my own two feet. And now I hear Joke's words, 'To say no alimony is scandalous.' To hell with alimony Jean. I want my twenty-three years back. I want all the me's that were, the way they were.

It's morning. I'm sitting on a train that's taking me to Italy, to my Italian sisters. Looking out at the Italian Alps I feel the beauty and my own fury. Last night I fell asleep in the compartment. A hand moved up my leg, then another hand. I'm having an erotic dream. The dream so real it startled me into awakening and seeing that those hands of my dream were attached to a body that sat opposite me. Two pair of male eyes were fascinated by the scene. Where in hell did they all come from? When the train took off I was alone in the compartment. I started screaming at the body with the hands while his face twisted into pain, rejection. And his buddies kept shushing me as if I were some demented child. Suddenly three pairs of arms were trying to soothe me. Christ, I'm going to kill those bastards.

I took my luggage and moved to another compartment. This time with a family, mother, father, two daughters all sleeping and a man who puffed away at a cigarette and ignored my entrance. I lifted my stuff to the shelves and went to sleep. No it can't be. Not a second time. It's not possible. His *mama mia* came at the exact moment my foot connected with his balls and suddenly the whole compartment was awake. Everybody screaming. Arms, hands, mouths gesturing.

He left immediately. The father, the daughters went back to sleep but the mother sat up with me. She couldn't speak English and you know how limited my Italian is but we communicated. Oh how we communicated.

THE ITALIAN WOMAN'S MOVEMENT

THE WOMAN'S MOVEMENT began in Milan on January 1970 when Serena Castaldi, just back from observing women's liberation in the States, gathered fifteen women in her living room to discuss feminism.

That same month a small group in Rome organized a debate about WL in the States. The debate turned into a seven week seminar on the condition of women. As a result three more groups were formed:

Movimento di Liberazione della Donna was conceived as a mixed group which gathered most of its members from the Radical Party.

Rivolte Femminile was formed by Elvira Banotti of Rome and Carla of Milan. They began meeting and in July 1970 wrote the manifesto for RF.

The Fourth World was started by Orietta Avenati. A mixed group it is also known as FILF, Fronte Italiano di Liberazione Femminile.

That summer Serena Castaldi travelled to Rome and discovered the other feminist groups. A meeting was held and this was the beginning of communication between the groups.

In March 1971 in Milan, the university women and the socialists who were part of Serena's group broke off and formed a new group. Their reason: They couldn't accept Serena's concept of sexual politics.

The following month in Rome an offshoot of Rivolte Femminile formed their own aggregation which they called Collettivo di Lotta Feminista.

Other feminist groups are meeting at the University of Trento, Florence, Turin and Venice. All maintain contact with one another.

MILAN

MILAN IS a phantom world. Buildings stretch upward without end. Fog choked streets fade into the distance only to be joined by other streets. People rush around, their vivid indoor hues fade as they cut through the haze. Cars screech forward, their yellow orange beams straining into the dark mist. A possessive grey film hovers over the city, swallowing everything.

For two days I walked in the Milanese rain, which never seemed to stop, past the Galleria Vittorio Emmanuele, the Duoma and La Scala to an apartment where I met with two feminists from Rivolte Femminile. Every night I walked in the rain back to the thirteenth century building where I stayed. My room belonged to an Italian feminist who was visiting her sisters in Paris.

RIVOLTE FEMMINILE

THEY REFUSE interviews with the media. Carla and Liliana ask me not to use their last names. — None of us are more important than the others. None of us are experts. The first experience for the feminist is to communicate with other women in the group. Alone she is isolated with her books and ideas. — In Milan and Rome members meet once or twice weekly for CR. Action will come when they are ready.

WILL WOMEN ALWAYS BE SEPARATED FROM EACH OTHER? WON'T THEY EVER FORM A UNITED BODY? This is the first line in the Rivolte Femminile manifesto.

EQUALITY IS AN IDEOLOGICAL ATTEMPT TO ENSLAVE THE WOMAN AT HIGHER LEVELS. They maintain that equal pay does not mean equality. Equal opportunity does not mean equality. Only when women are free to express their own sense of existence will they be on their way to equality.

VIRGINITY, CHASTITY, FIDELITY ARE NOT VIRTUES BUT CHAINS TO FORM AND MAINTAIN THE FAMILY. RF feminists emphasize that men have glorified motherhood as *the creativity for women.* Yet this same woman is not allowed to give her creation her name.

UP UNTIL NOW THE MAN HAS USED THE MYTH OF COMPLEMENTARY ROLES TO JUSTIFY HIS POWER. Most men work for an employer. For his labor he receives a salary. These same men become employers in their own homes. Their wives receive free bed and board for their labor. Economically the man is the power. This concept extends to her sexual life as well. Man gives. Woman receives. Or does she?

Carla tells me, — When you are a girl you are told you have to grow up and develop beyond the clitoral experience. Masturbation is immature. Vaginal orgasm is adult. But vaginal orgasm fits the patriarchal world because it keeps the woman passive. —

When woman's sexuality was brought up in Carla and Liliana's CR group it was just another topic, so they thought, until so many of the women expressed dissatisfaction with their sex lives. They wanted to know why. The women discovered that without exception all were concerned with their mates' sexual pleasure rather than their own. As a result they were anxious about their sexual performance. After all, wasn't the woman responsible for the satisfaction of the man? Their answer: NO.

— We not only think of our pleasure now, about our different sexual appetites but we refuse to have sex unless it is pleasurable for us. Although the clitoris is the only female sexual organ equipped to have sexual climax, the male has refused to recognize this. We have been discussing the pleasure of clitoral sex with or without a man. It is important for man to understand what sex is for a woman but it is up to the woman to make this clear. —

THE NEGATION OF THE LIBERTY TO ABORT IS PART OF THE GLOBAL VETO OF THE AUTONOMY OF THE WOMAN. Yet last year when RF was confronted with abortion, they refused to fight for any action against the existing law. Carla explains, — If an abortion law is passed we know it will have conditions on it for incest, the very young, the raped, women having many children, if your mind or life is endangered. These conditions are not in accord with feminist goals. Our problem is to find out why women become pregnant. Why should you have an abortion when you didn't even have the pleasure in the sexual act? —

THE STRENGTH OF MAN IS HIS IDENTIFYING HIMSELF WITH THE CULTURE. OUR STRENGTH IS TO REFUSE IT. RF argues that male culture, which is considered *the culture* has no relation to the female. She has practically no say in it and very little choice. However, since it is the only culture offered, women out of necessity are part of it. The women in RF do not participate as they once did. For example, Carla who is an art critic refuses to join in the opening exhibition of an artist. She reviews the show on the second or third day. She tells me, — I once felt I could achieve liberation through art but feminism has made me realize this isn't possible. As a critic you are essentially an observer, rather than a participator. The painter, when he is painting, is liberating himself, not others. —

IN MATRIMONY WE RECOGNIZE THE INSTITUTION THAT HAS SUBORDINATED THE WOMAN TO THE MAN. RF is against marriage. Yet almost half the women in this particular CR group are married. Now it is my turn to question. How can they separate from the male culture and remain with men? Carla, who is no longer with her husband answers, — We consider this problem a point that must be resolved. But we feel there is a difference. In our personal lives we can achieve equality. And since RF all our marriages have changed for the better. We cannot work in this society as it is now, but on a one-to-one basis it is possible to express yourself and if you manage to do this it is worthwhile to stay and not leave. —

It was the second interview and we talked late into the night. The RF manifesto was very clear to me but I kept going back to their repudiating marriage and the culture but still living with men. Carla looked wearily at Liliana, at me and then said, — Bonnie if we leave everything we'll take a little boat in the Pacific and go with the wind. —

A NEW GROUP

I WAS the first American feminist to meet with this new group [the women who left the Castaldi group]. Liliana and Paula, the Italian women whom I interviewed in London, spent a week with this group and told them about our dialogue. — We want to hear more about Ireland. . . . You don't mean they're not for abortion? . . . . .Is it true the Dutch feminists are meeting without men? . . . . What are the American feminists going to do on Abortion Day? . . . Mijo called from Paris and said you're going to see the feminists in Spain. You don't really believe anything is happening there, do you? . . . But then imagine a movement in Ireland . . . . . Oh yes did you know Betty Friedan is coming here? —

The women from this new group discussed why they broke off from the Castaldi group. — Most of us are university women, socialists. We think of ourselves as emancipated so it was difficult to understand the concept of sexual politics. The leftist men believed in our liberation. They said they wanted the customs broken which meant that after we licked the stamps we were free to have sex with them. When we saw this we began our own consciousness raising. —

Marinella added, — We'd already broken with Serena but for the first time we understood what she'd been talking about. —

Pia spoke. — In Italy we're not used to thinking about our feelings so discussion about feelings, even related to the society, is not accepted. We tend to intellectualize.

— Italy has a history of demonstrations but here there is always the working class, the middle class and the capitalists. These classes have always been removed from one another and there is little communication between them, so it becomes difficult to separate politics even from feminist groups. We've tried to have dialogue with the communist and socialist women. They keep telling us that it is up to the working class women to make the revolution and we tell them it is important for all women to participate in their liberation. The political women's groups don't represent feminism. They have no real understanding of woman's oppression. —

Although membership is growing they are having trouble reaching the successful woman in Italy who insists there is no such thing as inequality. [The Professional Woman's Syndrome again.] Then there is the religious Catholic woman who is adamant that contraception and abortion are sinful. Marinella tells me, — Contraception is legal now but the church still considers it a mortal sin so many religious women are confused. But the law is important because once something becomes legal it eventually becomes moral. —

New members are mainly university women but recently women from all walks of life are becoming curious. How to integrate these women into the new group is a problem. After much discussion they agree that open CR is the best idea. Two months later in Spain I received a letter from Marinella, — The movement goes very well. I tell you this because at our last meeting there were more than eighty new members. Do you remember you were talking about open CR meetings when you came to our group? That's what we're doing. —

As for International Abortion Day they have mixed feelings about demonstrating. They maintain that abortion is a feminist fight and as long as the political groups are in they want out. The American woman's fight for abortion is something they disapprove of since it is the individual State that legislates rather than the women themselves. No, they will not march on International Abortion Day. But two days before the march I telephone Marinella from Rome and discover they've been in contact with Paris and they will demonstrate. Their arguments remain intact but she tells me they can't in all conscience do nothing when their sisters are dying from illegal abortions.

Action: The new group is running a feminist nursery where mothers of the children are full participants. The school, modelled after one already in existence is loosely structured, nonauthoritarian. The area chosen is a slum because of the obvious need and because women in these areas are unaware of contraception and abortion. The objects: An egalitarian school and the formation of autonomous women's groups. The school will set a low maximum fee and if the mothers cannot afford this, the feminists will help defray the costs. This is to be the first in a series of feminist nursery schools.

SERENA CASTALDO

In the middle is an empty hole

MARINELLA WAS apprehensive when she called Serena and invited her to her apartment to meet me. She hadn't seen Serena since she'd left to form the new group. Would Serena come? How did she feel? She telephoned from the apartment and within seconds I watched Marinella's face light up. Not only was Serena breaking an appointment to join us but she was apparently thrilled to hear from Marinella and wanted to know all about the new group.

Serena Castaldi spent the winter of 1969-70 in New York intending to write a thesis on the Black Revolution. She explains, — Within a short time I realized I was facing a different reality and was completely outside of the black situation. And the blacks refused to let me work with them because I was white. —

She discovered women's liberation but found the ideology hard to accept. Still she went to groups and observed. She tells me that before going to feminist groups she felt that Americans were cold compared to Italians. She was made to feel embarrassed when she touched people or kissed them. This was not true of the feminist women who impressed her with their warmth and feelings of sisterhood.

In Philadelphia, at the opening of Kate Millett's husband's sculpture exhibition she met Diane Alstad who told her she'd started in the black movement but found the women's movement more important to her. Diane suggested Serena write her thesis on the feminist movement. Serena began collecting documents.

— When I returned to Milan I wondered what WL could mean to Italy. At the University of Milan I began to notice things that became unbearable. For example I was talking to a man and another male friend came over to talk. He started caressing me. I was so furious I couldn't react. Suddenly I couldn't function anymore. —

Her fury led to the first feminist meeting which she held in her apartment. She tells me that as the women sat around in a circle rapping she noticed that the Marxist-oriented university students had a fixed point of view. The other women were more open, freer to talk of their personal experiences. Serena laughs and says she really understood the leftist women. — In New York I actually said 'the woman's problem doesn't exist.'

— In Italy politics is abstract, connected to a specific political organization, to a historical background such as the Russian Revolution or the Chinese Revolution. This is the point of reference here, rather than a specific situation. It's a vicious circle because even if you understand something is wrong in your private life, the only way to come out of your own problem is to join a political group. You have to jump from your own experience and identify with something that has to do with your situation. One side is the political theory. The other side is you. But in the middle is an empty hole. Yet when it is the only alternative, you identify with it. —

The women in Serena's group refused to work as feminists. Feminism to them was an insulting word. Serena shrugs, — The contradiction was they agreed that women didn't have any definition but they refused to lin their problem with the feminist movement. We talked about women's problems but never on a personal level. It was very different from the small groups in America. The political women talked so much theory which cut off others who had no political background. Some women left. Others came back. —

The Castaldi group is no longer political. They meet for CR and action. They translate feminist material from all over into Italian. Their paper goes to other groups and nonaffiliated women. Day care centers are planned for the future. They have rented a villa which is functioning as a rehabilitation center for women. There professional women give counselling not as experts but as sisters.

Serena speaks about herself. — When I was younger I thought of women as a put down, something uninteresting, nothing very attractive. I identified with men. I felt equal to them but when I was the girlfriend of some man I felt different. Male chauvinism comes out in the female-male relationship. In the relationships with the Italian man you're put into the mother role. They want you as supportive, understanding. You must be down and at the same time strong. You have to be there when they need you and shutup when they need to be alone. —

In June, in Milan, the Italian feminist groups had a convention. And again it was the political women and the feminists. The situation broke when an unwed mother talked about her problems. A woman rose and stated emphatically, 'I don't think these are our problems.'

Serena says, — That started a very angry alive dialogue between both factions. The next day the political group started their official talking again and I couldn't stand it anymore. I told the women, there's a garden outside. I'm going to sit out there and if anybody wants to join me, they can. —

At 3:30 am Marinella, Serena and I said goodbye. As Serena got into her car I looked around at grey blanketed Milan and said, — This city is unreal. I'm never quite sure I'm here. —

Serena burst out laughing. — Everybody talks about the smog in New York. When I was in New York it was like living in the mountains. — She waved goodbye from her car, both disappearing into the fogworld before I got my goodbye out.

ROME

ROME IS a very exciting city for a woman if she happens to be a nymphomaniac who likes pigs. My second day in a hotel near the station, I found myself being smothered by a hotel clerk who threw his oversexed body on top of mine.

I arrived on Sunday night, was given a room that faced a lovely frosty garden. No heat. I almost became another statue in Rome. The second night my room was in the main part of the hotel. No windows but plenty of heat. In a freezing Rome perspiration came from every pore in my body. The next morning I was given a room with a window and heat. As I unpacked for the third time in two days I discovered my robe was missing. The hotel clerk unlocked the door and we searched. Realizing my robe had fallen from the bed and landed next to the wall I leaned over the bed to retrieve it. Only to find myself pinned to the bed by this panting twenty-three-year-old clerk.

Now, if you're a twenty-three-year-old woman and this happens you tell the pig to get off, you complain to the hotel manager and although you may be silently accused of asking for it you do have a fifty-fifty chance. But face it. What twenty-three-year-old kid would want a forty-five-year-old woman. If he's on top of her she led him on. If she reports him it has to be that she propositioned him and he refused. Because in a situation like that the man rarely loses and when the woman is older he's a sure winner.

I told this primeval animal what I thought of him but didn't complain to anybody until I saw Julienne. She turned red, rushed from my room to the desk and told the clerk if it ever happened again she would personally see to it that he is prosecuted. He looked at her as if she were mad and said nothing.

The next day I told Giovanna. Giovanna who has another life style went storming downstairs, threatened to flatten him out, make his head spin from her blows. — How dare you? — she screamed at the top of her lungs. The guests in the lobby suddenly became an audience. How could anyone believe such a thing of him he said. I'm only twenty-three. He gave Giovanna a 'look at her and look at me' look. Ah here it comes, I thought. This is it. Eyes downcast he said, — What would I be doing with a woman that age? I'm a boy. — I turned to Giovanna. — What did I tell you? —

Giovanna screamed, — Are you accusing my friend of lying? — He looked like he was going to faint. — I could never do such a thing. Never. Why would I do such a thing? I'm engaged. — The housekeeper suddenly became part of the act. She looked from the clerk to me to Giovanna. — He's a boy, — she said. — Why would he do such a thing? —

Giovanna's words came fast. — Because he's a man. — To the clerk. — Because you're an animal. — To me. — You're leaving this minute. — To the clerk. — Get my friend's bill ready. —

I spoke. — And I will not pay for today. —

— The law says you're supposed to check out at 12:00. It's 2:00. —

ME: The law? Are we going to talk about the law now?
GIOVANNA: Yes, tell us about the law.
CLERK: All right. I shall prove I am a gentleman and only have my guests' interest at heart. You do not have to pay for today.

Two minutes later we were downstairs. Giovanna swept dramatically to the door and said her last words in Italian. I didn't get what she said but from the look on ex-sexy's face I've got a strong feeling it will hamper his style for a long time to come.

JULIENNE TRAVERS

It's a free world. You can leave.

SHE CAME to Rome from the States when she married an Italian and then when the marriage failed decided to stay. — When I separated from my husband I had to either accept that what had happened to me was due to my personal inability or I had to find some other answer. After I reflected for a long time I found that my relationship with my husband belonged to a general social context. I wanted to find out if there were other women who were alone like me and who had reached the same conclusions. —

Julienne Travers spent a year interviewing ten women. This culminated in a book published in 1968. — My aim was to present a living portrait of each woman. When I wrote the book women had not yet begun to get together. These women expressed the reality of that time. We were women who had to fight alone, as we could, against the society.

It isn't the book I'd write today. —

Julienne was at the first meeting of Rivolte Femminile. She became an active member. She was also one of the women instrumental in starting Collettivo. She talks about statements she made before she became a feminist, particularly those pertaining to homosexual women. — I'd say everybody's life is their own and it's their problem. What a person does is their affair and what I do is my affair. —

At FEMØ in Stockholm she and other feminists were confronted by a homosexual who said that women were ignoring the fact that sexual relationships between women and men were oppressive. She felt that women did this to deny the possibility of having sexual relationships with women.

— For me it was a shattering experience. I had to face the fact that I am fighting against certain aspects of an individual man. And at the same time I'm going to bed with that man. I'd always taken it for granted that on all levels you fight with the man but afterwards you go to bed with him. The other attitude is you can exploit him for sex so I'll just use him for sex but that's a negation of all feminist values. One way is not to think about it as I had always done. But we want to create a society in which relationships have an authentic deep value so what does it mean as a feminist to go to bed with a man just to exploit him. —

Julienne Travers tells me her personal background is absent of male oppression. Her grandmother divorced her grandfather and brought up Julienne's mother by herself. Julienne's mother divorced her husband when Julienne was three so she too was brought up without a male authority. Their religion was Christian Science, whose leader and founder is Mary Baker Eddy. Ms. Travers went to schools in America and England and every school had a woman at the head. She believes her private background is responsible for her always having good women friends.

She talks about her mother, describes her as a spontaneous person, totally nonoppressive. — My mother was a real feminist even though she'd never even heard the word. — But she goes on to say that her mother suffered from men and the male world, that she was a person who lived with her feelings and this was responsible for the terrible hurt she suffered. — I learned a lesson from my mother. I never wanted to take the blows my mother had in life and I felt the way to attain this was to be totally rational.

— There were these two elements. I'd always been with women so it was the most natural thing for me. On the other hand I never had relationships where we talked on a feeling level. This rationale has been the instrument of my life until recently. I wanted to protect myself from the suffering that I saw in my mother's life. —

I saw Julienne at least six times; at meetings, demonstrations, privately, publicly, in her business office, at her apartment. We discovered we were both admirers of Saul Bellow.

Julienne covered countless subjects, talked of her life, related many incidents. One that disturbed her greatly took place in her apartment. An Israeli couple, good friends of hers, were visiting. The man, she says, is a philosopher — so in many ways as a human being he fascinated me. But I couldn't stand the way he kept oppressing his wife. Finally I told him he only lived to suppress his wife, he wanted a woman to serve his spiritual and material needs. He said 'If you don't want to do this for a man you don't have to have a man. It's a free world. You can leave.' I was so infuriated by what he said I found it impossible to answer. It's like the nineteenth century factory owner who said in essence: 'You don't have to do this. You don't have to work for me sixteen hours a day in the most appalling conditions. You can leave if you want to. It's a free world.' —

Another incident. Recently Julienne and other feminists were present at a taping of a TV special called, *Is A Woman A Slave?* She says, — It was a chance to say the word feminism which is a breakthrough because Italy has no history of feminism. Just for an Italian woman to hear another woman say I am a feminist is something. It was very bad because there was this media priest there who discusses woman's problems. We call him the Dear Abby Priest. On the program were also the Catholic Action Family Groups. But the ones we feared the most were the shiny magazine Dear Abbys. The most famous one came in dressed very elegantly, very self-assured and she immediately sat herself next to the Dear Abby Priest. We waited and said what is she going to say because she's considered an authority and when this woman speaks all the women drink it in. Before the program began we saw her bend down and speak to a friend of hers in the audience. We heard her say 'Should I do it? Dare I do it?'

— The program began and several participants expressed their views. She asked to speak and then the priest said, 'I think we ought to let her talk because she's the expert on feminine attitudes.' We thought, oh here it comes. And she said, 'I just want to say this. I have never been allowed to write the truth at any time and that's all I have to say.' —

Before dropping me off at Alma Sabatini's, Julienne said, — Remind me to tell you about my last conversation with my husband. —

The next time I saw her I asked, — Well what did he say? — She smiled, told me they'd been arguing — and I asked him, who do you think you are, which is really a rhetorical question and he said I'm just a man who wants peace and quiet. And then I had one of those feminist breakthroughs. Whenever he'd said this before it had the enormous power of raising in me a terrible sense of guilt. All the masochism which has been indoctrinated in us and then I'd think, this poor man who's had to live with a shrew, when any other woman could have given him some happiness and he had to have the misfortune of finding me. And he asked for so little. Only a little peace and quiet. But then I had this feminist breakthrough and I said to him, do you know what they call peace and quiet nowadays? It's known as law and order. And you just happened to meet somebody who wasn't going to accept your law and order. And it wasn't very peaceful for you, was it? —

YOU'RE A WOMAN ALONE

Man, this is Italy

STANDING ON what is probably the only obscure corner in Florence, talking to three Israeli students I hear, — There's the Italian version of Bonnie. — Turning, I begin screaming. The Haileys scream.

Betsy and Oliver Hailey insist they only saw my back and didn't know it was me. Oliver, with his flair for drama, swears they've been looking all over Europe for me, that he's followed redheads in every city.

They shlep me all over Florence, appalled that I've been in so many countries just to see feminists. We go back to their hotel. Before dinner Oliver uses one phone. I use the other. He is calling California, New York, London. I am calling feminists in the immediate area.

Later at a restaurant I say something that starts us laughing. Oliver says, — Write comedy will you? Why are you writing serious stuff and women's lib yet. —

— Draw my bath, — I say.

— I knew it. As soon as I said it, I thought, she's going to pick up on that. —

— Draw my bath Betsy. Really Oliver! —

— She always draws my bath, don't you Betsy? (Betsy nods) She likes it, don't you Betsy? —

— No I don't, — she says.

— Male chauvinist, — I say.

— I'm a male chauvinist! — Oliver has a shocked expression on his face. — Betsy, that funny lady we loved is gone ..... Aha, but why are you having dinner with a male chauvinist? —

— How could I refuse after you read the description of the restaurant? —

— Because I go to Europe like an intelligent person. I read everything before I left. Betsy and I have only been here three weeks and *we've seen* Europe. Everybody goes to the British Museum to see it, but you go to find the bathroom. Look, here's the telephone number of our hotel in Rome. I'll just ignore that remark about male chauvinism. We'll be there tomorrow so when you get there call ...... Betsy, isn't this dessert unbelievable! Bonnie, don't start licking the plate. You're with class now. —

Oliver Hailey and I received grants with the New Dramatists at the same time. While he went on to win the Vernon Rice award for his play *Anyone Can Whistle,* had two plays produced on Broadway, another off-Broadway and countless plays produced all over the States, not to mention his TV scripts. While he went on to bigger and bigger things I had one play produced, played wife and mother, and in my spare time, when it was convenient for everybody, wrote.

I was told by Jules Irving of the Lincoln Repertory Theatre, — I would really like to have you on this production but you do have three children and I need somebody dependable. — However, I did work with him.

I am in Rome. Having dinner with the Haileys before I go to my first meeting at Collettivo Lotta Feminista. We enter another one of Oliver's carefully chosen restaurants and again the food is excellent. We talk about the theatre, the New Dramatists. We keep topping one another and laugh hysterically through the meal, while the other patrons, dressed to the teeth, leftovers from a drawing room comedy, steal delicate glances at us, their eyebrows reaching for the ceiling.

— Come to California, — Oliver says. — New York is dead. You can't make it there anymore. Half the people you know are on the coast. You'll love it. —

— I lived there once, remember, and I didn't love it. —

— Listen for a change. Comedy is what you're meant to write. Why are you writing about a damned bunch of feminists? —

Leaving the restaurant Oliver decides to have Italian pastry in another place, but settles for the creamy ice cream. He refuses me a taste when I tell him I have to leave for the feminist meeting.

OLIVER: Come with us. You haven't seen a damned thing. What are you going to tell everybody when they ask you about Europe? Nothing. If it weren't for us you wouldn't have seen a thing.

BONNIE: Oh sure. Great! You took me to that church with all those damned skeletons.

OLIVER: That church happens to be one of the wonders of the world. It used to be one of the seven wonders until they replaced it with something else . . . . . Bonnie, it's 10:30. Those women aren't going to be there.

BONNIE: Of course they will.

OLIVER: Then at least take a cab.

BONNIE: I'm taking a bus.

OLIVER: Betsy, talk to her. She doesn't know where she's going, she can't speak the language and she's going. Why, of all the fascinating people did we have to bump into this one. *[pushing me away]* Get your female hands off my ice cream. You can't have any if you're going to leave us like this . . . . Bonnie, don't go. You can't even speak the language.

As I board the bus I hear Oliver's exasperated voice, — You're a woman alone. Man, this is Italy. Get off that damned bus. —

As I laugh from the back of the bus, I see four arms go up in resignation as Betsy and Oliver laugh back at me.

COLLETTIVO LOTTA FEMINISTA

A society without culture heroes or leaders

I ARRIVE after 11:00 at their headquarters, 94 Via Pompeo Magno. And the feminists are there. As soon as I enter I hear, — We've been in contact with rue de Canette. One of our members is there now. We called Milan and some of the women are coming here. —

This first abortion march in Rome was a last minute decision, too late for the feminists to get a police permit, they tell me. And then — Don't take any papers with you. —

— Maybe you'd better not demonstrate on Saturday. If you're arrested you won't make the Betty Friedan thing, that's if she'll show. I understand Alma hasn't reached her yet. —

Somebody complains, — Why is Alma holding a special demonstration? The press won't give us any coverage with or without Betty Friedan. —

Collettivo Lotta Feminista is the newest feminist group in Italy. Most of the members were with Rivolte Femminile from July 1970 until April 1971. On abortion they are in complete agreement with RF. They are marching because they cannot tolerate the senseless deaths of their sisters.

The figure for illegal abortions in Italy varies from 1,500,000 to 3,500,000. Even if one accepts the smaller figure it is staggering. CLF states, — This system couldn't do without clandestine abortions because millions and millions of lire can be earned and circulated throughout Italy. The doctors can and do collect enormous amounts of money because they claim it is dangerous for them. —

The feminists in CLF work in small study and CR groups. Their papers are distributed to universities to inform and encourage new members. Collettivo repudiates the claim that women's problems are personal and states, — Since her privation is political, i.e., her relegation to the private world of the family and her exclusion from the rest of society, we consider this a political fact based on a power situation. Since women have been separated into individual ghettoes her situation appears to be personal. However, when you multiply this personal complaint it is a societal situation which applies to all women. In order to find her identity a woman must discover it with other women. When oppression goes really deep historically and psychologically it appears to be a *natural condition* and obliterates woman's real situation. We are not only discovering our own identity but trying to discover a new language since the one we use is not ours.

— We are trying to create together a new society with totally new relationships where no human being ever looks to another to find her identity or to use another to acquire an identity. A society without culture heroes or leaders. —

One month after Collettivo was organized they held a Mother's Day Exhibition at Piazza Navona. The exhibit had three sections. One showed the media. I saw an ad where a boy had one hand on his mother's belly, another on her breast and the caption read, *How Beautiful You Are.* What was the ad for? Bras naturally. An ad for maternity clothes showed a three-year-old girl lying on her back holding what else but a doll. But the prize for instant nausea was a naked girl holding a beer bottle close to her breast with the caption, *How I love you.* The ad was for beer, not jock straps.

The second section showed actual photographs of women. The reality. Women working at home, as professionals, business women, factory workers, domestics, wives, mothers.

In the center of the display was a support with feminist sayings.

In the works: A contraception and abortion information center without the usual authoritarian structure, but one that will stress human relations.

GIOVANNA CAPUTO

The so-called difference is balls

SHE FOUGHT with fascists in front of the Teatro Eliseo. She went on two abortion marches, danced with the feminists at Piazza Navona in the pouring rain. Nobody has to define sisterhood for Giovanna Caputo.* She lives it. Working all day as an interpreter, she would leave work, meet me, interpret for me. She knew all the feminists and moved from group to group comfortably.

One feminist being interviewed realized her English was not too bad after all so we spoke in English only to be interrupted by Giovanna's

Italian. – Giovanna, – I complained, – we're talking in English. – In another interview at 3:00 a.m., utterly exhausted, she yelled, the woman being interviewed yelled and I yelled. Giovanna was asking question after question. – Who's doing the interviewing you or me? – I asked. She was furious. – But you don't understand. It's important that I understand so you can understand. – – But it's perfectly clear to me. – She stared at me. – Well it's not clear to me. –

The following is just a brief glimpse of Giovanna Caputo. We spoke much during the time I lived in her apartment. Everything she said interested me. She tells me her life is not typical of Italian girls, that she was given the freedom of a boy. At age twelve she spent all day alone on a boat. When she was fifteen her father saw her in the bathtub and realizing she was fully developed put a stop to her freedom. That same year she stopped going to confession. – I had nothing to confess. Anyhow even then I couldn't believe that making love was a sin.– When she was sixteen she refused to leave a party with her cousin and came home with a boy. Her father was furious and hit her. – I was under the blanket so it didn't really hurt but I yelled you'll have to kill me before you stop me from doing what I want. –

Giovanna, a born rebel, had difficulty in school as well. There she refused to accept the authority of a teacher and studied other books related to her studies. To add insult to injury, she persistently expressed her own opinion and those of other authorities rather than paraphrase her teacher's thought. Once she had to write her comments on a poem about a woman who kept a lock of her mother's hair in her locket. Giovanna stated the poem was sweety, pathetic, and that real love or affection for one's parents had nothing to do with sentimentalism. After this incident the teacher called her mother and told her Giovanna was a cynical and depraved girl.

When she was in high school there was a contest for the best essay written about the UN. A trip to Paris was the first prize. Giovanna says, – For a start it was a way to find out about your political ideas and your family's ideas. I was furious because this essay wasn't supposed to be compulsory and then I was compelled to do it. If I wrote that the UN was a political alliance amongst the big powers for economical reasons I would have been labeled a communist and you don't have to be a communist to think this. At that time one got a job through the recommendation of the parish priest and the priests were preaching politics from the pulpit, politicizing for the Christian-Democrat party. They were very anti-communist. —

She knew she wouldn't win, didn't give a damn, so she purposely wrote it badly and decided as an extra bonus to eliminate all punctuation. Her punishment was to repeat Italian, which she did. The next year she was told she couldn't register for high school. She went directly to the headmaster and shouted, — If you think that you can throw me out of school because I think with my own brain, and because there's an old conformist teacher who's stupid and illiterate, you're wrong. Now I'm going down and registering. — And register she did, even at the refusal of the registrar. — I've spoken to the headmaster, — she stated. — Now register me. —

But, according to Giovanna, all these incidents left their mark. Disgusted with the educational system she refused to go to the university and instead chose a language school. It is a decision she regrets. — Going to the language school was an escape for me. School, everyday life, living in a family in that particular society meant I was never free to do what I wanted. I always had to compromise and I suffered much from it. I felt I was half a person because I was a girl and I knew if I'd been a boy it would have been very different. I was so oppressed that I was not strong enough to understand what I really felt. So I would rebel in a specific situation. I wasn't really trying to build something. I was only reacting.

— Those early years marked me. I never got out of it really, and now since I've joined Collettivo I go back with my thoughts to those years and I start to understand why I acted in a certain way. I remember saying to myself live by the day and now that I'm almost forty I'm trying for the first time to build something or coordinate my existence towards some aim, rather than survival and getting about. —

She talks about her first abortion when she was twenty-three. — If I had any feelings they certainly weren't feelings of guilt. When I was eighteen or perhaps until I was twenty-one I thought about having a child but long before the abortion I grew out of that entirely. I stopped thinking that a woman realizes herself in motherhood. Although I do like children very much because of their natural spontaneity. —

After the abortion she had complications and had to have surgery. — Before the operation I went to church even though I hadn't gone for years. And although I was convinced I hadn't done anything wrong I went to confession out of cowardice or fear I would die. I told the priest I made love with my boyfriend and that I was in love with him and therefore was not confessing it as a sin. And that I didn't believe making love was a sin so I couldn't repent and promise not to do it again and that for me to believe in God had nothing to do with things like lovemaking. And I also told him I couldn't believe in the God of the Bible who was a God of violence but I only believe in a God of love.— Giovanna laughs her contagious laugh. — I was absolved. —

Two more abortions followed. One was performed in London where she lived for some time. The third was done in Rome.

— The way I was brought up, which is similar to the way a lot of women are brought up, is to refer to some male authority whether it be a father, a teacher or a priest. I think if a woman is logical and strong and does things which society thinks are masculine, it is evidence not that I am masculine but the so-called difference is balls. There's no reason why a woman couldn't be equally successful as an engineer or a scientist if they didn't dress her in pink and push a doll in her hands and say this is her lot in life. —

ALMA SABATINI

You must be autonomous

— I THINK IT is illusory to believe that women will get together in the very near future to change everything and overthrow the governments. It is only possible for women to carry on their revolutionary themes if they realize it's a situation we're not going to have in Italy for some time. —

I first read about Alma Sabatini in an article in The New York Times on July 20, 1971. I learned that Ms. Sabatini and twenty members of Movimento di Liberazione della Donna were actively campaigning for free and legal abortions in a country where one year ago the word abortion was taboo.

Alma Sabatini feels the right to legalized abortion is the main fight. They are trying to get a bill passed through popular initiative which means they must obtain at least 50,000 signatures. She explains, —Getting signatures is a marvellous opportunity to speak to women and open the debate in the country. — Ms. Sabatini and other members of MLD are gaining most of the signatures in the poor sections. They are also creating a feminist nucleus in each district.

— People must learn to fight for their own rights. They have to learn they can't leave politics in the hands of other people and this goes for women. The woman in the worst situation is the poor woman. I think the turning point will be when we bring the movement from the restricted circle of the elite to the masses. —

Alma Sabatini was one of the panelists on the TV show *Is a Woman a Slave?* She tells me, — I spoke very clearly about abortion and what we wanted and the Media Priest jumped up and screamed, 'Now I know what it means. Now things are clear. You have become radicalized. All you women are murderers.'— Ms. Sabatini is not disturbed when she's called a murderer since this insult is hurled at her every time she goes out to get the abortion signatures.

There are many factions blocking abortion in Italy. She explains that in April 1972 the Communist Party *(Commissione Femminiolo del Partito Communista)* met. They maintained abortion couldn't be an issue for the Communist Party because it would alienate the Catholic masses. — It's mystifying when we know the Catholic masses are the poor women whose signatures we are collecting by the thousands. It is not these people they are afraid of alienating but the top people who make the line. These they don't want to alienate. —

Another political party also in the act, according to Alma, is the P.S.I., the Socialist Party. They've introduced a law for therapeutic abortion. This means abortion in case of malformation of the fetus, psychological or physical illness of the woman, after the woman has five children, or if the woman is over forty-five.

MLD rejects this proposed law because of the conditions and because the decision will be made by a committee composed of a gynecologist, a social worker, a neuro-psychiatrist. — They will be mostly men appointed by the hospitals. The management of these state hospitals is in the hand of the clericals and it is terrible, corrupted. We also know that the gynecologists are reactionary as a whole. They earn their living from delivering children. The neuro-psychiatrists are so backward we still have electric shock treatments and strait jackets in our hospitals. —

The feminists know few women will receive abortions under this system and if the woman is rejected by the committee and still wants an abortion, everybody will know it. As it is illegal she can be prosecuted.

Aside from the crucial abortion problem, Alma is concerned with the forces who are trying to repeal the recent divorce law. — Divorce is the first step in freeing women. Now we see that the communists are practically bartering the divorce law for openings into power, to get to the government together with the Christian Democrats. When this is finished we will have ten to twenty years where any kind of libertarian struggle will be practically impossible. —

The situation becomes complex because the Christian Democrats propose divorce only for those who marry in a civil court. However, since 1929, when the Concordate Pact was signed between Mussolini and the Vatican, the marriage was practically left in the hands of the church. After the war, approximately 1948, the Communists voted for the introduction of the Concordat into the new Constitution. — Although few married in civil ceremonies before 1929 it was at least separate. Now that it's linked together the problem is practically insoluble. The point is that all the other problems will be fucked. We are going on with our struggle for abortion but we know the communists and Christian Democrats form another front. —

I ask Alma why she was instrumental in starting MLD, and why a mixed group. She says she is aware that MLD has been criticized for having men as members but adds, — I understand the women who say in the beginning we have to be alone, to work without men, but it is not my choice. If it is going to be a real woman's liberation it will be a liberation of everybody. The fact that we can't have an authentic relationship with a man because of our different roles is also true for the men. The men will have much to gain but they will have to give up a lot of their own personality. The problem is a serious one. Freedom is not fucking whenever you want to. This is not freedom. You must be autonomous. You can be sexually free on one hand and, once you are emotionally involved, revert backwards to the dependency role. I think that the problem is one of love and not sex. And that's what fucks up women. —

NOVEMBER 18

Afternoon

AT MLD HEADQUARTERS plans are being made for the second abortion demonstration on November 24 at 5:00 p.m. In the midst of sending a telegram to Ms. Friedan in Trent, talking to feminists who come in and out of the office, Alma Sabatini answers the questions of two feminists from the States. They are writing about the movement in Italy from a sociological point of view. The phones never stop ringing. Alma says to me, — It would be wonderful it you could give your speech in Italian. Do you think you could do it? — She is talking about the speech I will give if Betty Friedan can't make it. Before I know it she has translated it into Italian. And the feminists keep interviewing her. She laughs, — It's a madhouse, isn't it? — Alma's still answering questions as she rushes off for a meeting. I'm on the phone when she comes back, sticks her head in the door, — Bonnie don't forget to be at my home tomorrow morning. I'm going to call Betty in Milan. —

NOVEMBER 18

Early evening

AT COLLETTIVO headquarters women are working on posters for the demonstration Saturday. An American feminist, Susan Dubiner, who's been working as an art teacher in Rome the past year and is a member of Collettivo, is on the floor putting finishing touches on posters. She turns to me. — What is it like in the States now? A year is a long time and I want to go home but . . . Let's get together before I leave ok? —

Somebody calls out, — Who's got the red poster color? — Ronnie, a recent emigrant from Greece, who now lives in Rome and is with Collettivo, constantly gripes for my benefit. — Americans are war mongers, capitalists. You people are crazy. — She is half teasing, half serious. — You are corrupt. —

Renata says, — We've got to get this thing settled. Are we going to demonstrate on Wednesday night too? I think it is ridiculous. International Abortion Day is the 20th. —

— But Friedan is coming on the 24th. —

— I thought we agreed the one thing we don't need is culture heroines. —

Anna comments, — She's important to the movement. —

— That's not the point, — a woman interjects. — We need to show solidarity. —

Ronnie complains, — Every country is marching on the twentieth and that's when I'm marching. —
— Ask Bonnie what she thinks, — a woman says.
— She's her friend. She'll say demonstrate naturally. —
— Ronnie, I don't know her. —
— You're an American. You'll say march. —

Twenty posters are finished so far. It is decided we will all congregate at Piazza San Cosimato at 2:30 on Saturday afternoon. As the media refuse to recognize the movement in Italy feminists will be on the phones contacting everybody.

Renata yells, — Are we or aren't we going to demonstrate on the twenty-fourth? —

Giovanna meets me at Collettivo and we go to Elvira Banotti's to discuss Rivolte Femminile.

ELVIRA BANOTTI

Men are afraid of their bodies

SITTING IN a restaurant I ask, — Elvira are you and Rivolte Femminile going to participate this Saturday?—

She answers, — I'm starving. You came so late. The veal scaloppini is very good here. Shall I order for all of us. Giovanna? — The food is ordered and Elvira continues. — I will speak to you in English but of course when things become complicated I will speak in Italian and Giovanna will translate. She knows all about Rivolte because she started with us. — Then, — You saw Carla in Milan so of course you know we won't demonstrate. As she must have told you we refuse to participate because of the conditions put on abortions and because we refuse to be a part of the society as it is now. —

Long before there was a feminist movement Ms. Banotti questioned the female-male relationship. She calls the heterosexual union —two faces of reality. — Carla and Elvira, long time friends, had many conversations about woman's predicament long before they formed RF. Elvira explains, — If you go inside the woman's problem you immediately discover all the people, the moral society who mean well. Take off the facade and you find the hypocrisy of men. They are wearing a mask. They say we mean well, we are humanitarian, we want to protect women. But if you scratch behind this mask you find what there is. —

She is adamant that what men call a love relationship is really a form of terrorism. — From the moment I became a feminist I had difficulty with men. Now I can only accept special situations, those men who show me they are removed from the patriarchal society. It's not easy to find men like this. Generally I don't like a long-lasting relationship because I need a deep sensation. Then after a certain time they ask you to play a certain role which is impossible for me. In all my experience I find men not able to have sexual relationships erotically, to move their bodies sensually. The first time is always amusing to me. Their bodies are not relaxed. They are not even able to move their hands. In their approach they are not what they say they are . . . the conquerors. They're clumsy, not creative sexually. —

She bursts out laughing. — They are always disoriented to find I am so free in my sexual attitude. The last thing they take off is their underpants. Men are afraid of their bodies. I was always in doubt about the self assurance that men have because I never felt the need to limit the freedom of other people. This to me was a key to their limitations and the absurdity of men's roles. —

Elvira explains that RF began with the premise that women cannot join the patriarchal society because they are removed from its history, which is a very violent one. — Men justify this in terms of their own exploitation but we cannot accept this. They look at their history as *the history* of the world. It is ridiculous for them to think that theirs is the only history. They not only ignore the experience of women in history but try to cancel it. They've forced a history which denied women's experiences and then deny their own defeat and decadence. —

On education: — All education is geared toward the male so that it cannot relate to women. Education forces women to absorb values which are borne against them. —

Elvira's particular group is studying the history of work. They believe that work has become a fixation in the male society and that this has destroyed any joy that work may have. — In the beginning man identified himself with his economic power, organized the culture which excluded women. Men consider work the thing they do. They do not consider work the thing that women do. This evaluation stems from the male culture and even after thousands of years the Marxists still exclude woman's work. It is their analysis, not ours. —

Ms. Banotti believes that man has sold out his humanity for economic power, political power. — This is pathological for me. The one-dimensional man. Another deceit is that this ideology pushes the woman to identify to the same abstraction. They expect us to find our freedom in the same form of alienation.

— Socialism, as it is now, is the last trap because it ties every member in the society to this economical abstraction. It does not allow people to find their own oppression but forces each one to adapt to the dialectic values of the society. Today, anyone who proposes her or his own liberation in terms of economic independence principally demonstrates to have assimilated the basic values of the patriarchal society. —

NOVEMBER 19

Morning

— YES ... YES. Please ask Ms. Friedan to call me here. — Alma hangs up the receiver, tells me, — Her plane is late. Do you have time? ... Good. We'll have lunch together. —

Then, — Now I'll answer your question. Yes there were those in Movimento who felt intimidated by the men in the beginning but there are those who are intimidated by men and women. You take the black people. They can very well live without whites but women can't completely live without men. They're always in their lives, either a father or a brother or an uncle, a husband, a lover. It's a reality of life and I think it important that we confront men and raise their consciousness whenever possible. —

— I don't agree. I think it's up to them to get their own heads together. —

— Take me. I have a love relationship now and it's certainly different from the others. It's more authentic, has a more genuine quality. I don't say that it's better or worse but it's certainly different. I'm playing no games and he's playing no games. —

— Alma, what really interests me is the way many men have changed since the new feminist movement. Now that we're discovering our own sexuality, man has turned from robot to super robot. He's reading all the books, perfecting his technique, but inside himself nothing much has changed. —

— It's funny that you mention that. I was discussing the question of technique the other night with my doctor and I said what is the point of technique? What does it mean? Supposing he kisses you on the mouth, on the nipple, stroking your clitoris. I could stay as cold as ice if this procedure is done in this technical way. You can have a man stroke your clitoris for hours but if it's done mechanically . . . . I could very well have sex without love and enjoy it, but there must be at the moment some other thing. If it's sex without attachment it's nothing. Then there are men who have an inquisitive attitude, and they say let's see how she'll react to this and that puts me off. The two persons have to be involved. —

— Alma, how about the man who's so intent on giving you clitoral satisfaction that you swear you're having a clitorectomy without anesthesia. —

We were laughing when the phone rang. — Betty, this is Alma Sabatini. Did you receive my telegram? . . . . Good. Will you be able to make it on Thursday? . . . . Marvellous. What hotel will you be staying in? . . . . . Yes I'll write it down . . . . . I have an American feminist who wants to greet you . . . . —

As I put down the receiver Alma sighs. — Now that that's settled we must send a press release immediately. —

JENNY

I hurt in all the erogenous zones

— I ONLY FEEL now that I'm being myself and that I have enough balance to go back to Holland. I'm now pleasing myself, being honest to myself, and this is the most important thing. If I'm not pleasing you, that's too bad. —

She is with Collettivo, was born in Amsterdam, came to Italy close to thirteen years ago, stayed when she married her husband, an Italian. When she was fourteen she received a scholarship which took her to New York where she was a student at a high school. She is well educated, comes from a wealthy family. Her husband had little education, was born to poverty.

Jenny* talks about him, his family. — These people are pure. They don't have all these preconceived ideas about how one must live life, what is good, what is bad. The trouble is you can't marry the peasant and it took me twelve years to discover it. It's not enough for me to see another person the same as myself but also the other person has to see me as being equal to himself. My husband was always trying to show that I was stupid so it wasn't so bad for him to be stupid. And it didn't help that I didn't think him stupid because I thought he was marvellous. —

Before her second anniversary she had her first child. And she began working. She organized a student hotel that was very successful. Her husband, on the other hand, worked spasmodically and once for a period of four years was unemployed. Her marriage started deteriorating and by the time Jenny had her third child the situation was terrible for her. Her salary was twice his and she was now receiving an inheritance from Holland. As manager of the hotel she was always in contact with people. This made her husband jealous. She said there was no communication and that their sex life which had always been good was finished.

— Here's the difference between the education of a woman and a man. A woman can only make love when she's happy. She's not only happy to have a man's body. She needs his company. He was never home, would wake me up for sex but I refused. The very moment he realized he had lost me he started oppressing me in such an awful way it just pushed me farther and farther from him until we had such a bad fight. He started beating me up one night when I refused to wake up to make love. The next night I had a terrible nightmare. —

She dreamed she committed suicide by jumping out of their fifth-floor apartment. When she woke up she decided she wasn't herself anymore and needed help. The analyst she chose told her she couldn't help her. — She said to me we're Christians here. You're Dutch. I could never advise you to leave your husband. Here, I will give you the name of a man in Holland. — Shortly afterwards she took a holiday in Holland and saw the Dutch neurologist.

Jenny tells me, — I hurt in all the erogenous zones, my breasts, my vagina, every part. I thought I had cancer. Now I realize I was hurt as a woman, so all my female parts were in pain. The doctor in Holland started hollering at me that a woman shouldn't think she can't raise children by herself. He hammered with his fist on the table because I said that isn't what I wanted. I didn't want to leave my husband. I just wanted to feel better. —

Back in Italy she tried to please her husband while she felt sicker and sicker, went from doctor to doctor. She asked one if her sexual desire would ever come back. — I loathed my husband, couldn't stand his touch. — The doctor said no. Another doctor, an analyst, told her to come three times a week for some outrageous sum. Jenny told him her children needed the money more than he and anyhow if she stayed with her husband she was sure to kill herself. — The doctor said I was cured. That's the funniest answer I ever got. —

It took a year for Jenny to find a lawyer who would represent her. The lawyers she sought told her that since her husband didn't drink, wasn't untrue, didn't gamble she didn't have a case and that it was her obligation to go to bed with him. She wanted out so badly that she asked for nothing but custody of the children. She tells me, — I made a terrible mistake when I asked for nothing. The mentality here is so different. They think that women are out to cheat men of everything and felt I didn't because of guilt. The court was a tragicomedy. My husband said he caught me in a locked room with a foreigner. The judge looked at me as if I was talking from the moon. —

— What does that mean? —

— It's an Italian expression that means loony. I said if it was a locked room how could he catch me? The judge insisted I give a serious answer but I simply refused because it was too ridiculous. It was as good as pleading guilty. — She didn't win a separation and for the next two years was equally unsuccessful. She finally found a new lawyer who advised her to sell everything (she'd bought property with her inheritance) and offer her husband full custody of the children. The lawyer insisted her husband only wanted the money.

Jenny says, — It was terrible for me. I had to fight myself because I had to emotionally release myself from the children. I didn't think he would take them from me but there was this small possibility that he would. — She talks about the possessions she had, how she had to give them all up. What stands out in her mind are the Dutch tiles she received as a small child. She'd saved them for years and finally placed them around an open fireplace in the home she'd designed and had built. — I had to sell the house with those tiles. They were important to me because they were my childhood and I'd placed them there because the hearth is the center of the house. When I was at the point where I could give up all these things I knew I was dead inside. But I knew I'd be alive for the children. —

She placed her children in a boarding school, had to have them baptized which was against her own religion. Why? She was accused of being a bad mother. — In Italy only Catholics are good mothers. — She won her separation three years ago. — I was free from him but he followed me in the beginning wherever I went. I was free but how could I be free when I trembled every time I saw him. —

Three months after the separation her pains disappeared. Jenny tells me she is not interested in men now. — I've had it. They're all the same. They drain you and that is all. They're not giving anything. They think with their pricks. I think there are some young emancipated men who feel differently. At least I hope so. Otherwise you just have to go out and shoot yourself. —

We had dinner with her children. Then talked well into the night while Jenny's children slept in another room.

NOVEMBER 20

International Abortion Day

GIOVANNA AND I sit by the potbellied stove drinking capuccino. She tells me the temperature has dropped to 35 degrees. The clothes I brought are for 75 degrees. I borrow a sweater, boots, leotards to wear under my jeans. My identification is put in a drawer. It's just a precaution Giovanna says. — They won't bother you because you're an American. But there's a good chance I'll be arrested and if I am you don't know anything. You don't know me and don't come back here right away. Go to Alma's or Jenny's or one of the other women. —

We lock the door, go out into a freezing Rome. At the Collettivo offices women are still working on posters. There is a tremendous feeling of excitement. I hear, — Can you believe? Our sisters will be marching in so many countries . . . . . . Has anybody seen Julienne? . . . Will somebody please help me put my poster on? — Susan is rushing around, putting last minute touches on the posters. Ronnie my Greek friend spots me, — Oh good. The American has arrived. Now we can have our march. —

— You know you love me Ronnie. —

— I could never love the bourgeoisie. I am certain you have at least twenty servants. —
— Thirty-two to be exact. —
Ronnie takes a deep breath and bursts into an aria from *Carmen*.
— Let's go. —
Forty of us move out of the Collettivo offices and into the street. We drive in cars to Piazza San Cosimata, an open market place. As we approach the Piazza we see clusters of women waiting in the bitter cold, holding signs, banners. People who are buying food from the stands stare at us, at our posters that denounce the church, the doctors, the government.
— Is the group from Milan here? —
— Yes. —
— Is Orietta and the Fourth World here? —
— They're meeting us at Piazza Navona. —
Two American feminists join us. One says, — I didn't even know there was a movement here. I wish I'd known. —
Onlookers are fingering our signs, reading them, snickering, passing remarks, some in utter amazement. A priest walks by and glares at us. A group of nuns glance quickly and then move away. By now there are hundreds of us. I try to count but it's impossible. One man points to my sign, says Americana and laughs with his friends.
— We'll leave in fifteen minutes. —
The temperature drops. We stamp our feet, jump up and down, flap our arms back and forth and talk to one another. Susan tells me she's glad she's here on this first abortion march, asks me if I realize how much courage it takes for Italian women to go on an abortion demonstration. At 3:00 p.m. our number has doubled and we begin our mile-and-a-half walk to the Piazza Navona.
As we go from Viale Trastevere to Ponte Garibaldi, up Via Arenula more women join us. Feminists from other groups. And women who are nonaffiliated. I speak to visiting feminists from France, England, Denmark, Sweden, Germany. We hand out leaflets as people cheer us on, shake their fists at us, call us murderers, lesbians, whores. Susan looks up at the winter sun and smiles, — Did you ever see such a golden light? Now you can understand the Italian Renaissance. There isn't any light to compare with it. —
One of the American feminists hands out leaflets to men. Someone asks her to stop. — Save them for the women. — Demonstrators go into

a bridal shop. In the doorway of a store are two women in their sixties, dressed completely in black. We hand them the leaflets. They read them, look up at us, their expressions blank. Then suddenly one yells, — Brava, brava. — The other woman joins her. — Brava. — They wave to us and smile from the doorway. A group of feminists break into women's liberation songs, and we march along singing, handing out pamphlets.

At Campo Dei Fiore, another open market, the merchants cheer us until they realize who we are. The comments are pathetic, funny, hilarious, serious, insulting. People run up to us, speak with us. One woman selling vegetables shakes her fist at us. A woman, her grey hair in a tight bun, studies the signs and says, — It's about time. — Another woman argues with her and she screams back. — Quiet. Keep quiet. If my husband wouldn't kill me I'd go with them. — A man gestures with his whole body. — What do women want now, what do they want? — A priest walks by as if he sees nothing.

At Piazza Navona, Orietta Avenati and the women from the Fourth World are demonstrating, their posters high. Giovanna points out Orietta. I move to her, — Orietta, I want to talk with you. — — Yes I know. They told me. Call the office on Monday. I have a girl who will interpret. My English is not good. —

By now we are frozen solid. Fifty of us go inside a cafe for coffee, tea, brandy, while the rest march in the Piazza. Men at the counter eye us up and down. It's a joke. It has to be a joke. We meet their smiles with stares. Their smiles rapidly disappear. We go to a large room downstairs. The waiter who is all of twenty doesn't know what to make of us. He smiles when we smile, is serious when we're serious. Periodically between taking orders he glances at a poster. He nervously takes our orders. Renata laughs. — Poor boy. He looks like we're going to attack him. He can't wait to leave. —

Our waiter isn't gone five minutes when the electricity fails. In the darkness one of the women breaks out into the feminist songs and we are all singing. We are singing about male pigs and liberty, about doctors who kill, the clergy, free abortion and how we will fight. Suddenly in the doorway we see a light. Our young waiter is standing, two lit candles in his hands. Ronnie bursts out laughing, — Our hero, our young hero with two lit phallic symbols. — The waiter grins sheepishly and comes into the room with his candles amidst a burst of applause. And the lights magically come on.

At Piazza Navona we demonstrate in the dark while onlookers take our pamphlets. The press is nowhere in sight. As expected they are ignoring the women's movement. Giovanna nudges me and points. I look and see the police. They question women. We watch Orietta go over to them and see them move to the side as we keep marching. Jenny comes over to us. — We are free to demonstrate. — — What happened? — I asked. Renata burst out laughing, — Orietta got a permit. —

At 6:30 we are marching back again. One-and-a-half miles to go. As we pass through the open market at Campo dei Fiore merchants cheer. A man buying fruit asks — Now what do they want? — He says something and the feminists burst out laughing. — What did he say? — I ask Julienne. — He said they just want to fuck in peace. —

JUDY WINTER

I don't consider myself a liberated woman

I MET HER during the demonstration. She came up to me. — Well what do you think of the Italian feminists? Aren't they beautiful? —

Judy Winter* came to Giovanna's apartment the following day. She told me she's from California, has been in Rome four years. An airline stewardess, she met Carlo* on her first flight to Italy. Four trips later he convinced her to live in Rome, with him naturally. He didn't speak much English. She couldn't speak any Italian. — I was completely disgusted with America anyhow and I wanted to get away. I figured it would be a fun affair and I gave it two weeks. —

When Judy came to Rome she got more than she bargained for. She lived with Carlo but had to accept his three housemates as well. — They weren't living together in any kind of commune. Just a group of men who were friends and lived together because it was cheaper. I tried to establish some kind of system where we all took turns with household tasks. They objected to systems and felt they could eat when they wanted, buy what they wanted. I couldn't see this boarding house arrangement. When it came to cleaning the house they said they didn't demand that I do it and they didn't care if the house was clean. If it bothered me I could do it. —

She tells me if ever she understood female oppression it was during the two-and-a-half years she lived in this situation. Carlo, who works in the film industry, and feels women should be decorative, didn't help. — Once he was expecting a friend. Carlo took one look at me and asked me to wear a different dress. He said he wanted me to look pretty for his friend. I screamed I wasn't an object. Then another time he came home late from work and was angry because dinner wasn't ready. He didn't share in any of the housework but I accepted it until I saw the dishes of his friends in the sink. At that time I fully accepted the traditional role of the woman. —

Judy points out that from the beginning she was disturbed by the relationships of the Italian couples they knew. In one case the husband went out every night, had affairs. At the same time he was jealous of his wife and locked her in the house. They were poor and he left little money for his wife and children. Judy tells me this is just one of many cases.

When Judy Winter had a pregnancy scare a few years ago she realized she didn't want children. At that time she sensed marriage wasn't what she wanted either. — I don't think we can really experience intense human relationships until we've had an experience living as a couple. But it shouldn't stop there. We should be able to have relationships with a lot of people. I am upset with the intense one-to-one relationship. It may be beautiful but it is also dangerous because the couples cut themselves off from others. —

Ms. Winter went back to California in April 1970. She planned to stay three weeks but stayed for two months. During that time she visited many of the women's groups. — I was very excited about it. When I came back I began looking for a movement here. That's when I joined Rivolte Femminile. — She became a member in November 1970, and was one of the women who went to Collettivo when they split. Consciousness raising had a strong effect on her.

— The day I realized I only existed as an appendage to Carlo I was very angry. I cried. It was the only time I felt suicidal. Carlo came home from work, saw I was sullen. As I talked to him he began to feel my personal oppression and he started to cry. — She tells me that day changed their relationship and they now try to share in everything. But there are problems.

She decided to go from journalist to camerawoman and began studying camera techniques. Carlo was furious, claimed she was unrealistic, that there weren't any camerawomen. — I said I'll choose what I want.

Even if it's a negative experience it will be my experience. — He suggested she do other work in filmmaking. The work didn't interest her and she screamed, — The reason you're insisting on it is you want to continue being my master, my ruler, my God. —

Judy talks about a couple who are close friends. The woman and she have established a very tight, warm friendship and the men constantly tease them, say the only thing they haven't done is have sex together. Recently both men were out of town on assignments and Judy and her friend found themselves at the same party. — I felt very depressed, out of it and I wanted to go home alone and work out my depression. My friend didn't want to leave me alone and insisted we go back to her apartment. There was another friend there, a man, and he said he wanted to go too. —

The three of them landed on the bed. They went from talking to touching to sex. After a while the man moved to Judy's friend. Judy got out of bed and went into the next room. — It was my first lesbian experience and I felt good about it. It was completely natural. —

— Hold it Judy. If you felt so good about it why were you the one who left the bed? —

— He went to her and there just wasn't any reason to stay. —

— Did your friend feel good about it too? —

— Yes I know she did. We're very close. —

— Then why didn't he get out of the bed? —

— I don't know. It was such a natural thing. —

— Why didn't you both tell him to leave? —

She shrugs. — This may seem funny but it just happened last night and I haven't seen my friend since. I'm going over there when you leave for Jenny's. I want to talk to her, see what she thinks. You know, I've been thinking about it all day. —

As we waited for Jenny to drive up she turned to me, — I don't consider myself a liberated woman. I don't think there's such a thing. Inside my house I'm very liberated but as soon as I walk out on the street I'm hassled. —

ORIETTA AVENATI

The Fourth World

IN 1965 ORIETTA AVENATI started the first center for contraception. She explains that the center was allowed because women came of their own volition. At the center Orietta and other women advised and educated those who came, and informed them that doctors were dispensing contraceptives. Again they were called cycle regulators.

Italian law forbids written material on contraception but this did not stop Orietta from adapting a book on the subject. The title: *Willful Procreation and Contraception Techniques.* It was written by Christopher Tietze and Richard Frank. As a result of the publication of this book Ms. Avenati and her publisher were tried in court. When she realized that written material was against the law, but the actual use of contraceptives was not, she and her lawyer decided to take the case before the Supreme Court.

I am told that the Italian court pushes press trials through but in Ms. Avenati's case it took three years for the preliminary trial and another two years to get it before the Supreme Court. Because of her persistence contraception became a legal fact in Italy on March 16, 1970.

All her books were confiscated at the time of the judgment, but after the case was settled she was able to get some of the books back. While I talk with the interpreter, Orietta leaves the room, comes back proudly displaying a book. She smiles, — It is the only one I have now and I would never part with it. —

When Serena Castaldi visited Rome in August 1970, the press was present and a number of women made statements. — At that time I said our class enemy is not the man. Our enemy is capitalism which pushes back the women in a situation similar to the sub-proletariat class. — This press release resulted in many calls and letters from Rome and other cities. She says, — Personally I was not very interested in a feminist movement but I was concerned about the condition of women. — However, she did start a feminist movement called FILF, Fronte Italiano di Liberazione Femminile.

Orietta Avenati is a member of the Socialist Party of Proletarian Unity, P.S.I.U.P. It was formed in 1965 and the members came out of the left of the Socialist Party. FILF started with the Italian League for Human Rights. — This league has helped all the leftist groups. Their experience was very important because they taught us how to build a movement that wouldn't split up into a thousand little groups after it started. From the start we developed a political line so people could either accept or reject it. —

There were seven women and three men present at the first meeting. All nine were at the seminar sponsored by the Radical Party. They refused to join Movimento because its ideology wasn't acceptable. — The line wasn't clear to us. They said liberty would come from a social change and then changed their line to sexual freedom. —

Actions: They are organizing militants who will form food cooperatives, housing for the public good, better school conditions, paved roads. I ask what this has to do with feminism and am told, — The very fact that we're mobilizing women into action is to us a feminist action because women do not participate in Italy. —

More action: In November 1971 they formed a Medical Clinic where the relationship between doctor and patient is on a humane level.

In the works: Convinced that the nuclear family is oppressive to all, particularly women, they are planning an egalitarian community. The complex will be self-contained, maintain all services such as medical, dental, stores, food cooperatives, nurseries and so forth. Each housing community will have four people who will mobilize the people politically.

I ask if she considers this a socialistic complex. I receive a no. Then what I ask? She says, — This line can't be defined in traditional terms. But we believe that every man and woman is responsible for the social reality in which she or he lives. The four people, for instance, would discuss the library or housing, internal or external problems in an antiauthoritarian way. Our hypothesis is that people can be educated to realize that if something is wrong it is their responsibility to right it and since there's more to be done in the case of women, we have more responsibility. —

FILF is organized like Group 8 in Stockholm. There is a central organization which coordinates the small groups. These groups are autonomous and can decide if they want to be all women's groups or mixed.

Their newspaper is called *The Fourth World*. I quote directly from the paper. — We speak of the Third World when we wish to indicate those countries that are oppressed and exploited by imperialism and neocolonialism. But in almost all countries, not only those of the Third World, there is a majority that is weighed down by a twofold oppression, intensified exploitation and unjust discrimination, not only by those who exercise power but by the exploited themselves, who willingly or unwillingly are the intermediaries and accomplices of the exploiters. We are speaking of the entire female population. We call this population the Fourth World.

— Female subjugation to the male has such antique roots that even women have difficulty in recognizing and rebelling against it. Women have been subjected to a millenary conditioning that has given this oppression a homogeneous and generalized quality; thus, women are a *class* and, as such, must have common goals.

— It is now time for European women and particularly Italian women, who until now were swept along by the irresponsible decisions of a dominant class selected according to patriarchal models, to realize the fact that, among the oppressed, they are the majority and that their interests coincide with the interests of all the oppressed and exploited in the world. —

As I left the FILF offices I turned to Orietta Avenati and told her I knew nothing about her personally. — Are you married? — I asked.

She smiled at me. — Are you? — — No but I was. — — So was I, — she answered, — but no more. — — Do you have children? — I asked. — Yes, two. Do you? — — Yes three. — We were both laughing as I walked down the stairs.

AN OPEN LETTER TO SAUL BELLOW

Dear Saul Bellow:

FIRST COMPLIMENTS and then a blast.

I was fascinated with *Herzog,* your brilliant self-indulgent protagonist. Or is the word self-destructive?

I too write imaginary letters so the first time I read *Herzog* I became so engrossed with my own letters I dropped your book. But I was drawn to *Herzog* once again, his world of ideas, his abstractions, his philosophical lovers, dead and alive, his preoccupation with the past. Not to mention dropping his pants for his real life lovers, refusing to face up to his own life. When he does so, in an anti-Kierkegaardian way, he is absolutely brilliant.

His family is so alive, I can see them, smell them, I am there with them. And I am envious because you write with such love, and I haven't reached that stage in my fiction, and perhaps I never will. When Herzog writes about his brothers and the dreams his parents had for all the boys, while his sister wasn't a *genius pianist,* I realize why my feelings aren't overflowing with that kind of love, although love I have. I wasn't the genius anything either. That position was reserved for my brother. And if somebody then admitted I was, I would be out to kick a Herzog in the face, right Saul? Inconceivable that a female just wants to make her own little niche in this *effing* world without trying to kill males in the process.

You are, nonetheless, a brilliant writer. But when you write about women, couldn't you try Buber's *I-Thou*?

I am a woman too. But unlike Ramona and Sono, I am not offering my body to some brilliant male God.

Dear Saul Bellow:
Is it ever possible for a man (particularly a sensitive one like you) to write it like it is. I mean the baths and the cooking bit! And what was Herzog's wife really like? How come a mental giant like Herzog always manages to come up with a woman who's willing to spray herself with perfume while he sprays her with sperms? And why must you envision these stereotypes whose minds barely peek out from the pages?

That's why I want to know the real Ms. Herzog. Because she's the only woman whose intelligence gets through. Also fascinating since she's the only one who rejects your Herzog. So how about it Saul? What really happened?

A fan,

(with reservations)

NOVEMBER 23

Evening

BETTY FRIEDAN came to Rome under the auspices of the literary society Martedi Letterati to speak at the Teatro Eliseo. I had to wait for a friend who was coming from Abruzzo so missed her talk but I came just in time to see the feminists accosted by fascists ouside the theatre. My friend Giovanna was in the middle of it all, screaming at them.

— What are they saying? — I asked. While other feminists argued with the men who were waving their fists, Giovanna turned to me, — We are depraved, murderers and lesbians and whores and God only knows what else. — She turned back to the men who were lunging forward, the veins in their throats standing out like overcooked strings of spaghetti. The feminists stood their ground and argued vehemently. Finally the men as if on cue stopped talking and began eyeing the feminists up and down. The women stared back and finally the men moved on.

A half-hour later I sat in the Collettivo headquarters while the women discussed whether they would demonstrate the following night. Some argued that it was unnecessary, anticlimactic. Others felt they should show solidarity with Alma and her group. At one point I was asked what I thought. When I said I agreed that solidarity was important Ronnie became furious. — We had our Abortion Day Demonstration. This is only being done for Betty Friedan's benefit. Maybe America needs its feminist stars but we don't. Every time we read about the movement in America we see the same faces and we're sick of it. Here in Italy, every woman is the movement. —

Two hours later when I left, the women were still debating.

NOVEMBER 24

Second Abortion Demonstration

ALMA AND I looked out of the Movimento windows but saw nothing. Rain was being thrown down in buckets. She sighed. — What a night! Never have I seen such a rain. — We stood at the entrance of the building as thunder and lightning raged in one big chorus. The smell of dampness was all around us as we ran for Alma's car.

Our wet clothes clung to us as we stood waiting for Betty Friedan in the lobby of the Forum Hotel. A half-hour later she arrived, apologizing that she'd been delayed at an interview. Anyhow, she said, who would come out on a night like this. She would gladly go with us if there were any feminists there but it's pouring she said. My toes made water designs inside my shoes as I listened to her. Alma and I went to the Piazza Navona to see what was happening. Alma burst out laughing as we ran to her car. — Look at us. We're like drowned rats. —

The car seemed to be floating down the street. Pale yellow droplets leaped from headlights, spreading pieces of sun on the car-filled streets. We got two blocks from the Piazza when Alma parked the car. — It's ridiculous. We'll never get there at this rate. I'll run for it. — Ten minutes later she came back drenched. — There are hundreds of women. I'm going to drive back and get Betty. You go to the demonstration and tell them we'll be right back. —

— Are they soaked? —

— No. They're across the street from the square. You know where the buildings, the stores, are, where they have the overhang. It doesn't matter. You can't miss them. The Collettivo women are there too. —

By the time I arrived the feminists had been waiting close to an hour. Ronnie spotted me. — I see your friend didn't come. — — She'll be here in less than fifteen minutes. Alma just went to get her. — Ronnie snickered, — I'll believe it when I see her. — A group of us ran out into the Piazza and danced in the rain. We were back protected by the overhang, talking to one another, singing feminist songs. At first we didn't notice what was happening and then suddenly everything stopped. — Fascists! — yelled Giovanna. They began throwing rocks at us, trying to break up the demonstration. Jennie screamed jubilantly. — Finally we are recognized. Now they know we are a threat to them. —

There were about twenty of them, men and women. It was so chaotic I only caught words here and there but I saw what was happening. Men were giving orders to the women who were shouting at us. The men moved their fists toward us but never on us. The rocks stopped as soon as they got our attention. And when the fascist women stopped speaking they were egged on by the men. Little by little the women stopped speaking and the men became the major spokespeople.

When Betty Friedan got out of Alma's car with her daughter Emily at her side, all she heard was the singing of feminist songs. The movement women came up to her car greeting her. Ms. Friedan broke out into a big smile. The platform was set. She stood there, went into her speech but didn't get beyond the opening when the fascists began screaming directly at her. Bewildered she bent down, asked, — Who are those people? — When she heard the word fascist she stopped, stared out at her assailants. She then gave an extemporaneous speech in a voice so loud nothing could drown her out. Giovanna, who acted as her interpreter matched her in sound. Although the fascist group continued screaming at Betty and the feminists, all that could be heard was Betty Friedan without a microphone, giving an impassioned speech. Giovanna interpreting just as passionately and hundreds of feminists cheering.

Ms. Friedan concluded her speech. — This is your threat. This is what you have to fight against. We have to stop the fascist forces because there is no such thing as a women's movement under a fascist regime. They are your enemy. —

As we moved on to the Movimento headquarters the word lesbian was chanted by the fascists. One woman held on to a man and screamed at us. — We are nothing without children. I have five children, five and I am proud. You are murderers. You are killers. Lesbians. —

I SAT WITH Emily while she talked about the beginning of NOW, how she and her brother spent week after week with their mother mimeographing material. A debate began between Ms. Friedan and the Collettivo women. Alma and Giovanna both interpreted.

QUEST: You said that in NOW right from the beginning it was assumed that men would be allowed in the movement. However, it was understood that the women would have the leadership position. But I want to ask you whether you considered the very problem of leadership itself?

BETTY: The pseudoradicals refuse the leadership roles. Everybody's the same but this is woman's hang-up. It's a lack of self-confidence. You have to demonstrate leadership where the leaders are elected to represent the people and when they don't represent you any longer you change your leaders.

QUEST: I think the difference between you and me is that you are working for a larger integration of women into the society as it is structured now and we refuse those very structures. I believe the real liberation of women will be in changing these structures.

BETTY: Well how are you going to achieve this?

QUEST: Through unity among all women. We don't want what happened in America to happen here as you were the first to point out in your book. You said that after the women got the vote they completely integrated into the society rather than change it.

BETTY: It happened in America because women didn't have a feminist awareness yet.

QUEST: We don't believe that this awareness is possible in a mixed group.

BETTY: Well what do you do?

QUEST: We are meeting in consciousness raising and study groups.

BETTY: The only thing is in changing society and not in a pseudoradical movement. If you want to go off by yourselves in little groups and waste your time that's all right with me but I call that mental masturbation.

QUEST: Many of us have come from the University of Trento where there is a strong leftist movement. These leftist men cannot understand women's oppression. And it is only now that we have begun to get together in small groups that we are beginning to understand.

BETTY: You can't just sit in your bedrooms and talk. How the hell do you expect to change society if you don't do anything to change it?

QUEST: We are a different country. The Italian feminists are not interested in taking action in the existing government. We want the government changed.

BETTY: Well what are you going to do about it?

QUEST: We are uniting all over Europe as a force, a force that will have to be listened to.

BETTY: But you must take political action.

QUEST: The thing I understand is that your fight in America is to move into the male society, into the male dominated government. We do not wish to integrate into the society or the government until we have changed it.

BETTY: It is not my place to change your society. It is your place to do this. There was a group of women in New York who had consciousness raising for years and they got bored with it and started taking action. Although in my book I only saw rights of women in individual terms, I realized later it has to be done in terms of society. I saw what the fascists did tonight. In my country, if you asked me today what I think is the most serious problem I would say it's the danger that my country will go fascist. There is no way for any woman to be liberated in a fascist country. As I define myself as a woman, it is in organizing to keep us from throwing hydrogen bombs all over the place. In organizing women to liberate themselves. It cannot be done by turning your backs on the forces of your country.

QUEST: We are not turning our backs. We plan to take political action. But we are positive that there is no possibility, absolutely no possibility for liberty for any woman in this society. And I would like to add that your statement before that we need leaders is a direct contradiction of the position of the feminist movement in Europe. Our struggle is to destroy all hierarchies, all leaders and to work for humanity.

BETTY: The fight is not to be afraid of speaking about power. Otherwise you'll be manipulated by power.

I SPENT the evening at Alma Sabatini's. Jenny picked me up the following morning and drove me to Giovanna's On the phone I said my goodbyes to the women from Collettivo, to Elvira Banotti. Giovanna took the day off and drove me around Rome, pointing out the sights, as she did that first night we met. At 10:00 p.m. Jenny drove me to the station. We sat in a familyfilled compartment. She promised to write, told me she was definitely going to take her children to Holland for a visit, perhaps for good. As she was leaving the train she said, — I did tell you I have gone with men since my separation, didn't I? I don't want you to think I'm frigid because I'm not but for the moment I'm masturbating. I have had it with men because they never satisfy me. —

She waved goodbye from outside the train. — Bonnie say hello to your sons when you write them. Let us hope they will be different. And write. — I waved as my train took off for Genoa. From Genoa I took a boat to Barcelona. From Barcelona a plane took me to Alicante. In Alicante I took a bus to Benidorm, then a cab to my flat. The weather was freezing and there was no heat in my apartment. The concierge told me it was the coldest weather they'd had in eighty years. I wondered what he'd say if he knew I'd just been in two abortion marches. I decided not to test him.

In my apartment I sat with my coat on, with a blanket around me. I looked over my notes, took out the pictures of the abortion march and wondered if there could possibly be a movement in Spain.

SPAIN

PORT-BOU

THE TRAIN taking me to Spain eight months ago stopped at Port-Bou, the Franco-Spanish border. After our passports were scrutinized, our baggage opened, we boarded another train. Three of us sat in a compartment playing guitars, singing. An enormous contingent of soldiers and policemen were seen boarding the train. The music stopped. The compartment door was opened and suddenly the racks opposite us were filled with rifles and baggage. Two grey uniforms sat down under the oppressive paraphernalia. Belts holding pistols circled their waists. From that time on wherever I went I saw policemen. In grey uniforms, in brown (these are replaced by blue in the winter). I learn the greys can stop anyone on the street and take them in for questioning. Reason doesn't matter since they are virtually gods and don't have to answer to anyone but Franco. The brown uniforms are friendly and don't seem to bother anyone. Then there are *Franco's informers,* who wear civilian clothes.

For the tourist Spain means a relatively cheap holiday with sun, beaches, sangria, paella, flamenco dancers (authentic or otherwise) and friendly people. The police don't bother tourists and the tourists are not bothered by the police. In Spain there is a famous saying: *En boca cerrada no entran las moscas,* which means 'flies don't enter a closed mouth.' And those of us who come here to write, to paint, to work, learn to take that saying seriously. If you want to remain here you keep your eyes open and your mouth shut. We all knew the police were around. So what! But so what only applies when you're an uninvolved person.

From Benidorm I took a bus to Alicante. It seemed ridiculous that I could live in Spain for eight months and never try to contact feminists. True, I'd received addresses in Paris. But my friend Hilary, who worked for the American Express in Benidorm, had looked them up for me. She said they weren't listed in the phone book. This I knew since I had already checked. But her Spanish was better than mine and I thought... maybe.

In the time I lived in Barcelona, Casteldafels, Mallorca and finally Benidorm ... in the places I travelled, I asked people about women's liberation. And always received strange looks. Here in Spain you don't go running to the nearest newspaper and ask about feminism. However, I did become friendly with a newspaper editor and he asked me to write a piece on feminism in the States. When I asked about feminism in Spain he looked at me, then explained he'd been working in Paris for two years, and this was his first time back. But he doubted it.

The truth is, I myself was convinced there couldn't be a women's movement here. But I was going home soon. And even if there was one isolated feminist it was worth a try.

I took the night train from Alicante to Madrid, knowing this was the last lap of my journey.

MADRID

AT THE tourist office in Madrid I was told the address was nonexistent. At my hotel, the same story. Both places X'd a similar address on two maps. Now what?

An hour-and-a-half later I was at the X'd address. A portier told me Simone G. didn't live there. I think she's foreign I said. No. She's English, she's American, she's Italian. No.

Another hour-and-a-half and I'm back at Avenida Jose Antonio. Now what?

I went to a restaurant, had lunch, tried to remember who gave me her name. Was it Mijo, Catherine, Giselle, who? And was she Spanish or foreign? I remembered nothing.

I went to the Prado. Spent hours in the worlds of Goya.

I walked through the old section of Madrid, past narrow stone streets, through archways to the cobblestoned Plaza Mayor. I watched children play while their mothers rocked baby carriages and talked to other mothers. A group of older women sat on a bench isolated from the rest of the people. They were dressed in black.

I saw boys no more than twelve practicing *machismo,* eyeing girls up and down, jabbing one another, passing remarks. The girls walked by, their eyes searching the ground. Older boys made 'ssst' noises through their teeth, grinning, leering, circling the women. *Guapa, guapa* [pretty, pretty].

The sky darkened. The windows of the apartments were quickly closed. Rain poured from the now-black sky. I rushed to the nearest cafe and to the phone booth.

The Madrid phone directory is arranged according to area. Under the area are street addresses with the occupants' names next to them. My fingers went from page to page. Suddenly I saw it, the address I'd been given in Paris. I knew Simone wasn't listed so I called all the occupants at the address. — We don't know her . . . She doesn't live here . . . No . . . No. — Nine no's. I sat down at a table, ordered a glass of wine. Looked at the clock on the wall. 7:30. I paid my bill, rushed out into the rain and boarded a bus.

One hour later I spoke to the night porter who assured me that nobody by that name lived in the building. I kept insisting. He kept saying no. As I left I thought if she was in France maybe she's French. I walked back in and was told take the elevator to the eighth floor. I stood at the door. — Simone? — A puzzled *si* came out. — Do you speak English? — Another *si.* — Simone, Mijo told me to look you up. — — I don't know any Mijo. — — Catherine? — Her expression was blank. — I'm sorry. There must be a mistake. —

— Simone, I was given your name at rue de Cannette. —

Her face broke into a smile. — No! Come in! — I told her about the different addresses, the calls, the night porter. She burst out laughing. She said had I come five minutes later she would have been gone. As for the phone, it was listed but under her married name. Her husband entered the room. She introduced us. — We can't go out tonight Miguel. Isn't this marvellous! Please sit down Bonnie. Tell me what's happening in Paris? Where have you been? Ireland? Impossible. Is there really a movement there? Oh this is marvellous. —

And now in case anybody thinks I've flipped . . . I know Simone is a French name but it isn't her real name. And she isn't French. In this section names, nationalities, professions, everything has been changed. Here is fascist Spain there is an active women's movement. But it is illegal and to avoid political harassment, everyone is anonymous but one.

Their dialogue is word for word.

Simone picked up the phone and dialed a number. — Chris, you'll never guess who I have here. —

THE MADRID WOMEN'S MOVEMENT

THERE ARE no headquarters, no members' names, addresses or phone numbers. Ask the average woman on the street and even if she's aware of the feminist movement she's completely unaware that it exists in Spain. Who are these feminists, where do they meet, what do they do?

Approximately half are married, half are single. A few are lesbians but they don't discuss it. Almost all the unmarrieds live away from home, which is unusual in Spain. The feminists are mainly from middle class and upper middle class families. They meet in each others' homes and constantly change their meeting place for security reasons. Like every political organization in Spain, other than The Falange, which is the official fascist party, women's liberation cannot declare itself. This would subject the women to immediate police investigation, which they are certain would lead to arrest, fines, and imprisonment. They are also certain that the police are aware of WL. Most of the members are already in the police files for previous political activities.

The Madrid Women's Liberation movement gets its members by direct confrontation with women they know. In the beginning everybody knew everybody else, but now even though they feel they've been discreet, they are frightened that informers have infiltrated. In spite of the complete lack of publicity and no contact with the media they get inquiries from prospective new members daily. They refuse to run MWL as the government runs Spain. So women are not screened which adds to the risk of infiltration. New members immediately form CR groups.

What do these women want? They want contraception, abortion, divorce, equal education, equal pay, more and better nursery schools. They would like to do something to initiate reforms, make the public more aware. But they know people have been jailed, exiled, lost jobs and passports for signing their names to a piece of paper.

A letter sent to the UN and the Minister of Information in Spain by three Basque priests exposing the denial of human rights in their province is responsible for their six-year prison sentence. This is one of many such cases.

Because freedom in Spain is nonexistent for all, many political women who are interested in feminism argue that first they should join with the men in the struggle for freedom and then fight for their own rights. Some of these women work with freedom organizations such as the Comisiones Obreros, the illegal trade union formed by dissatisfied workers. However, they have discovered that although the men talk about equality for all, in reality a woman's position in this organization is far from equal. As a result, within the past year MWL has attracted a number of militant working class women. They all admit they were reluctant to join a women's group, certain it would be uninteresting and ineffective. They've discovered they were wrong.

THE SPANISH WOMAN

Divorce: The Catholic church forbids divorce.

Contraception: Shades of Ireland. We again have the cycle regulator.

Abortion: 30% of the women I interviewed had had at least one abortion. This was done illegally since abortion is punishable often by death (coathanger method) or imprisonment.

Education: Few Spanish girls attended institutions of higher learning (senior high) until the '60s. The majority rarely go beyond the required age of fourteen. Not more than 8% of the total university enrollment finish college. This applies to men as well.

Equal pay: Women do not receive equal pay for equal work in any profession. The average salary for a woman who's a college graduate is $150.00 a month. A salesgirl or factory worker earns between $50.00 and $60.00 a month. Even for Spain this is not a living wage.

Nursery schools: All are run by the government and there are not nearly enough to accommodate women who need them. Furthermore, the hours of 10:00 to 5:00 force many women to work as maids since these are not the hours for the average worker. The conditions, moreover, are so substandard that most mothers refuse to send their children.

Exclusively Spanish: Before July 1972, a woman under twenty-five could not legally leave her parental home without her father's permission. The legal age is now twenty-one.

The population explosion receives a Spanish award: Spain gives special awards and citations to exceptionally large families. Even with this great incentive, the Spanish family remains small. The feminists claim rhythm is not popular in Spain, but onanism is.

Marriage: When you marry in Spain you are required to give your money and property to your husband. As a consolation prize you keep your maiden name on your papers, your passport, your driver's license.

Passport: The husband must give permission for his wife to have her own passport.

Voting: The people can vote for one third of the Cortes (Parliament). Those who vote must be heads of families so even if you are fifty-five years old and living at home you cannot vote. In other words, you must have a separate residence. As a woman you can vote if you're widowed or single and live alone. However, since the only people on the ballot are those approved by the government, your vote doesn't really mean that much.

Law: There is no trial by jury. There is a judge, the defense attorney and the prosecutor. In Madrid there is only one woman judge. She presides over the juvenile court.

The only branch of law where the woman does the actual defending is in political crimes. In all other branches of law the woman is the one who prepares the briefs for the male lawyers. Since there is a daily page in the newspapers with *orden publico* (political crimes) these women are kept quite busy. But in Spain any lawyer who defends those who have committed political crimes is unpopular.

Actions: Aside from CR groups, the Spanish feminists are taking definite actions which are proving quite effective. It would make an exciting part of this section but I cannot record any of it since it would set the feminists back and impede any future action.

SIMONE

Nobody's liberated here

I LEFT MY hotel, went to the cafe across the street, had coffee, took the bus to Simone's. I keep telling myself it isn't so. Am I being followed? Tell Simone. Don't be ridiculous. Why should I be followed? Tell Simone. I knocked on her door and said nothing.

Simone spoke. — It's very difficult in Spain. I'm living here five or six years. Before I was more optimistic but now I don't know. You're always waiting for a change in Spain. Some are waiting for thirty years. There was always some women's movement here, some democratic movement but they weren't revolutionary. Even the university women. What I mean is women never got together to consider their position. These groups still exist and they're very happy with what they think and do. I think these women are quite conscious of the woman's situation but they don't want to lose what they have: a big house, their position in the society. I would prefer not to say that but sometimes you have to. Nobody's liberated here. If we have the head out it's quite good. —

Simone joined the woman's movement in Madrid four months after it was formed. — It was positive for all of us I think. I am really on the outside because I am not from Madrid. I think some of the problems were that the women in the groups knew each other too well. They'd been friends for so long. I would not like to say if the experience here in Spain is positive or not. But I think the little you do is positive. —

Simone left the movement 'temporarily' she tells me. Her reason: — You have a meeting at 7:00. The first woman arrives at 7:30. The second arrives at 8:00. The sixth arrives at 9:00 and she forgot the paper. I demanded responsibility and we often discussed why we weren't more responsible. And we said we cannot expect women who haven't been treated responsibly to change in two weeks. I am trying to express what happened to me in the group, why I left. I don't know if it's a real problem with the group or a problem with me. For example, you're in a group with all that sisterhood and the feeling of helping each other. And then you go out and feel that for other women. But maybe the other woman feels contrary; she doesn't respond.

— To speak about Spain is so complicated. I could speak for a year. For instance, if you go on the street to buy something in the store you can't walk without men looking at you or telling you things. —

— What things? — I asked.

— They tell you I would like to go to bed with you but I think if you said *vamos* [let's go] the poor man would be in shock. —

— I haven't lived here as long as you Simone but I doubt that the men I've met would go into shock. —

— But you're a foreigner. You know all the Spanish boys are looking to pick up the foreign girls because the Spanish girls don't go to bed. When I say shock I mean the man who does construction, the laborer, the office worker, the average man. They're all talking about women and looking at them but they're not capable. The ones who are out looking for it, of course, are different. —

— Simone, for me that's not the point. In Benidorm, I go for a walk every day and every day I'm bothered by some stupid creeps who either go *ssst* or make some dumb remark. I start off feeling good and I end up wanting to sock somebody. One day I was walking along the sea feeling fantastic when two men (and I use the term loosely) began following me, making those *sst* sounds. First they were in back of me, then in front of me leering, blocking my way. Finally I'd had it. I waited till they got in front of me and then I crouched and stared at the ringleader's penis. And I followed, crouching, staring all the way. He looked at me like I was insane. Then both of them began to run away from me. That night I told my friend Hilary and she couldn't stop laughing. But it wasn't funny to me. I was close to tears when it happened. —

— I love to walk, but like you say, here it's impossible. I can't walk freely. I was walking in the park with a lot of people around and there were women and children and still I couldn't walk for fifty meters without a car stopping or a man stopping. They're not accustomed to seeing a woman alone in Spain. The role for the woman is so defined here that they can't think of a normal woman just walking. I'm sure it was worse ten years ago. But even though it has changed a little, they still think it's funny if a woman walks alone at two in the afternoon. How can I explain that? It's like if I'm in the house and I want to go to a movie and my husband says I don't feel like it, then I can't go to a movie. You can't go alone. Everybody would look at you. They can't accept that a woman is there because she wants to go to a movie at eleven at night. She has to be there for something else. —

Simone points out that if she stayed with the intelligentsia, the people she knows, her life would be different. — If I want to forget all the society around me, the men on the street, the politics, all the problems the Spanish society makes I could be very happy. If I could forget everything and keep myself in my own little nest maybe I could be happy. This country can't give you anything but frustration. Here people don't let you live your life, from the concierge to the people upstairs. You're not free. I mean, the more advanced you are in your life, the more freedom you want. —

SIMONE PICKED me up in front of my hotel the next day. The same two men were standing there as we drove away. She explained that although she felt France was not the most advanced country it certainly was different from Spain. — The terror is not the same. In France the feminists will find a solution. Everything is illegal in Spain. Yet if you want contraceptives or feminist books you can get them, if you know the right people. —

I asked her what she thought of MLF in Paris. She smiled, — I think they're wonderful. All the groups were really working . . . . It seemed to me they were very organized and efficient. When I was there they were all so active and rushing and the phone kept ringing. And they want contact with everybody. They want an international movement. Everybody was always so busy there. Isn't it so Bonnie? — She signed. —*Estoy harto.* Do you know what that means? It means I'm fed up. —

We were stopped in the middle of Avenida Jose Antonio. The honking of horns was deafening. — Everything is so impossible here. Even to drive your car. *Mon Dieu.* We'll be old and grey by the time we get there. —

CARMEN AND WL

Just work and be mono

CHRIS IS an American married to a Spaniard. She is the only American in the movement. She introduces me to Carmen who is the founder of the feminist movement in Madrid. The tape recorder is set up. We sit in the dining room, have lunch and talk.

Carmen tells me she started the movement with twenty of her friends. Four months later, after meeting twice a week, they made their first contacts with feminists in other countries. By then they had sixty members.

BONNIE: How can you have political action?
CHRIS: You can't really. That's one of the big problems. Our work is strictly underground. There are too few who are willing to take the risk and it's hard to organize women for a big demonstration because you cannot contact people. And then it's illegal for more than twenty people to meet anywhere.
CARMEN: That's not the only problem. We are not interested in public demonstrations now. When we made contact with feminists in

other countries we realized we have the same feelings. The French movement wrote us the date of the International Abortion March and they wrote us, encouraging us to demonstrate here but it is impossible for us you know. It is very good for us to have contact but we cannot do any more.

SIMONE: We can't participate in the international demonstrations...

CHRIS: ...because you would simply spend your life in jail. Everything depends on political change here.

SIMONE: For the women here everything is forbidden and to change the situation of the women you would have to change the government because the government isn't just fascistic. It's Catholic.

CARMEN: We even have a bishop in Parliament. In the beginning we only had consciousness raising and we knew everybody. Now we have the work groups and the study groups.

SIMONE: We don't know who some of the women are, if it's dangerous or not.

CARMEN: For the first time I am very afraid but I don't think we have the right as feminists to question the new members and say who are you. The general meetings are so large and we don't know all the women any more.

CHRIS: A year ago an American feminist wanted to interview us but we didn't trust her so we refused to talk with her. She said she lectured all over but we thought her knowledge on feminism was very superficial.

CARMEN: You have to understand that even to talk on the phone is dangerous.

CHRIS: Nobody says anything on the telephone that could get you or your friends into trouble because you never know when they're listening. It's not likely unless you're politically involved that your phone will be tapped but you never know so you never say anything specific. We think all telegrams are monitored. For instance, we sent a telegram in coded English to a person in Ibiza asking him to speak at a political demonstration. The telegram was intercepted and the man was arrested. The American Embassy is obviously exchanging information with the Spanish government.

BONNIE: Are you sure?

CHRIS: Oh we know, we know. I was picked up that same night. While they were questioning me I asked, are you people in contact with the American Embassy and the man, obviously caught off guard, said yes daily. When our friend from Ibiza was being interrogated he said I won't say a word until a member of my embassy is here and no sooner did he say it when a representative from the American Embassy walked in and said, 'Oh, what has to be done here.' There's complete cooperation between the Spanish government and the American Embassy. You know about the American woman who was thrown out a month ago, don't you? She was writing a book on censorship. They escorted her directly to Barajas. She wasn't even allowed to call the embassy. I wouldn't tell people you're a writer. I wouldn't tell them anything. Say you're a tourist or you came here to buy jewelry in Toledo.

BONNIE: Carmen, since the movement started a year-and-a-half ago have there been any changes?

CARMEN: Yes. There have been changes in public opinion.

BONNIE: But nobody knows you're here.

CARMEN: [laughing] Oh yes, everybody knows.

CHRIS: And the police know who we are but since we haven't gone out into the streets yet they're not bothering us. If they wanted to they could but it's not convenient for them now. They don't like the idea that we're here but they've got too many other things to worry about now. And since whatever Franco wants is the law, there is no justice because you can be arrested for anything.

SIMONE: We couldn't make a demonstration here.

CHRIS: It would be such a useless sacrifice. You wouldn't get far enough to make an impression.

BONNIE: Carmen, what do you discuss in your CR groups?

CARMEN: All the feminist topics but you have to understand we talk little about sex. In Spain nobody talks about sex so just to go into a feminist group and even mention sex is a big thing. I don't know if you can understand that. The big problem with the couples here is the relationship. We know there is a discussion on clitoral and vaginal orgasm in the United States but it is different there. Here it's enough to discuss sex in general.

BONNIE: Simone tells me there are workers in some of the groups.

CARMEN: Yes we have some. They came from the Communist Party. We would like to get together with more workers but it is a problem.

CHRIS: They live far from us where many of the workers live and they cannot come here because of physical things such as the hours they work. They live a different kind of life. They can't leave their children, even with their husbands.

BONNIE: Why not go to them?

CHRIS: They're not convinced that it's a feminist problem and then it's dangerous. They also see us as very privileged. They think what do those women need to be freed from? And in a way it's a pity that you need to have a position of luxury before you can enjoy being a feminist. The economic problem here is so different from the U.S. Take a maid. She works full time for 50 or 60 dollars a month. She thinks in terms of freeing herself economically because how can she be free unless she frees herself economically and this lends itself much more to political action.

CARMEN: Yes but professional women are oppressed as well. I worked in very good position but there was no possibility of change. The salary was very bad, about 110 dollars a month. When I quit my boss told me they are going to hire another woman for the position. I speak French, English, Spanish. They said they would have to pay a man with my qualifications much more. I quit not only because of the money but the people there treated me like a girl. I worked in a publishing house and whenever I had an original idea they said don't worry about it. You are so nice, that's not a problem for you. We'll do the thinking. It's not for you to think. Just work and be *mono*.

BONNIE: That means cute.

CARMEN: Yes, that's right. Work and be cute.

SIMONE: And shut up.

CARMEN: Yes, when I have an original idea.

BONNIE: Carmen, you're single and you live away from home. I understand this is unusual.

CARMEN: It is difficult because the family thinks you want to live away so you can have men. I was twenty-one when I left home. My family felt disgraced and I didn't go home for a year-and-a-half.

BONNIE: Did you have a job before you left home?

CARMEN: Yes, I found the job one month and I left home the next month. It was very difficult to do and I had many problems in my job because my boss knew the difficulty I had leaving home. I stayed for three years because you cannot be that independent here. When you are, you are forced to go back to your family. Legally my parents could have made me come home but they did nothing because they didn't want the scandal.

BONNIE: Carmen, what do you think will happen with the feminist movement in Spain?

CARMEN: Right now I think it would be good to do something fabulous but it's more necessary to speak with women, to show that the women stick together. We're taking more chances but we have to. I hope the regime will change. Then it will be possible to do things differently, to write and make propaganda.

CHRIS: I think everybody here is waiting to see what's going to happen. Franco can't last for too many years and something's bound to change.

CARMEN: We are no longer twenty women and we are now well organized. When the time comes we will be ready.

SIMONE DROVE me back to the hotel. She parked the car and we went to a nearby cafe. She warned me to be careful, to make my phone calls from an outside phone rather than the one in my hotel room and to say little. — The police have confidants everywhere. It's like a second police and they know everything that's going on. —

We sipped our coffee. Simone looked around carefully, spoke as if she read my mind. — It's all right. We're not being watched. — Then as if she said nothing, — Of course I am a feminist and I will start going to meetings again. I don't know if the difficulty I see in front of me is . . . like saying here we can't do anything so why bother or it's because I'm not activist enough to do anything else. I don't know which it is.

— Listen Simone, I think I'm being followed. —

— Really? Today? —

— No, for two days. —

— Be careful and watch the tapes or it will be bad for all of us. —

HE WAS standing at the desk when I got my key. The same man. It's not your imagination this time. He's talking to you. You're American aren't you? How do you like Madrid?

Play stupid. Play smiling happy bubbly tourist. Oh how I do love Madrid. All those Goyas at the Prado Aren't they fantastic, aren't they marvellous! Imagine one man having such talent. I love *paella.* I just love the Spanish people. You're all so warm and friendly. Oh yes, I do intend to go to Segovia and Toledo and all those wonderful places.

He's looking at you totally bewildered. You wave and walk to the elevator. He doesn't wave and follows you. The tapes are in your bag.

You get on the elevator and without looking you know he's there too. Two people get off the elevator. Two people walk to your door and you keep on talking. It's so tiring being a tourist. I'm half asleep before I even reach my room but I love Madrid. You put the key in the door. It was a pleasure meeting you you say. His hand reaches out for the key. Let him be a pig. You know how to handle a pig.

He tells you the night is young. You're hoping he'll break out into song and you'll applaud and leave. But he breaks out into a smile that never leaves his face. He tells you he wants to talk with you. He's a writer. Some of his best friends are writers. Bonnie he says, won't you join me for a drink. He knows your name, your profession. What else does he know? Join me for a drink he says. Thankyou but no thanks. I leave for Segovia at eight. He's insisting. His smile is no longer friendly. All right. Give me a minute to wash up. Wash up! Who in hell washes up for a drink? You turn the key, open the door. Your smile vanishes with the closing door. Get rid of the tapes. Do something with the tapes. You search the room. Everything is so obvious. Put it in your luggage and then lock it. No. In a baggie inside the toilet bowl. No. There's a knock at your door. One minute you sing out. The tapes go into your boots. Thank God you have big feet.

You stand in his room and sip your drink. He's talking about Spain, politics. What do you think of the politics here? Do you have friends here? Do you know writers here? You're playing Billie in *Born Yesterday*. Billie in the first act. No you're not playing her. You are her. And he's giving you the business but you don't know from nothing. He's talking about Solzhenitsyn. Don't you think he's political he asks. Next he's going to give you books to read. Who played that part? Night after night and you don't remember his name. You don't remember anything.

My stomach is pushing up to my throat. It's separating into sections and rushing up there. He's next to me but something's happened. I'm playing the part technically. I feel nothing but my body. Oh Christ, I'm going to vomit while he stands there feeding me lines. What's that about Vietnam? Does he think I personally started that war. I put my drink down and move to the door. He's saying something about Spain and no wars and no freedom. I'm trying to stop the lock on my door from swimming. He's opening the door, standing there. Where is his smile? What's he saying? Help? I don't need help. He's pushing in the door with you. Get him out. Take a deep breath and push him out.

You hear him outside the door. You lock it and rush towards the bathroom while your insides fall in big chunks on the floor. You join your insides. You hear sounds outside the door. Somebody's knocking. Through the night you hear sounds. Voices are replaced with other voices. You don't know if they're real or you're delirious.

I SNEAKED out of my room the next day, bolted down the stairs, took the first cab I saw and had him stop in less than five minutes. I told him straight ahead. Follow that road. My eyes drove backwards. Nobody there. Where were the two men this morning? I went into a cafe, had coffee, took the metro to Chris' apartment. Was I paranoid or was I being followed? I clutched the tapes in my bag.

I made up my mind to tell Chris but as soon as the door opened the whole thing seemed bizarre. What actually happened? A man who was there when the map was X'd and happened to be there every time I went in and out of the hotel asked me question after question. I got violently ill after one drink. Me, the boozer. So? And the two men outside the hotel that liked to walk when I walked. So?

Chris introduced me to Rosa, the woman I'd come to interview. We were talking a few minutes when the phone rang. It was Carmen. Had she told me that they met with feminists from Barcelona in February? Would I like an address there? — When you're there contact Maria Campmany if you can. She is going to Rome and may not be back before you leave but try. She's not with the movement but you'll find her very interesting. Chris said, — Campmany is from Catalon. In Barcelona if you're not a Catalonian you're considered a peasant. I came here with the idea that all Spaniards are Spaniards but they're not. They're Catalonians, Andalusians, Valencianos . . . . . —

ROSA

They said a girl dedicated to the virgin should not dance with a boy

HER STORY is not typical she says. Born in a small Andalusian village she went to a school for boys and girls until she was twelve. She was most influenced by an atheist teacher who didn't believe girls should be treated differently from boys. At twelve, against her father's wishes, but at the insistence of a very strong grandfather, she went to Seville to further her studies.

She boarded at a girls' school run by nuns. Aside from her regular studies, she was required to go to Mass daily and pray three times a day. — The nuns gave me so much moral advice but it wasn't really necessary because I'd already assimilated the ideas of Catholicism. The best teacher we had was a nun who taught literature. She was a very cultured person, very attractive and was the confidant of many of the students. When she left they told us she was sick and had to leave. I didn't really know she was a lesbian until I graduated from the school. I went to Seville for a visit and saw her dressed in regular clothes. She talked to me, confided in me. I learned she was thrown out.

— I know there are a lot of lesbians in the nunnery but it's ignored unless it becomes a problem. I myself had a friend who was a lesbian. I was only ten and she was twenty. —

Chris and I reacted together. — She was twenty! —

— Yes it's true. The priest found out she was my friend and forbid me to talk with her. I didn't listen to him and we remained friends until I was twelve. I didn't want her to touch me because when she did I felt something. I was very attracted to her but nothing ever happened. —

In the boarding school Rosa was taught what she calls — sex in abstract. We were told you must be pure, dedicated to the Virgin. You must be clean. They said a girl dedicated to the Virgin should not dance with a boy. We were allowed to do folk dancing because we never danced close to each other. —

When Rosa was fifteen the Archbishop of Seville forbade social dancing in the province of Seville. This continued for years. She tells me her life in school was miserable. — The nuns occupied all of our time with praying and studying and I was never left alone. For me there was always this search for silence. — Miserable as she was she knew if her parents found out she would be taken out of the school. — On holidays I always cried when I had to return to school but never in front of my mother and father. —

She finished the *collegio* and went on to the university where she majored in science, minored in Greek and Latin. Science to her was the highest level of knowledge. She changed her mind when she graduated and went on to study sociology. She is now working in her field, earning an exceptional salary. Chris explains that Rosa was the top student all through school.

Rosa continues, — I became interested in the problem of women when I was twenty-one years old because up to that time my life was ordered. I went to school. I thought I would marry my boyfriend, have children. Then when I broke off with him I found myself . . . —

— Don't talk. — Chris' eyes darted to the open window. — We're being watched, — she whispered. Rosa stared at her. The sofa where we sat was next to the window. — For how long? — I asked Chris.

— I didn't want to say anything when you came but my home's been watched all day, since early this morning. —

Rosa's hands were pressed tightly together. — Did I say anything? —

The bell rang, a man stood at the doorway, said he'd come to do home repairs. Antonio walked down the stairs, talked to the man, said he hadn't called for any repairs. The man looked around, his eyes landed on Rosa and me. Then he turned and left. Chris asked Antonio, — Is there any reason why you should be watched? —

— None that I know of, — he answered.

— Nothing's been going on? You know what I mean. —

— Nothing at all. Why? —

— I didn't want to worry you but when I got up this morning I saw this man across the street but I didn't think anything of it and when I looked . . . . . . —

— The man who was just here? — he asked.

— No, somebody else. He was joined by the man who was here. They've been standing outside five or six hours. Why? —

Antonio shrugged. Chris turned to him. — I did contact a number of people for Bonnie and when I couldn't reach Pablo I went to his office and put a note under the door. You don't suppose it was found? —

Antonio nonchalantly looked out the window. — They're still there. I'm closing the window. Chris, why did you leave a note? You know that's dangerous. —

— I didn't actually say anything. Just that Bonnie was here and needed information. —

— They're leaving, — he said.

I blurted, — I think I'm being followed. I'm suspicious of the man next door. — My brilliant statement broke the tension and all three burst out laughing.

— Oh forget it. I know it sounds absurd but there are also two men who wait outside the hotel. —

Chris laughed. — All Spanish men are suspicious. Am I not right Antonio? —

— Of course. It's in the blood, our poor children. — He went back upstairs. Chris opened the front door. — They're gone. Now where were we? —

— How can you live like this? — I asked.

Chris answered, — You get used to it. And you know it is quite possible that you are being watched. It wouldn't surprise me. They're quite interested in us. Now what was Rosa saying? —

— Chris, just a minute. What about the tapes? —

— Obviously you'll have to work on them here and use anonymous names. This is Spain. —

— Ok. Rosa, you said I thought I would marry my boyfriend and then when I broke off with him I found myself . . . —

Rosa looked at me bewildered. — What? Oh yes. Please don't use my name and delete that part about ————. — She took a deep breath and continued. — I thought I would marry my boyfriend and then when I broke off with him I found myself alone and everything was different. I didn't want to go back to my family so I came to Madrid, lived in a pensionne and worked until I found a place with friends. The problem of living alone made me think about the problems of women. There was no movement then so I did nothing, but the first day the feminists met in Madrid I was there. I think the only possibility now is to make Spanish women conscious of the problems. It's hard to make anything happen because everything is forbidden. —

Chris spoke. — We have to be careful how far we go. You need permission for every conference and a policeman always goes to the meetings. We were at a conference and the discussion turned very aggressive. We, I mean the feminists, provoked a violent discussion about women and abortion. —

I asked her why they pushed the issue and she answered, — It just snowballed. It just happened. There were police there but they did nothing. We know they're observing and writing reports and they could always stop the meeting. You never know. You couldn't organize a conference with the title, *Sexual Life of Women in Spain,* or *Birth Control,* so the titles are vague. This particular conference was called *Mothers.* —

— I think, — Rosa said, — the women in all the world are objects for consumption. The women who are most conscious reject their position as a consumer object. The women who are less conscious of the problem use sex as their goal. But in most women there is the tendency for both. Even though you're conscious of your situation you tend to use your femininity. Even if you don't want to. So these two tendencies are always present in contradiction. It's an internal conflict between the efforts a woman has to make to achieve certain goals through work and by means of an easier way. Instead of studying twenty years and doing something through your own efforts you let the man do it. These two alternatives are not separate. One way or another they are together in the same person, even the most advanced women. They go after social, economic and cultural objectives through a man, maintaining in that way what has been learned. That a man is superior to her and that he should give her support and protection.

— I have many personal ambitions. Some way or another I want the guarantee that in the future there will be things in my life that will fulfill me independent of my sentimental relations. —

I asked what she meant by sentimental relations and discovered she is married. Her reason for getting married was certainly different. — I got married to get over the problem marriage presented. I have no unity with my husband now and I could leave him at any moment. I don't think the relationship will last very long but it doesn't matter to me now. I wanted to get rid of the problem of marriage. — She explained, — There was always the question of stability in my relationships. I wondered if this was due to my not being married so I got married to see if I could sustain a stable relationship. I wanted to get rid of the idea of marriage so it wouldn't obsess me and I could devote my time to more important things. —

I SPENT the rest of the day transcribing the tapes. Chris spent the day erasing them. The original idea that I would take the tapes back to the States was finished.

Very late at night, over coffee at a cafe, Chris motioned for me to be quiet. We discussed historical places of interest. Our observer was so obvious, it looked like a badly directed movie. As we left I told Chris that even though pseudonyms were substituted for real names I was nervous. Could they break into my apartment in Benidorm and confiscate the rest of the book? — I keep thinking of the American writer. —

— Well it does happen. Maybe you shouldn't come to my place tomorrow. Why don't you play tourist for a couple of days? Go to Segovia. You'll love it. —

— It's too far. I have an appointment with Marina tomorrow night. I think I'll go to Toledo. —

At my hotel my writer friend was waiting. I grabbed the keys, mumbled something about a long distance call, and bounded up the stairs two at a time.

Morning. My walking buddies have split up. The heavy set one is standing outside the hotel. I jog to the metro, then stop short to look in a store. He's moving on. Good. I walk briskly, turn the corner and spot my buddy standing in a doorway tying his shoelace. At the station platform I wait for my train. Should I say *buenas* to him? I move slowly up the stairs. Eight stairs down to the platform. I don't have to look. I feel his presence. A subway is a subway is a subway I tell myself as the train pulls in and I hear the car doors open. Now count. I get to eight and bound down the stairs just before the doors close. As the train moves I see a pair of legs running. I never find out who they belong to but they look strangely familiar. Is this for real or am I dreaming it?

MARINA

The honesty is that we can't be honest

I WAS VERY vague on the phone, didn't want to interview her in my room. I kept thinking the room was bugged and at this point it didn't matter if it was true or not. I was uncomfortable. My imagination took me alternately to the airport where officials of the Spanish government shoved me on a jet or to prison where I would remain for life. One good thing about Spanish prisons is that you can get your food brought in. Simone's husband was a good cook. Maybe he'd bring me a meal once in a while.

We met in the lobby and went to a Chinese restaurant. The menu was in Spanish. — What the hell is lechee nuts in Spanish? — I asked. Marina laughed. — Why shouldn't we have a Chinese menu in Spanish. You have it in English. — The waiter came over and when I told her I ate everything she ordered in Spanish. The waiter was Chinese. It was all too much for me.

Marina went to college in the States. Her parents didn't believe in Catholicism so she was not brought up in Catholic schools and received no religious training. Yet she claims the Catholic dogma seeps through.
— Sex has always been such a hidden thing here because of religious tradition. You must never talk or think about it. It's all dirty. I was brought up to be pretty and nice, to study and never compete and to stay a virgin until I had a husband. —

— Simone tells me that although she knows some of the feminists are lesbians they never mention it, refuse to talk about it. Why is that? —

I've heard this happens but for me it was a first. I'd had dialogues where feminists hesitated or were reluctant at first but Marina totally turned off. All the warmth and chattiness disappeared. She rose, said she forgot to make a phone call and left the table. Shortly afterwards she returned and as I started to speak she said, — I really must go. I have to get up very early tomorrow. —

— But you agreed to a dialogue. —

— I didn't know you wanted me for the book. I just thought you were a feminist who wanted to talk to other feminists. —

— Marina, you knew I wanted to interview you for the book. You knew about Carmen and Rosa and the others. Look, if it was the lesbian . . . —

She was charming and guarded. — It hasn't anything to do with anything. I just didn't realize this was going to be put in a book. —

— You can talk about anything you wish. All I ask is honesty. —

She smiled, then turned serious, her face hard. —Maybe you should put in your book that the honesty is we can't be honest. That we're afraid, that we're brought up in such an atmosphere that honesty is impossible. I'm really sorry but it is late. —

What can I write about Marina? In the beginning she asked me about the feminists in Europe. What are they doing, what are they like, do you really think things will change for women? She asked many questions about the book. Why was I writing it, who had I spoken to? She had such enthusiasm and warmth that when she changed it was shocking.

Although she was in a tremendous hurry to get home she sat in the restaurant with me for another hour. Without words, I understood I wasn't to ask any questions. We spoke about feminism intellectually. Once outside, she insisted on driving me to the hotel which was close by. She parked her car in front and then proceeded to ask me more about the book. I started to apologize because I felt bad about the interview.

She interrupted me, — It's important what you're doing. I believe in it because the feminists are talking for themselves. —

— Then why didn't you talk? —

— I don't know. I honestly don't know. —

— But you did know I wouldn't press the interview. —

— Yes. I sensed that immediately. Maybe I can't be honest. Maybe I'd like to and want to but something inside, because of the politics here, because of the terrible repression you suffer as a girl here . . . . Maybe this is what you should say about me. That I wanted to meet you and talk with you but when you asked me about me, even though I believe what you're doing is good, I just couldn't talk. I'm sorry. I really am sorry. —

CHRIS

The only thing I own is my car

THE NEXT day I went to see Chris. She gave me an article on Spanish WL, said she wanted to send it to *Ms.* What did I think?

She told me, — I was not in tune with what my generation was doing. For instance I came in at the beginning of the Civil Rights Movement. I was sympathetic but I didn't do anything. I did join two anti-war demonstrations. Basically I was not aware of life. I really feel it's important to participate in the history of your time. The feminist movement is important to me in two ways. First from a personal viewpoint and then it's a way of joining in the progression of the world.

— This year I've felt a tremendous hostility towards men. I also felt that I cheated myself when I was younger by being so repressed. Although in my personal life I have been lucky. I didn't come across any men who used me. I'm speaking sexually. I don't think I've been exploited by any men. —

Chris claims she has a typical American feeling, what she terms a 'service complex.' She feels Americans are brought up to do social good in the world. — I've almost tried to rid myself of the complex as if it were a disease. —

On marriage: — I'm married but I don't believe in the family as an exclusive institution but at this time my alternative to live separately is less desirable than living with my husband. I would like to be financially independent. I feel very coerced because I am supported by my husband. The only thing I own is my car. I would like to be financially independent but I don't have the means. I can't make more than $150 a month in any job here. Rosa is the only woman I personally know who can support herself. The rest, even the professors, get help from their families. — The reality that she cannot support herself in Spain but could in America disturbs her.

As she drove me to the hotel she told me, — I often use the excuse that I'm inactive here because of the politics and I think if I were in the U.S. I'd be a very active feminist. [She's discussing public demonstrations, because she works constantly for the movement.] And I also feel an increasing need to accomplish something on some front. I find that very egotistical too. Why should everybody have to have recognition? I think the importance of being recognized is something we've absorbed from the male culture. Bonnie, are you a Catholic? —

I shook my head.

— I left the church when I was twenty because I thought it repressive. Then I was mostly concerned with sexual repression. Now I'm very anti-Catholic and I get angry with what the church is doing in the world. I find it a very destructive force. —

She waved from her car and said, — Call me if you need anything and write to me from the States. I'm anxious to know how *Ms.* is doing. You can leave my article with the desk clerk. Let me know what you think. — [The article is in the October 1972 issue of *Ms.*]

SIMONE ANSWERS my phone call. — Of course you cannot leave it with the desk clerk. That would be foolish. Is Antonio home? Well never mind. Bring it here and I will see that Chris gets it. We'll have lunch together. You don't mind eating at four o'clock do you? When does your train leave? Oh good. Then you have time. Adios. —

The lunch was Spanish. The dialogue was English.

— Listen it's true. I've been followed. It's not my imagination. I mean the first time ok, but it's no longer funny. I'm just hoping I get on that train. I keep thinking about my apartment in Benidorm. Who's to stop them from going in and getting everything? —

Miguel answered, — I don't doubt that you're being followed. Your

mistake was to say you're a writer. And then all of us are politically involved which doesn't help. —
— I'm completely paranoid now. I can't wait to leave Spain. I have nightmares my book's going to be confiscated. —
Simone made a clicking noise. — It won't. I'm telling you we're not a threat now. We don't make enough trouble. —
— Yes but that woman who was writing on censorship. —
— Well we don't know all the facts, — she answered.
— The truth is I'm now suspicious of everybody. I mean everybody. Even you. —
Miguel and Simone were hysterical with laughter. Together they said — Us? — Then Miguel, — You are suspicious of us? —
Simone stopped laughing. — You see. That's how you get. Really we live in constant fear. Sometimes we're very cautious and other times we just say to hell with it and we take all sorts of chances. — She sighed. — Now you know Spain. You trust nobody here. But not to trust us is a little too much. — She burst out laughing again.
Miguel said, — Your world is so different Bonnie. I don't know that you can understand us or I should say me because I am Spanish. As you know I speak many languages fluently. I have a number of degrees. I have money so why should I stay here in Spain and be a political activist. Why? I stay because I was born here, my friends are here. We are all the same. We are all politically active and we are waiting for the time when we can really act. If I leave what will happen to Antonio, to Vicente, to Pablo, to all my friends. I will have deserted them. Many times I think, go, go anywhere, to America. I've been there you know but I don't like your politics either. Yes, it's much better than here but it's not good for me you understand. I believe in liberty for all. I'm happy Simone is active in the women's movement. —
— You really believe in equality for women. —
— I like to think yes. I suppose there are elements of machismo in me. There have to be. You can't be brought up in Spain and not have some of this machismo. Simone and I share, but in our professional life she is not a threat. She can't be. A woman in Spain has a very difficult time earning a living. For that matter, a man doesn't have it easy either. But I think liberation for a woman means women getting together and demanding what they want. Men will not give them liberty. It is the women who will do it. —
— I believe the same, — Simone replied. — In all the countries it is

the solidarity of women that matters. –

BENIDORM

I TOOK the night train from Madrid to Alicante. In Alicante I took the bus to Benidorm and then a cab to my flat. I looked around the room and thought I'm home, only to realize I was going to leave that home in two days. Was it possible I'd spent a year in Europe, eight months of it in Benidorm? I stood on the terrace overlooking the sea and decided to climb the mountain for the last time. I picked wildflowers as I had done many times before, sat on a rock looking out over the royal blue sea, remembering all the women I'd spoken with. They numbered over one hundred and fifty. One hundred and fifty parts of me. I sat until it was dark and then went home.

The next day I packed all my belongings, went into one of the bars where the artists and writers hung out. To say goodbye. I went into the shops of the people I knew and said goodbye. In the old section of Benidorm where the sea lashed against the rocks I looked at the twin beaches, at the island of Benidorm, and waited for the sun to set.

I left Benidorm at one o'clock in the morning and drove straight through to Barcelona. I cried when I left my apartment. I didn't think I would but I did. After all what was it? One room, a tiny kitchen, a bathroom. I hadn't chosen the furnishings. Actually, all that was mine was my clothing, my books, my typewriter and some photographs. But there was more of me in that one room than any place I'd ever lived. The first apartment I'd ever had. I thought of Virginia Woolf's *A Room of One's Own* and really understood what she meant. Waking up in the morning. Smiling. I never smiled in the morning. Realizing this is my day. When did I every have a day before?

But then I could always do what I wanted, couldn't I? My former husband always said, who's stopping you. If you really wanted to write, you'd write. But there was always a child who needed to be fed, diapers to be changed, clothes to wash, a crying child. There was food shopping, visits to the dentist, the doctor. My life was being swallowed in day to day living.

Then they were all in school and their father said, — Now who's stopping you? — and even as he said it he was half out the door on one of his numerous business trips. With three there was always one home sick with something. So you read to them, play games with them, talk with them, doctor them. Mom, I'm thirsty, I'm hungry, it hurts, I don't feel good. After a while you're positive they're doing it for spite. They're getting sick to stop you from writing. And there are teachers' conferences and PTA meetings. Holidays where you shlepped them to museums, concerts, picnics. Friends of theirs who come after school and stay for dinner. How can you deprive them? Stop it you want to yell. I can't concentrate. But how can you stop the natural noises of childhood. So I stopped the natural feelings inside me instead.

When I left Philadelphia I wondered if I was capable of writing all day. Was my former husband right? Had I used him and my sons as my built in excuse? The thought of living in a strange country was frightening enough. The realization that I might not function was shattering. The only encouragement I got was from my sons and my sisters in consciousness raising. The voices of doom fed my vulnerability. — Oh come-on, you don't actually think you're going to write a book over there. You've never been to Europe before. Are you going to tell me you're going to lock yourself in a room and write? You'll play tourist. You'll bum around. Everybody does. I fought these voices but inside myself my own voice kept saying, — What if they're right? What if they're *all* right? —

But they were wrong. I came to write and write I did. I came to find myself and that I did in part. And now I'm going home. To reality I heard. You had those children. They're there. You're responsible. Why'd you have them if you didn't want the responsibility. Reality? The only reality is that there is no reality. Go home. It will be all right. You're not the same person.

BARCELONA

10:00 AM. THE statue of Columbus is standing in a square, pointing, as I drive my rented car to the Plaza duque de Medinacelli. Everything is being checked, put away, including my book. As I wait for my receipt I hear, — Is that Bonnie?...... No it can't be. — I turn and see my Barcelona friends standing outside the office window. We go into a screaming, hugging, kissing act. — What are you doing here?...... How's the book coming?..... You can't be going back. You just got here. — I met them when I lived in Casteldafels, a suburb of Barcelona. Artists, writers, sculptors from the States, England and France, they are now living in Spain and working. We sit in a bar eating tapas, drinking wine. One hour later I say goodbye, take my baggage on wheels and check into a residencia near Via Leyetana and the American Express. Now starts the search for the three feminists I have in my book.

The address Carmen gave me is nonexistent. I look through the phone directory, check at the tourist office. Nothing. I find the other two addresses on a map but the phone book has no listing. Are the names theirs or their husbands'?

That whole thing always confused me. You get married, you say I do, he says I do and suddenly you've lost your name. From the former Jane Smith you become the present Mrs. John Jones. Is it your name that's former, you, or what? And if I want to locate the former Jane Smith how do I do it unless her parents are living or I know her husband's name. In Spain the woman loses everything but her name. At the same time I discover that although her name is on all her papers it's conspicuously absent from her mailbox, the phone directory, from her doorbell. Rosita's address includes an apartment number. The man who answers turns out to be her husband. No she isn't home. She's at work but will be home later. He takes my phone number, hands me his.

At the second address the concierge tells me there is no Marta M. Are you sure? Positivo, he says. It's her maiden name I tell him. He shrugs. I stand there refusing to move. I know she lives here. No, he says. Then she moved I say. She moved? Why didn't you say so? He searches through his papers and hands me a phone number.

I go to the nearest phone booth and wait while two men complete with buckets, soap and rags wash it. They motion me inside and I dial while I watch the bubbles making patterns on the door.

— Is this Marta? — I ask.
— Yes. —
— Really! —
— Who is this? —
— My name is Bonnie. I'm with the feminist movement in the States. — Now it's her turn. — Are you serious?—

The men are still throwing soapy water on the door of the booth as I leave with her address in my hand. Bubbles are floating in the street as they stop and eye me up and down, give me their sexiest looks. — *Hola guapa, guapa.* — I answer, — *Adios animales. Piense con su cojones.* — Translated this means, hello beautiful. Goodbye animals! You think with your balls. I would have said prick but I never learned that word in Spanish.

MARTA

I have nothing to do here

— HOW DID you find me? Where did you get my address?... Did you speak with Mijo, with Danielle? Did you meet the feminist from Chile? ... You didn't know I moved? You just guessed it? That's very funny. I'm so glad you came. — She sits on the sofa, stops talking, stops smiling. — You know you met me at a bad moment. For the last six months I'm going through a crisis. I have nothing to do here. I suppose I'm afraid to break the bourgeois life I'm leading and I know if I go by myself I couldn't afford anything like this. Even if I could I wouldn't. Why would I need this size house if I were alone. But it's not just that. It's being alone I think of. But when my husband travels I like to stay alone. All the same being alone for a few days is not the same. We're made to be so dependent. —

Marta and her husband came here from South America when he received an exceptional job offer. She holds two degrees, is fluent in four languages but has been unable to find satisfactory work. This is not half so disturbing as her statement, — Maybe I'm not as capable as I think I am. — She tells me this is the first time she's spoken so freely. I ask her why she doesn't speak to the other feminists in Barcelona. She stares at me. — Did you think there was a movement here? There is nothing here. I'm afraid you came for nothing. —

Madrid? Oh yes she knows there's a movement there. Rosita? She must be like me. — I am here two years and if there was a movement I would know. —

Marta, who received an advance to write an article on feminism for a South American magazine, tells me she's been with the feminists in London, at the FEMØ Camp in Denmark, in Paris. Since there was no abortion march in Spain she travelled to Paris to participate. She says, — I turned around at one point and there I was standing next to Simone de Beauvoir. She was with a group of women and seemed such a warm person. We went from the Plaza de Republique to I don't remember where. Anyhow we passed in front of a church just as the wedding party was beginning to enter. Some of the feminists went inside too. Can you imagine what it was like for the bride on her wedding day? —

Marta believes that women's secondary position is tied to the economy, that the economy is dependent on their free labor. — Imagine what would happen if they had to pay all the women. The economy would collapse. Why should half of humanity live at the expense of the other half? It is ridiculous. Women are expected to exist merely to help men in their way of life. —

While we spoke her husband came home with a friend. Over dinner we discussed politics in Spain, in South America, in France where their friend lives. As Marta's husband and friend retired to another room she said, — You can see how nice he is. I love him but how can I stay when there is nothing for me to do and how can I expect him to leave for me. I have a friend here. She's fifty-six years old. She was a communist in the Civil War. During the war she fell in love with another man and she left her husband and two children. You can't imagine what this was like in Spain thirty years ago. She suffered so much. She always says, Marta you shouldn't leave your husband or you'll end up with another man and it will be exactly the same. —

She discusses machismo in Spain, in South America, stating that both countries base their system on the cult of male power and sexual strength. She likes the Anglo-Saxon countries and hopes to go either to England or Holland. — There you feel freer, you can go in blue jeans. You can go anywhere you want. There you feel free because men don't look at you, don't say things. — She pauses. — But really at the core it's not different, is it Bonnie? Men feel the same way even if they don't react. To the way we dress, the way we look. Here it seems more important and that's the danger. When you go to other countries you just fool yourself. —

We phoned Rosita who was evasive but set up a date. As I said goodbye to Marta she called out, — Don't forget to call Natalia. She wants to talk with you. —

NATALIA

Where are the men?

WE WATCHED the folk dancers at Plaza San Jaime. Had dinner facing the waterfront at an unpretentious restaurant that served marvellous seafood. We ignored the Spanish men who constantly harassed us as we walked and then finally told them where to go. One of the men furiously said that ladies did not say such things. How could we? He made our day and we walked down the Ramblas, arm in arm, roaring with laughter.

The next evening I met Natalia at work. We took the metro to her home where we had dinner with her children.

Natalia is separated from her husband. She manages an elegant boutique in Madrid. Her salary is good but not good enough to support her two children. She is helped financially by her mother and her husband's parents. What did Natalia do before marriage? She studied in Spain, in England, in France. She wanted to learn about life and did the hard way. She left home because her stepfather decided he was free sexually. This included his wife and her daughter. Nothing ever happened but the situation became unbearable for Natalia and her mother.

Men promised her love, gave her babies. After two abortions...
— the pain was horrible. The *comadronas* used long needles and no anesthesia, — she decided she'd had it and married her childhood sweetheart. Her marriage turned out to be another disaster. Once after her husband broke her nose she went to the police, only to be told, 'You have children. You have to take care of them and your husband. You are young.' — I went to the police for help. I thought they would help me but I was wrong.

— The trouble is I treated my husband like an adult but he was a child. Where are the men? I don't think there are any real men. It's a myth, a story like Santa Claus. My husband never argued with me, so like little children when they can't say anything they hit. And children know that adults express themselves better so it makes them mad. He was a child. They say the woman is not finished, she is not complete, but I think it is not the woman but the man. You could say a dog is a dog and a man is a man but it's not the same. I mean there is a dog, a cat, a fly, a woman and a man. A woman grows and becomes mature but a man keeps a part of himself that's a child and it's the worst part. He still expects everything for himself. My boy is not the same as my girl. He's more selfish than she.

– In Spain the men are impotent in every way. I think they are very insecure inside but they behave like egoists just the same. They want their wives to be virgins even after they're married. They don't know anything. We have a hole and that's all they know. They don't care. The world is for them, –

Natalia's husband was also educated abroad and did not hesitate to share in the housework. He told her he didn't want to be like Spanish men. But when it came to his sex life he felt different. After having affairs with a number of women he settled on a woman much older than himself. Natalia says, – He felt big because a woman of forty fell in love with him. He felt important when people said, 'Oh you have a nice wife and girlfriend too.' I felt like I was swimming in the sky, not the sea. –

When Natalia found her present job she did not say she had been married or that she had children because she knew she wouldn't be hired. – They think if you have children you won't go to work, but that's not true. The rest of the staff always stays home for some reason but I never do. –

She enjoys her children but at the same time feels frustrated. Natalia explains, – It's terrible because when I am with them I'm always in a hurry. In the morning and at night I have to hurry because they need twelve hours sleep. For that reason on Sunday I spend the day with them because if I spend one free afternoon with somebody else I feel like I'm taking time away from them. I'm either with my children or at work. I don't look for men.

– The terrible thing in Spain is they make you unhappy even if you're not. They say poor girl when they know you are separated and have children. It's why I now think I might go to England or any place out of Spain because a young woman here . . . well they look at you differently. They think you can't do anything. The minds here are all archaic. Today I overheard somebody say, 'Did you hear about abortions? That is really to kill. It's worse than the drugs.' —

ROSITA

Barcelona Women's Liberation

ROSITA SPOKE for close to a half-hour with Marta translating so I heard what she said twice. Once from Rosita, once from Marta and both times I got the message that there had been a feminist movement in Barcelona but it no longer existed. That yes Rosita knew some women in Barcelona had contacted the group in Madrid but she didn't know who. Did she know a Marci? No. Carmen had said she was one of the women but the address I had was nonexistent. Rosita said she was sorry but she couldn't help. Finally I said to Marta, — Ask her why there is no longer a movement. — I see Rosita's smile, hear her words in Spanish before they are translated. — Of course there is a movement here. What I mean is, it is illegal so we don't say we have a movement. —

Rosita and five other women started women's liberation in Barcelona in February 1971, three months after the movement started in Madrid. She had lived in Paris as a student, had observed the 1968 French Revolution, had been there when MLF was formed. She explains that in Barcelona there was a problem from the beginning because there were two opposing factions. Rosita's groups believed that sexism was connected with the political system. The other group maintained that men were directly responsible for women's position. The result: Two groups were formed. They were not only autonomous but totally isolated from one another. I am sorry to say I never met with the other group since there wasn't any way of knowing who they were.

Rosita says, — Here it is much different than in France and other countries. Spanish women are not yet conscious of their situation. In France the women knew they needed to be free. Once you realize this need you can move not only politically but in your private life as well. —

The group is small, approximately twenty women but keeps growing. In the beginning they were confronted with the problem of how to meet other women. Rosita points out that Spain does not have women's clubs, that the women stay in their homes, are isolated from one another.

After months of extensive study the Barcelona feminists decided to meet in poor urban neighborhoods in order to form autonomous groups. Their stated intent: To meet and discuss neighborhood problems and to help women with the issues one encounters in these urban neighborhoods. Their real intent: To make women aware of women's problems and to show them that all women share much in common.

How do they do this? The feminists usually start with a newspaper story that relates to women and follow it with group discussion. Recently they read an article about two Spanish doctors who received prison sentences for performing abortions. Rosita tells me — The immediate reaction of the group is agreement with the official viewpoint of the government and church. They say this is all right because abortion is bad. After the women express their feelings we lead a discussion where we ask if they didn't think abortion might be positive. We talk until women realize that in certain conditions it is wrong for a woman to have a child and that the woman should decide whether she should have a child or not.

— I myself think the woman should be the only one to decide but I don't say that to them. We discuss the children these women have, if all their children are wanted, how they feel about having them.

— We would prefer not to have leaders but when we tried leaderless groups nobody spoke when it came to their own personal situations. We lead but we are still part of the group. If there were no one to lead, the group would collapse. Women here are not used to talking about themselves. Doctors don't give information on birth control. I know a girl who took three pills at once because she hadn't any idea of how many to take. There are so many taboos in Spain.

— We know we take chances when we go to these neighborhoods but as long as we don't act nothing will happen. Once we do, there will be problems. —

Rosita is a scientist, rare for a woman in Spain. Her salary is just average, respect in her field sub-average. — For instance, I was doing research with a man. I got along fine with him but when the work was finished my part of the project was shorter than his. He laughed and said it was because I am a woman. I thought it was a foolish commentary but it shows they're always conscious that you're a woman. If my work had been longer I'm certain he would have made the same comment. You can't be equal professionally because anything you do differently they attribute to your being a woman. There are lots of things that continually emphasize these differences. And my capabilities are constantly questioned. Often when I'm spoken to in a condescending way I think, he wouldn't dare speak like that to a man. If a man makes a mistake it has nothing to do with his sex. But anytime I make a mistake they attribute it to my being a woman. —

TERESA

Here the man is king

TERESA AND I spoke together months before I knew there was a woman's movement in Spain. — I wish there was women's liberation in Spain. Of course I would join but there isn't anything here. —

My friend Peter introduced me to Jeffrey who told me all about Teresa. She was a beautiful person, they were going to get married, they'd known each other for over a year. Jeffrey was from Leeds. He accepted Teresa, said she told him everything. Even though Teresa and I spoke together often I insisted we spend two afternoons together so I could record what she said, rather than trust to memory.

Long before this, it became apparent to me that the Teresa I knew and the Teresa Jeffrey knew were two different people. After the first recorded dialogue Jeffrey, Teresa, Peter and I went out for dinner and dancing. We were doing the samba when Peter remarked that it was beautiful how Teresa and Jeffrey were so honest with each other. I opened my mouth only to smile. Later Jeffrey danced with me, prodded,
— Comeon love, just what did Teresa reveal? Any marvellous secrets I should know? Of course I'm joshing. There isn't a thing I don't know about Teresa. She has a child you know. Did she tell you about him?—

He knew about the child she had out of wedlock but he didn't know about her three abortions. He also didn't know her feelings about their forthcoming marriage. Teresa had asked me to be a witness and then confided, — We're getting married by a judge which is nothing in Spain. The only marriage they recognize is a church wedding. Jeffrey's the one who wants to get married and I'm doing it to make him happy and keep him quiet. —

She tells me her first abortion was done in Barcelona in 1965. — The woman stuck a needle there and I got sick, very sick. I ran a fever and began to hemorrhage and my boyfriend who was with me rushed me to the clinic. The doctor completed the abortion and afterwards I felt all right. —

I asked her how the doctor could finish the abortion and she explains, — He saw I was hemorrhaging and anyhow everybody knows the *comadronas* [mid-wives] and doctors work together. I paid the *comadrona* 5000 pesetas [approximately $80.00] but didn't have to pay anything to the clinic. —

Her second and third abortions were done in Madrid. She grimaces and says all three abortions were very painful because no anesthesia is used. The reason: — They want you to leave immediately and they're afraid you won't go fast enough. The whole procedure takes twenty minutes. It was horrible for me. —

Teresa has taken the pill, which she insists is available if you're married and have the money, but it is bad for her because her body swells and she becomes nervous. The church's stand against contraception is a hypocrisy to Teresa who maintains the people are not religious.
— They're Catholics but they're not Catholics. They go to church because it is an obligation but here, in the heart, inside, they don't feel. — She blames woman's condition on the government and the church. She is convinced that everything will change in Spain when Franco dies and Juan Carlo, who she likes, will take his place.

The family's relationship with its children is, according to Teresa, another problem. — Here in Spain the family doesn't speak with the children. They never discuss sex and of course it is never mentioned in the schools. When I was nineteen and had my baby the people said, 'Of course, it is natural for her. She is bad. She goes out until one, two in the morning.' But I wanted the baby and nobody thought of that. In Spain I think I am brave. Why is it necessary for me to marry the father when I don't love him? —

She talks about the church. — Here in Spain they think a man, married or not, can do anything. But a woman is holy. This is the church's attitude, believe me. The man can go with another woman and still say my wife is sacred. They come home two, three, six in the morning and all the friends know about it. For him it's not bad but for the woman...

— I will tell you something that happened to me when I was thirteen. I cannot forget it. The priest asked me one day when I went to confession, do you go with boys? I don't understand what he is saying because I am very young, so I say I don't know what you're asking. He says, tell me, don't the boys touch your breasts? I turn very red and I think even then, he says something bad because he has a sex mentality. — Teresa owns her own business. She prefers working with women. — They are very intelligent and interesting but also they are very frustrated. They never say anything because here the man is king. They think they're kings but they're stupid fools. It is impossible for me to talk to a man about my feelings. Always when I am with men they talk, they're gentle, they agree but why? Because they think it's possible I'll go to bed with them. You can't have a man friend because of the sex. Friendship is natural for women even if they're lesbians because all their life they have the same problems.

— If you want to know what I think is most important for a woman it is financial independence. Without this she has no independence. Women have to fight for this right. They have to get out of the kitchen and out of their beds and fight. And to learn. I never know enough. It is not important for me to be with a man when I have my work and my hobbies, the things I am interested in. Oh yes something very important. For me it is impossible to be satisfied sexually unless the clitoris is stimulated. It is so very important but I know that women here don't even know about this. They are not prepared for life. They don't even understand their own bodies. —

Teresa left Valencia one week after the last dialogue. We were all together the night before she left. She assured Jeffrey she would return for the wedding the following week but she never did. I wasn't surprised because at one point she took me aside, said goodbye and confided she doubted she would come back. — I cannot be tied to one man and to live with a man is the same as marriage. I must be free. —

Months later, when I was getting ready to leave Spain I went to see Jeffrey at the bar he managed. He had become very hostile and connected Teresa's disappearance with me. His hostility took the form of attacking feminism and calling me 'one of those.' He eyed every woman in the bar as if she were there for the taking. He told me he hadn't the vaguest idea of where Teresa was and — I don't give a shit. I'm balling every night. — He went to the end of the bar, sat with a young woman, laughed loudly. A few minutes later he was next to me saying, — Jesus love, give me a break. What did she say to you? —

— Jeff, you know damned well I'm not going to tell you. —

— What are you, a priest in the confessional? — Then laughing, — Do I have to buy your goddamned book to find out? — Then grinning, as if nothing had happened. — Well love have a good trip and tell your people to stop their war in Vietnam. It's giving all of you a bloody lousy name. — He kissed me on the cheek. — And don't drive everybody potty with your women's lib thing. —

He looked at me for a moment. The laughter went out of his face. The mask was gone. — I wish to God I'd never introduced you to Terry. —

MARIA AURELIA CAMPMANY

The penis is a visiting card that opens every door

IN 1971 **MARIA AURELIA CAMPMANY**** was invited to a Congress of Women Journalists in Washington, D.C. As her passport was confiscated in 1967, she went to the police with the invitation and requested her passport be returned. She received her passport too late for the conference, but she smiles and says, — Thanks to the Congress of Women Journalists I received my passport back. — When I asked why her passport was taken she said she said she couldn't answer.

Her shelves are filled with books, many of them written by herself. She is a novelist, a non-fiction writer. Since 1966 she has devoted her time to books about women, feminists, although she is not part of the women's movement.

In 1966 *The Women in Catalonia* was published. It is a sociological study about a small group of women, their alienation from the society. It deals with the women's work, their progress within their work, their independence and attitudes, their feelings about feminism.

El Feminismo Iberico is her book about suffragists, their influence in Spain and Catalonia. She points out that Catalonia has a social life and culture much different from the rest of Spain. — The influence of feminism in Barcelona is much different than Madrid. In Catalonia the power is in the middle class. In Madrid it is in the hands of the rich. —

I was surprised to learn that Spain had an active woman's movement in the early 1900s. The feminists then fought for the rights of women in their work, to enter certain professions which were dominated by men. The nursing, secretarial and teaching professions were but a few. They fought against the Spanish Civil Code which was degrading to women. During the Republic (1931 to 1939) they succeeded in getting the vote for women. However, since the education of women in Spain was very limited, the majority voted on the right. They realized this reactionary vote was bad for the public and blamed it on the strong influence of the Catholic church. In spite of this, the women did get more rights. Ms. Campmany points out that the feminists gave lectures in educational institutions, in Parliament. However, they never fought on the streets like the American or British feminists.

BONNIE: Why has there never been anything written about the suffrage movement in Spain?
MARIA: [laughing] I'm writing about it. [serious] The whole cultural world ignores Spain, not only in feminism but in everything. We were even in contact with women in Belgium and France, in England with Christabel Pankhurst. I even believe Emmeline Pankhurst was in Barcelona.
BONNIE: How long was the suffrage movement in Spain?
MARIA: From the 1890s to 1926. I'm talking about an organized movement.

Maria Campmany spoke to me that first day about feminism, about the feminist magazines. She explained that in 1907 there were four feminist magazines. The first one was started by a Catalonian woman named Carmen Carr. Some of the magazines had a short life and then started again. The movement grew in Madrid, Barcelona and Valencia but the rest of Spain did not react. − This difference is still true. The woman who works in the country is conditioned to her mode of life which is the same as one hundred years ago. Another point is that feminism in Spain always stays in the intellectual world. −

She spoke about her education at the Instituto Escuela de la General Idad de Cataluna which was run by the autonomous government of Catalonia. She explains that education for boys and girls was identical and added, − Afterwards the Falange introduced courses that were strictly for girls such as how to cook, sew, etc. These are still courses in high school that all girls must pass. −

She tells me she was a privileged person, being the third generation of intellectuals. In her home she was never made to feel that being a woman would exclude her from any activities. − I was treated by my father as a friend. He would explain what he was doing and ask me for help. My mother was intellectual, very bright. −

Maria Aurelia Campmany spoke for an hour-and-a-half and then excused herself. She was privileged, she did not experience prejudice as a woman. I asked for another interview and she agreed. I left with Marta, thoroughly deflated. Aside from her academic life, from her books, what did I know about Campmany the woman? I wondered what I had failed to do. Sitting upstairs at the Cortes Ingles overlooking Montserrat, Tibidabo and much of Barcelona, Marta and I had warm *churros* and rich hot chocolate. I thought about the interview. — I can't believe she's never experienced prejudice. — Marta looked at me, shrugged. — That's what she said. —

I came the second time prepared to the teeth with over thirty questions. I also decided that I would do as much of the interview as I could in Spanish. I asked the first question. Ms. Campmany answered, said she preferred questions. But I never asked another question. We spoke in Spanish, English. Maria spoke Catalon when she was excited which neither Marta nor I understood. — Maria,— I said, — I cannot believe that you've never experienced prejudice. —

She smiled at me. — I didn't say that. I said I was an equal at home. After the Civil War there was a strong reaction against women and the first time I was treated as a 'woman' was at the University of Madrid. I always say that the female characteristic decided by Freud to be penis envy is something I discovered for myself in April 1939, which was the day of the victory for the Nationalists. It is an ironical joke. It is natural for a woman who finds herself discriminated against to envy the characteristics of the one in power. As a fact, in all of the nineteenth century and up to today the penis is a visiting card that opens every door.

— When I entered the university I suddenly found myself in a completely hostile world. I will tell you an anecdote. In 1942 I received my Masters of Philosophy. In my class we got the best grades. I myself graduated at the top of the class. One of the boys in my class took me aside and told me he felt very bad about my having the best grades. He said it made the boys feel less important. He was very serious. Since a woman was capable of doing the same it made it not worthwhile for them he said.

— The most important thing for me was writing. University honors didn't mean much to me. I spent three years as an assistant professor at the University of Barcelona and the professor chose me because of my work. He respected me but I was never interested. I wanted to write. —

Maria Campmany reflected, lit a cigarette and then said, — I want it well understood that if I wanted to make a career as a university professor I would have met with lots of difficulties. In becoming a writer I didn't face the problem because as a writer the distinction of status is not a clear one. Virginia Woolf said no one could keep a woman from taking a pen and paper and she could go to a place at her home and write. But for a woman to be a doctor she has to pass a series of tests. The writer is always on the outside. The doctor, the lawyer, the minister, the bank manager are all people who are integrated into the system. That is why women find it easier to be writers. —

She explains she is unaffected by public opinion or what society expects of people. She feels her parents are greatly responsible. Although it was expected that women get married her parents never demanded this of her. And she never married. But she did manage to get engaged a number of times. Her relationship with men has always been on the basis of equality — which doesn't mean they weren't conflicting. For instance, when I was young and they expected me to assume the role most women play I didn't and this created conflict. When I had a professional relationship it didn't matter. But in dealing with passion and feelings, this of course created difficulties. I always felt equal but there were conflicts because men of this country and of my generation felt this freedom as a threat to their ability because they had the impression their virility gave them authority over women. —

She turned to me hopefully. — I think women have developed in these last years in spite of all their difficulties. You can see a will in young girls to react as responsible persons. For example you can notice a lessening of the religious influence, a freedom of women they themselves have acquired. Yet I have noticed, for instance, that at the university girls find it difficult to act in university activities, to be elected at an assembly even when the public recognizes that a girl is more capable than a boy. The majority in the university have a very traditional attitude towards women. These girls feel a tremendous frustration.

— There's a girl from Madrid who wrote a song about women's oppression. It is about a girl who runs away from home because at home they don't consider her a person but an object. When she goes away her parents say to her, 'Carmencita come home, come home. You won't be better off anywhere else.' She falls in love with a boy who is also very liberated. He is a leftist and she is happy with him until she realizes she has become an object with this boy as well. She runs away again and the boy sings to her 'Carmencita come home.' —

I went to her bookshelves, looked at the enormous amount of books she's written. I told her I thoroughly enjoyed her anecdotes. She laughed, asked if I wanted to hear another one. — Yes, *absolumente*. —

— A short time ago I gave a lecture on the feminist question in a small town in Mallorca. After the lecture there were questions. Most of the people were young boys from the village, very aggressive and yet repressed. One of them asked, 'Why do women speak so much about their freedom and they never get it.' Then one girl from the village, about twenty-two or twenty-three years old spontaneously answered before I could, 'Because they put before us all sorts of difficulties.'

— The reaction of the boys in the group was to laugh at her. I took advantage of the situation and told her, — You see, this is the greatest difficulty you will find, because the reactionary spirit uses laughter in order to ridicule those who think a change in the way of life is possible. Of course there is no argument against laughter.' And I told the girls from this village that you need great courage to resist the malicious laughter of the boys of your generation and others as well. —

I have recorded just a portion of my dialogue with Maria Aurelia Campmany. The rest is recorded permanently in my head.

— BONNIE BLUH? —

— Yes. —

— This is Senõr Lopez* of the American Export Company. I am calling to tell you the S. S. Young America is at the port and will leave tonight. You are to be on board no later than five tonight. —

— Are all my things on the ship?—

He laughs. — Yes, yes. I told you not to worry. I personally saw to it that everything was put in your room. Your novel is safe. —

My novel. What an irony. I came to Europe to write a novel and now I'm pretending I have.

It is afternoon. I take a bus to the Ramblas. And walk. I pull my typewriter and bag on wheels, as I'd done all through Europe.

The Ramblas is a very wide boulevard with all kinds of stores on either side. In the center island, merchants sell flowers, birds and other things. So I'm told. I have never seen anything other than flowers and birds. The Ramblas. An elite Spanish theatre where the actors, elegant looking Catalonians parade up and down, talking softly among themselves. While we, the audience watch, totally ignored.

In the Spain of summer, flowers, fruits, centuries of ancient buildings combine. The air is hot and sweet. I could close my eyes and know I'm here.

I wanted to call the feminists but decided I couldn't take another chance. For their sake. So I walked through part of my life. Remembering. The endless waiting that summer before to the day when the bagpipes played. And now it is gone. I have three hours before I leave for the States.

There are eleven of us on the S.S. Young America. I hear the blasting moan of the horn, rush out on deck to stand by myself. The gulls linger above. The blue of the Mediterranean turns royal at sunset. My eyes see Barcelona get smaller and smaller. Somebody tells me dinner is being served. I stay on deck.

We are passing Alicante. Remembering. How many times did I make the trip from Benidorm to Alicante? Alicante to Benidorm. I see the twin islands of Benidorm.

Remembering. My room. No longer mine.

The sea turns black. The sky is alive with stars while sea stars move in and out of the water, playing round the ship.

I am going home. I am going home.

An officer is standing beside me, grinning. — How're you doing? —

— All right. —

— Is your room ok? —

— Fantastic. —

— How come you missed dinner? —

I shrug. He looks at me. A special vein that only males have goes into action. He keeps looking at me. — They're nuts. I told them they're nuts.—

I don't want to ask who. I don't want to talk to anyone. Why doesn't he go away?

— You're a feminist. —

I nod and wait.

— They told me about you before you got on board. She's a feminist they said. A lesbian. And you know what I said when I saw you. I said, man are they crazy. That's a real woman. I know a real woman when I see one. So how're you doing? —

Welcome home Bonnie. Welcome home.

BROOKLYN

BROOKLYN

September 24, 1974

HOW TO END this book!

In the two years I'm home I've been visited by many European sisters. And I've received letters. Some of the groups are no longer in existence. Others have emerged. Some have changed their names. Feminists have moved to other groups. Some have dropped out. Hopefully they will return. But even if they don't, the changes in their personal lives will undoubtedly affect those around them. Just as the changes in me have made a difference to the people I know.

How to end this book without ending it!

When I decided to publish *Woman to Woman* in June, I thought the best thing would be to write most of the women I spoke with and let them speak of their changes. Some of the women answered. Other letters came back. Address unknown. Others I heard about through feminists I've remained friends with. Some didn't answer at all.

I would like to share the letters with you. And some experiences.

IRELAND – July 11, 1974

Dear Bonnie:

I never received your last letter due to a change of address. A significant change occurred in my life three weeks ago, just six years after I became involved in the northern war, and four years after I became involved in women's liberation. I voted in the local government elections here in the south and I was faced with a choice. Either to use the local government vote against the government on national issues by voting Provisional or Official Sinn Fein, or vote for women in the interests of women.

I voted all the way for women. I figured I had spent long enough on the north-south issue, which has little relevance to women, and that it was time I stood on feminist issues. I devote proportionately more of my time now in politics to women.

The most significant change since I became a feminist however is the psychological one. Whereas before I sometimes felt, and was always treated as a freak, for pursuing paths not considered 'feminine' I can now pursue those paths in the knowledge of complete justification. We are recognized as oppressed. We are supported by each other. I taste freedom all the time in my search for freedom.

There are no social pressures on me from my family to get married. I don't have to worry about reaction when I say I'm not having any babies. I don't give a damn about going anywhere alone, and I'm no longer expected to be escorted. I'm recognized as oppressed but also recognized as fighting the oppression. And I have no guilt at all about treating men as my political enemy. Bonnie, I enjoy being a girl.

Also my paper leaves it up to me whether or not I write about issues previously regarded as the woman's field. Naturally I don't write fuck all. I do my own column.

Love to you sister,
Nell [McCafferty]

IRELAND – September 5, 1974

Dear Bonnie:

Sorry for not writing before now. Things have been a jumble here and I'm just beginning to sort myself out.

As it happens I did leave Ireland for a short time. However, my mother died just a month after I arrived and I didn't stay as long or get as much from America as I had hoped. I came back far too early. I can see that now and I'm trying to work out when or how I can afford to go back for a year.

The movement is in ribbons here, nothing is happening, splits and counter splits. The little that is being done is being done by middle class women not on a feminist basis but more to help others. The charity myth.

Yes, of course, feminism has changed my life, but living in Ireland doesn't help me to grow or develop my feminist consciousness. I find that it's difficult to talk to women here without being defensive—areas which I am trying to explore—like psychology and psychoanalysis—are areas no women are into here ...

This is all very depressing but it will give you an idea of what's happening .... The problems of women are continaully put down as secondary to the problems of the north-south entanglement. Unless something happens soon, the women's question will die a death here.

Will write more when there's something constructive to tell you.

Love,
Mary [Anderson]

ENGLAND

I'D BEEN corresponding with Phyllis Jordan* but lost contact unfortunately. Through her I learn, while still in Spain, that Jane Martin* miscarried.

On feminism Phyllis wrote: — The consciousness raising group went quite well after you left but Jane and I both feel the time has come to join more active or at least more outlooking groups. —

Anne Sharpley is still extremely active and still rushing around the world covering the news stories. Her letters are whirlwinds .... In haste, as I just got your letter and I should be getting on a plane ...

You must forgive me for being so brief as I've just got in from Japan and am now off again after only a day to clear mail and change my clothes.

Good luck,
Anne [Sharpley]

LONDON – July 21, 1974

Dear Bonnie:

Yes, I do have some more news for you. First the bad news. British TV still does not have a female newsreader. My main reason for wanting one is that I feel the children of this country are growing up to believe that only a man can tell them about matters of national or political significance. We did have a great break a week ago however (I hope you note acidity in my voice) when a woman, Sheila Tracy was actually allowed to read the national news on radio (BBC). It happened because the male newsreader was taken ill suddenly and Sheila was the only person on hand. Her boss had long been saying that women were not suited to reading the national news, but when it came to the crunch look what happened. Sheila, according to the newspapers read the news 'faultlessly.' Big Deal—she's a real professional and has been reading news on local TV for years . . . .

Now for some news about me. I have for the past year been co-presenting my own show on Capital Radio, London's first ever commercial radio station. The programme runs for three hours, from nine to twelve noon and it's live. I provide feature material, information bits and do the interviewing in between pop records. I am glad to say that commercial radio is providing new opportunities for women in broadcasting. Capital Radio has two female newsreaders and several other women presenters and interviewers . . .

Things are looking up in the media, but I still think this country has a long way to go before we lose the patronizing attitude that has been shown towards the female sex for centuries.

Do hope that you are well and that your book is a great success.

All the best,
Joan [Shenton]

LONDON – September 12, 1974

Dear Bonnie:

It was very nice to hear from you and I only regret that the pressure of Parliamentary work prevented me from writing to you straight away.

I am delighted to know that you are publishing your book and I do hope it will be a great success.

The Bill finally got a second reading and was then referred to a Select Committee of the House of Commons. The last government then announced that it would introduce legislation itself and brought in a *Green Paper* on discrimination, just before the 1974 general election.

The present Labour Government has now introduced a *White Paper* and has promised that legislation will be introduced to coincide with the full implementation of the Equal Pay Act by the end of next year. So we still have nothing on the *Statute Book* and we have to wait for the result of the anticipated election before we know how things are likely to go.

With all good wishes,
Joyce Butler, M.P.

AMSTERDAM – July 14, 1974

Dear Bonnie:

I am surprised and happy that you wrote. Since we saw each other things have changed very much in my life. I am trying to remember what I told you. I know I was then unhappy and did not really know what to do with my life, because almost up to that moment it had been filled with husband and children. It seemed empty and has taken a long time to refind myself as an individual.

I met a man, a nice and attractive man. We are very good and intimate friends. We have travelled together the last two winters, living for six months at the Costa Blanca. As I had hardly seen anything outside Holland before that time, it does me a lot of good.

I must tell you I am now divorced of my husband and I am glad of it . . .

It strikes me that we are living an entirely different life. I looked at the sea and I looked and looked and dreamed. I try to deepen the knowledge of the foreign languages I already knew and I am learning Spanish. I like to write too; and music, my great passion, it all comes back, gradually.

My daughter Anne, has another friend now. She is doing well at art school, is one of the best pupils.

Please Bonnie, let us be friends. I also have often thought about our being together that day.

Love,
Diane*

AMSTERDAM – August 22, 1974

Dear Bonnie:
 I found your letter, returning from a long and marvellous vacation in France. Great fun to hear from you, must be something telepathic in it, because I had been thinking all of a sudden on my French mountain: What would have become of that American woman who interviewed me in that Damrak cafe and who wanted to do a book on European women? I had not the slightest idea anymore about your name and your whereabouts in America but I kept wondering. Has she written her book by now? And the funny thing is that me too, I can remember us sitting there, although I have been interviewed so many times and in so many places. Was that waiter mad when we wanted so many coffees when he was serving lunches and we did not want one of his overcreamed and overmayonnaised dishes which the Dutch always think the Americans are so fond of.
 Well I'm very happy to hear that you managed to write it and that it will be published soon. I'm looking forward very much to reading it; I'm so curious to know which kind of women you got together on your long trips through Europe. I must say I do admire you, doing such a lot of work.
 Yes indeed, I stopped working. In the summer of 1972 our government fell to pieces and new elections were proposed. That left me with making up my mind; did I want to run again and this time probably for a four year period and my own dear socialists in office, or did I want to retire. It took me about six weeks to decide. On the one side it would be fun to work in Parliament with my own people in office after that long period in opposition. On the other hand I was nearly 60, my husband nearly 70 and our days are anyhow counted. And if I stayed, there would have been the temptation not to stay as a simple MP but to take on a job in government, if we managed to get into it. Which would have meant a Sunday-afternoon marriage. Now the feminist in you will no doubt cry out: So what! But I counted my blessings on the fingers of my hands and found out that it had not only pleased the Lord to fit me out with enough gifts to do very satisfying work but also to send me that

very rare gem: a marvellous partnership with a very nice fellow. And that part of my life had been neglected for a long time and I decided that before going in for eternity I wanted to make the most of it. And so I did.

I do not regret it. Of course there are nostalgic moments, certainly when I see (on TV) my former colleagues busy and I grind my teeth because I find that they say things so complicated that nobody who has not been to university can understand it. But to have time to do things one never could do is marvellous after more than 40 years of intensive working.

Of course I started to write a book right away. About the formation of that government, which took nearly five months! It was well received and sold out in six weeks . . . . .

This winter I will take part in a TV program (monthly) on consumer problems and somewhere in the hidden parts of my mind another book is stirring, but I'm afraid I am too lazy by now to pay much attention to it. Although one never knows . . .

Keep well. My kindest regards,
Gerda [Brautigam]

PARIS, FRANCE — July 13, 1974

I do remember you Bonnie, and the stairs up to your room and the talk we had . . . And having heard no more from you since you left France, leaving no address, or maybe I lost it, I thought that one day, a book would come from any part of the States, and would be signed by you.

And then it's a letter I read when climbing four stairs home, and am answering now next to an open windown on a nice fresh July day. All things that make me feel quite lyrical, and happy too. Will you use that for an epilogue?

[Then she writes about the possibility of translating the book, which I asked her to do.]

Anyhow, I was more than happy to hear of you and wanted to send you my love as fast as possible. Which I do.

With love and sisterhood,

Cathy [Bernheim]

PARIS — July 25, 1974

Dear Bonnie:

I received your letter a little late since I was not in Paris. I remember you very well in fact and expect to read your book very soon.

[In my letter to her I talk about Jeanine Richette.* I'd heard through the women from Book des Femmes, when I saw them in June, that Jeanine was living with feminists and is separated from her husband.]

Giselle writes that Jeanine is separated from her husband but . . .

Jeanine does not live with other feminists, though she's most active in the MLF but she lives alone with her two daughters.

As for myself, it is hard to sum up what happened. I have not been working for nearly a year although I receive my salary for a training at the university. I parted from my husband and live alone with my two children. In October I shall move and share a house in Paris with four other people. I expect a lot from living in a community.

This is a very short summing up of two years but maybe you will be back in Paris one day and we shall resume our talking.

Good luck on your book and to you.
Kisses,
Giselle [Vaguelsey]

PARIS — August 13, 1974

This is Paris life; you tell somebody that you'll write at the end of the week . . . . then weeks pass by and you have not written yet.

You asked me about the French movement and then I realized that it was quite a job to find out what happened these past years, and to tell you clearly what is happening now!

When you came to France and we met, the women's movement was at its beginning here. I personally had not thought it over; all was going fast, we were in action and thought we could take time for ourselves later. Selves were very collective; we had things to learn together. It was just as if we had begun another life. At least for me, and indeed it made me begin another life. We did have a lot of actions; as women, as lesbians and as revolutionaries at the same time. Every woman's experience could be ours, and we thought it would be that way for the rest of the time.

It was the time of discovery; our own discovery of ourselves, and the society's discovery of women. You know, it has always been the same explosion through centuries; we were discovering that we have an 'herstory' (as you say; we have no translation for that word here) that had been hidden for times, that we had things to say and to act on this world-wide masculine machinery. We were appearing as 'le MLF' and this was a shock in everybody's conscience . . . . For the first time the medias began to speak of women's liberation as if the only women that could liberate themselves and other women were the women of the MLF. We had to say every time we appeared that liberation was each woman and all women's problems at the same time.

Now, women's liberation is part of the French society as well. You can't open a paper without seeing something on the subject, mostly written by women, and sometimes by men. You may even read in the horoscope of fashion papers: *Today girls will feel they are in an MLF mood.* The problem is, for us, that liberation is not a mood but a way of life. We try to deal with everyday life. Women's collectives appear everywhere and we can't say at all how large the movement is.

As to each one's life, the feeling of having sisters throughout the city and even through the world is a great support.

I now live in a small sunny apartment, two rooms where I can work on a new book, a novel, do some translations to earn my living, draw a little for pleasure, and develop pictures in a kind of collective lab that takes place in a kind of closet here. Women often come. Some are sisters I know for a long time. One of them has been my lover for three years and she still is. I did find out that loving women was not only making love with them, then feeling strangers to them when it's finished. Can you feel that?

I'll try to send you a special issue of 'les Temps Modernes' (Simone deBeauvoir's review) we took over, before leaving. Please let me know when your book comes out and do let me hear from you soon.

With love and sisterhood,
Cathy [Bernheim]

PARIS – September 4, 1974

Dear Bonnie:

Oh no, I have not forgotten you! Often, during these two years, I thought of you and regretted so much that I had not your address. So I am really very happy to hear from you.

Here are the answers to your questions:

— Yes, I am still the conductor of my own choir and orchestra. Why not? I am the founder.

— Yes, during these last years, I paid back almost the whole sum of the big deficit for our three concerts from the year 1968, the tenth birthday of our society. Since one month, I have my own bed. It's no more necessary to sleep on the floor.

— Naturally, I am still working 54 hours every week and next year, I think, it will be yet a little bit more. But after that, all will be paid.

Yes, I wrote to the address of the women's liberation movement in Paris but Bonnie, try to understand me, please. I cannot take part here. Look, I was coming from the East, twenty years ago. Really, I know what communism is and I am not a communist. I am *absolutely convinced* that the fact, the necessity of women's liberation has nothing, really nothing to do with politics. This is one of the main questions for me.

I would like to take part nevertheless, just to help change a little bit but to struggle still more than I have to already . . . I am really too tired. That's a pity I know.

On the other hand, I am sorry I never found the time to answer to New York, because the *Prime Time* [an excellent monthly paper run by Marjorie Collins and which I sent to Ingeborg] is not only very interesting but often I would like to discuss things with several of these sisters. These are my problems too. We could understand each other very well.

You know where I am going now? Direction: East Germany, to see my parents the second time. Last year, it was the first time, after twenty years, thanks to Willy Brandt. I think it is impossible to feel what such an event means if you had never experienced it yourself.

Yes, who knows? I am projecting too, to go one day to New York with my choir and orchestra, to give a series of concerts there. I will be back in Paris about the 20th of September.

Yours,

Ingeborg [Rawolle]

ROME, ITALY – September 16, 1974

Dear Bonnie:

Your letter has been lying in my handbag for a month at least. Every day I mean to answer it but I am always very busy and then I hate writing.

Jenny* lives in Holland, in the Hague. Julienne does not come to the group anymore. I know nothing of her. As for Alma, I have not seen her for a long time.

I am now part of a group made up of many left wing women. It is called Collettivo Feminista Comunista. There are many groups like ours in Italy, women militant in political groups are now being *infected* by feminist disease!

The old Collettivo Lotta Feminista has merged with other groups and is now called Movimento Feminista Romano, with the same address. As for us, we are temporarily meeting in a cellar, but are now looking for a new place.

As for new actions, yes, we gathered together with a trial case on abortion. A feminist girl was involved and we turned the case into a political one. Just now MLD is, with the support of others, launching a campaign for compelling the Parliament to discuss the new law on abortion presented by a socialist deputy, Fortuna. Our aim is to compel people to talk and think about this problem, as the country is ready for it. When the referendum for divorce was at stake, even the Communist Party did not believe that people and women would vote in favor of divorce and the abortion one is even more compelling. Some 240 women are now waiting for trial and I think the movement will gain in strength, so I hope. On the surface there is not much change, but ideas are spreading fast.

I went in August to a feminist camp in Denmark and met Jill Johnston, the author of *Lesbian Nation.* I have not read the book but I was told it is good. Do you know it?

I am surprised at the lot of things you manage to do. Congratulations. [I could hear Giovanna laugh as I read this.] I don't have the energy or rather I put them in other things, leisure and sunshine. My big work is talking, never stop.

A friend of mine, Marina ——— is now in New York and I gave her your address. If she rings or writes, she is a very charming person.
Back to work now. I am glad you got in touch and hope you write soon. I will answer, promise.

Love,
Giovanna [Caputo]

AMSTERDAM, HOLLAND – August 30, 1974

Dearest Bonnie:
My neighbor's friend came to Holland and he brought your letter with him. That was so good to hear from you. Now I have your address again and I can answer. I wrote to your address in Spain, [Jenny* and I had been writing but lost touch when we both moved] with the idea it would be forwarded. Anyhow, the knot is tied again.

I am in Holland now. I meant to stay for two years but the kids like it here and it is not good to change schools so I suppose that at least for another three years I'll be here.

I went to Rome one week in May. I saw many of the Collettivo women in a play. Giovanna was also in it and it was a production of the whole group. I thought it was very good.

I am studying at the university trying to become a teacher as I'm tired of men who are twice as stupid and who earn twice as much. On top of that I'm now collaborating in the system of profit. Being a teacher I can be mostly myself and put some of my own ideas into children, the population least spoiled.

I could write much more but I want this letter to give you quick answers for the moment. Write soon again. I'm still very much interested in your book and as far as I'm concerned you can write anything with name and surname.

Lots of love,
Jenny

I WAIT AT the Court Street station. On Montague Street. For Giovanna Pala who is visiting from Rome. Earlier in the day she called to say Alma

Sabatini gave her my address and phone number.

The minute we meet we realize we know each other. That first abortion march. We both laugh, talk at once.

— I didn't know it was you. We kept your sign for so long. —

— How is Alma? —

— Didn't you receive her letter? She said she wrote. —

We walk toward my apartment, me, Carol (a feminist from Boston) and Giovanna. She tells me about about the erratic post offices in Italy and then asks me who I heard from.

— Giovanna Caputo? She's no longer with us but I suppose she wrote you that. Of course we see her. You know we are no longer called Collettivo. There were so many groups called Lotta Feminista so we changed our name to Movimento Feminista Romano. And then most of the groups called Lotta Feminista fight mainly for housewives. —

— I'm not sure what you mean. Are you talking about women who earn their living as housekeepers? —

She makes a clicking noise with her tongue. — Anyone who does housework. We think here in America you don't talk enough about married women's work. We think it important that women be paid for their work. —

At my apartment I show my photographs of that first abortion march. We speak of the excitement of that first time, the newness. The freezing cold. The cafe where we went to warm up.

Giovanna shows me photographs of another demonstration. On March 8, 1972, less than four months after the first demonstration. Again the women are at Campo dei Fiore, but this time it is different. One photo shows the feminists standing talking among themselves, talking with their children. Another photo shows the Chief of Police and his men, also standing. Then a photo of the chief draping some fabric around himself.

Photo: Feminists fleeing with frantic expressions on their faces.

Photo: Policemen assaulting the women.

Photo: Alma Sabatini, her dazed expression looking out of the glossy picture. Something dark covers part of her face.

Photo: Alma being aided by other feminists.

— Giovanna, I don't understand. That first march was so peaceful. —

— Yes of course. Because they didn't know who we were then. We were a joke. Silly girls. —

— Why did Alma get beaten? —

— She was standing there, not thinking anything would happen when the Chief of Police gave orders. He has to say in the name of the Italian people ... something official like that, and then he drapes the colors of the Italian flag on him. See. — She points to one of the photos.

— And then the police charge. Women ran but Alma stayed because she couldn't believe they could beat women. Did she never write you about this? —

— No. —

— You know the market Bonnie. You were there. You know how easy it is to be trapped. There was no exit. —

My mind is racing. To that first time, to the women shopping in the market. — If my husband wouldn't kill me I'd go with them.— — What do women want now? What do they want? —

Giovanna continues. — I went with my daughter Susanna. I had many posters I wanted to put in the car. When I came back the police had started to charge. I can't find my daughter and I am so frightened.—

Giovanna tells me that Ronnie, the feminist from Greece now with Movimento Feminista Romano took movies of the entire incident. — In the movies you can see my daughter Susanna grab the microphone and scream into it, 'We are without guns and you wear guns so this means you are afraid of us.'

— My daughter. She is something. I think the Chief of Police went crazy because he was humiliated by an eight year old child. When I found Susanna she was screaming at him.

— We were all women, we had no guns, no weapons. We had daughters, sons, children. The police had helmets and rifles. They were there like they were ready for war. Alma's head was broken open. We took her to the hospital. She had to have many stitches. —

I couldn't look at the pictures, couldn't concentrate on what Giovanna was saying. Remembering. Alma and me, talking in her apartment, laughing, having lunch, running through the pouring rain to the Piazza Navona. On January 25, 1972, less than six weeks before the incident, in Spain, I received a letter from Alma. Here it is in part.

Dearest Bonnie:

This time it's my turn to apologize for the delay in answering, but something important has happened and I had to explain it to you (not just a hasty answer) and you know how hectic my life is.

The important thing is that I left MLD. The fact that you were in

Rome and came to the movement will make it less difficult for you to understand. I think you realized how very little 'feminist' MLD had become. They kept repeating all the time that our movement was 'political' and couldn't really be concerned with finding out, investigating what women's liberation was. They maintained that the only way of raising women's consciousness was to mobilize them about the abortion issue.

Moreover the atmosphere had become very heavy, tense, full of suspicion towards the 'thinking people' as they despisingly described me and other women such as Danielle Pacco (the one who was at dinner with us and Betty Friedan).

It all exploded when I, trying to recover the feeling of solidarity among the women in the MLD proposed to have some sessions among women. To talk about and confront our experiences. The reaction was disproportionate. They said that it meant betraying our document (which was absolutely untrue) and of course that it was unpolitical so they called for a vote (If Alma wants to have groups of women she can do it outside the movement they said) and with a majority vote they ruled out any possibility of changing MLD. As you realize I had no alternative but to leave. What a sense of relief, dear Bonnie. As long as I stayed in MLD I was feeling not free. Danielle left with me and a few more. We now have an autonomous group of about twelve women meeting once a week to discuss our problems but also having projects of work . . . . . .

I TELL GIOVANNA PALA about that letter and she informs me that Alma and her group are now part of the new Movimento.

And that Julienne is writing a feminist book.

Judy Winter* is with the Collettivo Cinema.

That Movimento (once Collettivo) has a feminist theatre, a street theatre that acts in markets, streets, parks. She shows me photos. Sometimes they advertise. Other times, they just go out there and the entire production is spontaneous.

That on March 8, 1974 at Piazza Navona the women from MLD collected their 50,000 signatures. The feminists fasted to bring attention to the abortion issue but their action was totally ignored by the newspapers. Infuriated, they went to the papers and continued hassling the people there until they printed what was happening.

In October of 1974 Parliament will discuss abortion.

For Italy this is an enormous step.

Giovanna gives me a copy of the MFR magazine called *Effe,* which comes out once a month, is written, edited, proofed and on and on by the feminists. Nobody receives any salary except for a small staff who coordinates everything. As a result, they do not need to have advertisers, who often dictate policy.

I learn that there is a woman's club called *Girlane* where they have a restaurant. The address: Via della Pelliecia 4A and it is in Trastevere.

I see a tremendous amount of photographs. Photographs of all the actions. Giovanna tells me everything is recorded; still photographs, video tapes, films.

— You wouldn't believe what is happening in Italy. We are now getting the mothers of the women. These women run away from home. They hear that we will help them so they come to us. This woman, she must be in her fifties, she ran away from her husband in Sicily. She came to my home. The first night she was there a group from the Movimento went out to dinner. You know Bonnie how we are all together a lot. The woman just looked. It must have seemed strange to her. All the women together like that. The way we are with each other. She stayed with me a week and we got her a job. —

— Doing what? —

— Taking care of a house. —

— You mean housework? — I groan.

— Yes. —

I want to cry but all I say is, — Is she happier now? —

— Oh yes. Of course. For her anything is better than to live with her husband. She is very happy. —

This is just one story. There are many others. Enough to fill another book.

How to end this book without ending it! Last summer Amanda Sebastyan visits me from London. She is part of the Radical Feminists, a group that was not in existence when I was there.

I receive a call that there are groups in Naples. Jean Zaleski, who lived there for a year-and-a-half and is back in New York ten months tells me there weren't any groups before. She is pleased and surprised.

BROOKLYN — September 20, 1974

CAROL CALLS from Boston. Giovanna wants to talk with me. Do I know the woman who is with the National Women's Health Coalition. Giovanna just received a call from Italy asking if the abortion stickers and posters will be sent to Italy. I call Merle Goldberg who tells me that two thousand stickers and posters were sent the week before.

The following week Lola Langley tells me that she and Merle met the Italian feminists in Bucharest at the World Population Conference. There Merle and Lola collected signatures supporting the *Woman's Manifesto* which is the right of women to control their own bodies through access to high quality medical care and medical education. That no woman should be the subject of medical research without her consent, etc.

At this conference the National Women's Health Coalition handed out buttons that said *My body belongs to me.* These buttons were made up in English, Spanish, French and Swahili.

Lola tells me they were told they couldn't distribute the buttons. Finally after much arguing, they were told they could hand out the buttons at the Athenee Palace, an old hotel. Lola says, — They felt it was too political because in Bucharest they don't give women contraceptive information until they have four children. —

I am just a woman in the movement. I am no more or less than anyone else. Others like me receive calls, letters.

There is no end.

As for me, in the little over two years I've been back, two of my sons, Kenn and Brian came to live with me again. Craig will be leaving for Europe tomorrow. I've discovered that the family, which was once so important to me, is one of the things that blocked my humanity. As a mother I still have ambivalent feelings. I feel guilty at times but not too often. I've come to think that mothers are important. How else can people excuse their own inadequacies.

I expect different things from myself. Yet periodically I slip back. How to rid myself of all the layers.

Like my friend Giovanna Caputo I won all the little battles but lost so many of the big ones. And like her, life left its mark. And like Giselle Vaguelsey I too want to be alone as much as I want people around me. And my friend Cathy Bernheim who said the whole life should be in one drawer so you could be a real person and not the divided person you think you are. Or Anneke van Baalen who spoke about loose parts. I still have them. And every time I put some together, others appear.

And maybe that's what being a woman is, in these times. Constant discovery, constant changes.

But I do understand myself better. And now that I do, I look at my own mother differently. And my sons. I do less around the house. My home doesn't look so fantastic anymore. Neither do I. I smile less but am happier. I am trying desperately not to exploit as I've been exploited but sometimes I forget and want somebody to make up for my lost years.

How to rid myself of the layers.

In the two years I've been back I finished writing *Woman to Woman*. I wrote a novel *Banana*. Worked for ten months in a printing plant. And miraculously, for me, am publishing my own book. If only my grandma Anna could see me now.

The women in this book, in speaking of themselves, really spoke for me as well. They touched me deeply. I only hope that in some way I touched them as well.

WOMEN'S CENTERS AND GROUPS

THE FOLLOWING is a list of some of the women's centers and groups in the six countries I visited. If you write to a sister, a center or a group in a foreign country it would be thoughtful to send an international postal reply coupon. And please don't forget to include your address.

Ireland

DUBLIN: Woman's Center: 32 Adai Flats, Sandymound Ave., Dublin 4
Woman's Center: 18 Fairbrook Lawn, Dublin 14

England

LONDON:
- Brent: 138 Minet Ave., London NW10 (01-965-3324). Open Mon.-Fri. 9:30 to 12:30 am. Wembley WL, International Socialist Women, Campaign for under fives (a pressure group for play facilities) and MUMS, a group of unsupported mothers (meets every Thursday night)
- Brixton Women's Centre: 207 Railton Rd., London SE24 (01-733-8663). Open Mon., Wed., 2:00 to 5:00 pm; Thurs. 6:00 to 8:00 pm; Sat. 10:00 am to 1:00 pm
- Brixton Women's Place: 80 Railton Rd., London (01-274-8498). Open daily 10:00 to 12:00 am; general women's meeting 8:00 pm; Thurs., CR group
- Crystal Palace/Anerly: 26 Anerly Station Rd., London SE20 (01-659-0924)
- Grafton Road: 158 Grafton Rd., London NW5
- Kingsgate Place: 1 Kingsgate Place, London NW6 (01-624-1952). Free pregnancy testing daily except Sunday. Medical self-help classes; one for newcomers, one closed. Anti-discrimination group, women on Ireland group. Open meeting for new women the first Monday of each month.
- South London: 14 Radnor Terrace, London SW8 (01-622-8495) AWARE meets here first Tues. in the month. Women's Art group is based here.

OTHER CITIES:
- Bristol: 11 Waverley Rd., Reedland, Bristol 6 (0272-38120). Open 10:00 to 12:00, 2:00 to 4:00 weekdays; 10:00 to 12:00 on Sat.; 8:00 to 10:00 pm on Mon., Wed., Thurs. Information service, meeting place, bookshop, library. Free pregnancy testing and abortion referrals Sat. am
- Cambridge: 48 Eden Street, Cambridge (Cam. 63886). Open meetings on Tues. night. Free pregnancy testing Sat. am
- Lancaster: 33 Primrose Street, Lancaster (0524-64785). Center is open at all times. Women living at the center. An information center, consciousness raising, self defense
- Liverpool: Merseyside WL, 49 Seel Street, Liverpool 1 (051-709-4141). Women living in. Meetings, free contraception information, pregnancy testing Sat. am
- Manchester: 218 Upper Brook Street, Manchester 13 (061-273-2287). Center acts as a focal point for the groups in Manchester area. Information on abortion, divorce, battered women, etc. Crash pad list for women passing through Manchester.

Holland

AMSTERDAM: Women's Center, Vrouwenhuis, Nieuwe Herengracht 95, Amsterdam. A large building for all the women's groups.

France

PARIS: Mouvement de Liberation de la Femme, 24 cite de Trevise, Paris 9
Bookstore des Femmes, 68 rue des St. Peres, Paris 7^e (222.02.08)
Maison de Femme, 2 rue de la Roquette, Paris 75011 (805-1754)

Italy

Bologna: Collettivo Feminista Bolognese, Via San Rocco 22/c. Meet every Tuesday.

Ferrara: Lotta Feminista, c/o Carolina Peverati, Via Scandiana, 5; or c/o Antonella Dei Mercato, Vicolo Parchetto, 9

Milano: Collettivo Feminista Milanese, c/o Giordana (tel: 26193) or Marina (tel: 865854)
  Rivolte Femminile: c/o Carla Lonzi, Via Monte di Pieta 1 (898-240)

Modena: c/o Giuliana Pompei, Via Morgagni 17 (350-416)

Naples: Le Nemesiache, c/o Mangiacapra, Via Posillipo 308.
  Movimento di Liberazione della Donna, c/o Tilde Romeo, via A. Falcone, Parco Lamaro 6 (866-1290)

Padova: Lotta Feminista (Group 1) c/o Sandra Busatta, Via Tommaseo 24.
  Lotta Feminista (Group 2) c/o Maria Rosa dalla Costa, Via B. Cristofori 35 (653016).

Porto Santo Stefano: Movimento Feminista Grossetano, Via Cuniberti, 11

Rome: Movimento Feminista Romano, Via Pompeo Magno 94 (386503). Meets Wednesday nights.
  Movimento Liberazione della Donna, Via di Torre Argentina, 18/c (651732, 653371).
  Collettivo Feminista Comunista, Via Pomponazzi, 33.
  FILF, Piazza SS, Apostoli 49.
  Rivolte Femminile, c/o Carla Arcardi (672359); Elvira Banotti, Pz. Sonnino 37 (581-1294).

Torino: Miglietti, Via Petrarca, 40 (658740).
  Rivolte Femminile, Via San Francesco d'Assisi, 11.

Trento: Clementina di Lernia, Via Marsala, 31.